STET!

Tricks of the Trade for Writers and Editors

Edited by
Bruce O. Boston

A collection of articles from *The Editorial Eye,* the newsletter on publications standards and practices.

EDITORIAL EXPERTS, INC.

ISBN 0-935012-07-9

Library of Congress Catalog Card Number 85-82111

Editorial Experts, Inc.
85 S. Bragg Street
Alexandria, VA 22312

Library of Congress Cataloging in Publication Data
Stet! : tricks of the trade for writers and editors.

"Collection of articles from The Editorial eye."
Includes index.
1. Editing—Handbooks, manuals, etc. 2. Publishers and publishing—Handbooks, manuals, etc. 3. English language—Rhetoric—Handbooks, manuals, etc. I. Boston, Bruce O. II. Editorial eye.
PN162.S74 1986 808′.02 85-82111
ISBN 0-935012-07-9

For Laura
(1943–1983)

Acknowledgments

"Editing Legalese" is reprinted with permission from *Across the Board,* published by The Conference Board, and with permission of Alan Siegel, Chairman of Siegel and Gale, Inc.

"Editor's Maze" by Ruth D. Hill and "By No Means" by Ethel Grodzins Romm are used with permission of *Editor and Publisher,* 11 W. 19th St., New York, NY 10011.

"Check Out Your Sexism" by Jean Ward is reprinted with permission from *Columbia Journalism Review,* May/June 1980.

"Common Proofreading Errors" is reprinted with permission from the October 1979 issue of *Modern Office Procedures* and copyrighted 1979 by Penton/IPC, a subsidiary of Pittway Corporation.

"Bring Back My Hyphen to Me" by Edward Bliss, Jr., is reprinted with permission from *The Quill,* the magazine of the Society of Professional Journalists, Sigma Delta Chi.

"Document Design" is reprinted with permission from *Simply Stated,* the monthly newsletter of the Document Design Center, American Institutes for Research, 1055 Thomas Jefferson St. NW, Washington, DC 20007.

"Tips on Proposal Writing" and "Proposal Production" are reprinted with permission from Michael Hough, *Professional Services Management Journal,* P.O. Box 11316, Newington, CT 06111.

"The Researcher's Writing Guide" is reprinted with permission of Mark Henry, Bend Research, 64550 Research Rd., Bend, OR 97701.

"On Readability Formulas" by Jefferson Bates is reprinted with permission from *Writing with Precision,* published by Acropolis Books, Washington, DC.

Stet! was designed by Lynne Komai of Watermark Design, Alexandria, VA. It was set in 10/12 ITC Garamond by Mid-Atlantic Photocomposition, Inc., of Baltimore, MD, and printed on 60-pound offset with a 10-point Carolina Coated cover by BookCrafters, Inc.

Table of Contents

PUBLICATIONS MANAGEMENT

I. RUNNING THE SHOP

II. PRODUCTIVITY STANDARDS

III. PRODUCTION

INDEXING

PROOFREADING

LEXICOGRAPHY

THE FINE POINTS

Other books from Editorial Experts, Inc.

Simplified Proofreading by Peggy Smith
Mark My Words: Instruction and Practice in Proofreading
by Peggy Smith
1987-88 Directory of Editorial Resources

Stet! Tricks of the Trade for Writers and Editors is a collection of articles from *The Editorial Eye*, a monthly newsletter on publications standards and practices. For a free sample copy of *The Editorial Eye*, write Editorial Experts, Inc., 85 S. Bragg St., Alexandria, VA 22312 or call 703/642-3040.

Introduction

Most journal anthologies try to keep two promises: (1) they offer long-time readers a chance to meander down memory lane, revisiting some favored pieces and recalling old pleasures; and (2) they offer more recent readers an evening or two around the campfire, as the editor trots out some of the old tales, by way of introducing some of the ancestral lore to a new member of the family.

This book tries to do both. In the case of the articles we have let stand (Latin: *stet*) in this collection, however, there is an added element. Since *The Editorial Eye* was launched by Editorial Experts in January 1978, its primary purpose has been to be useful. As noted in the first issue, *The Eye* wanted to help its readers "produce publications of the highest quality in the most efficient and economical way." That goal has been the primary selection criterion here as well. There have been others, of course. Along the way, *The Eye* has tried not just to inform and instruct but to amuse, divert, tease, test, and challenge its readers.

The pieces chosen for inclusion here were not just the ones the editor and his colleagues liked, but the ones that seemed to have worn well, those that bore repeating because someone could still benefit from them. Sections of the book are arranged topically. The material in the first 120 issues appears to fall into roughly the following categories of reader interest: editing; writing; publications management; indexing; proofreading; lexicography; and a kind of catch-all section dealing with spelling, grammar, and points of usage.

Two of *The Eye's* most popular features, "Test Yourself" and "Black Eyes," have been scattered throughout the book to provide resting places and diversions from weightier matters. Some conference report items have been included on grounds of their usefulness, even though they may seem somewhat dated. (A note on the form of citation: At the end of each article, the issue number and date of its first appearance in *The Eye* appear in parentheses.)

The Eye has undergone many changes since it began. As befits a publication finding its way, the first three issues were labeled variously *ee eye*, *The Eye*, and finally, *The Editorial Eye*, which stuck to the masthead; colloquially,

"The Eye" endures. A mark of both the uncertainty and the hope surrounding the initial venture is that Issues 2 and 3 were labeled "prototype"; only at Issue 4 did *The Editorial Eye* catch its stride.

Historically, *The Eye* has always been edited by a member of the staff of Editorial Experts and written by staff workers. There have been six editors. Susan Ellicott, who oversaw the prototype issues, was followed by Marguerite Lenz, who edited Issues 4-20. Peggy Smith, an associate editor since Issue 1, edited Issues 21-58; Charlene Semer was editor for Issues 59-71; Priscilla Taylor, Issues 72-97; and Bruce Boston (the first non-staff editor) was broken in on Issue 98 and currently serves. Each has placed a personal stamp on the newsletter, but not so deep an impression that the basic character of *The Eye* has changed.

The debts of any publication are many. Certainly *The Eye* owes much to its editors, who continually wrestle with the question of what kind of newsletter it should be. But *The Eye* owes an equal debt to its readers, whose lively and penetrating letters have often amused, sometimes embarrassed, but never bored. *The Eye* thanks you.

Six editors in almost 8 years might betoken a lack of continuity and editorial perspective, but for Laura Horowitz. From the beginning, she was the driving force behind *The Eye*, as with everything else Editorial Experts did. As publisher until her death in 1983, she provided the policy, perspective, and energy that transformed *The Eye* into the widely read and, we think, highly regarded newsletter it has become. Through all the changes in format, features, and editors, Laura insisted simply that *The Eye* uphold the highest professional standards. Where there were standards, we would try to adhere to them. Where there were none, we would help create them. Always, the prime goal was to serve readers. Everything else was secondary. After the early years, Laura didn't write much for *The Eye*, but everything in it passed under her own (merciless) editorial eye, and the newsletter was always better for it.

We hope you enjoy the pieces we have selected for you here. They stand for what *The Editorial Eye* has always espoused: the highest standards in publications work. *Stet!*

—Bruce O. Boston, Editor
The Editorial Eye

EDITING

I. ON BEING AN EDITOR

Dictionaries define "editing" as something like "revising and preparing a manuscript for publication." That's a little like defining "cooking" as "preparing food for eating." Both definitions have the virtue of economy, but no one who either edits or cooks for a living believes either one.

The reality, of course, is that the meaning of "preparing" in both definitions is boundless. Like cooking, editing is part art and part science, part drudgery and part exhilaration, part sound judgment and part flaming intuition. Like the serious cook, the editor approaches his or her vocation by trying to please the reader's palate without doing violence to the materials at hand. Regrettably, these goals have been known to conflict radically. Moreover, both cook and editor have a variety of expectations laid on them by people who don't understand the work very well, but who are sure to have definite tastes, whether grammatical or gastronomical. And as any experienced editor can tell you, what goes for cooks and the broth goes double for editors and the manuscript.

Nevertheless, both are noble callings pursued by noble beings. For the truly great practitioners of both professions, there is something profoundly satisfying about the process of bringing each creation to the peak of its potential, and serving it up as it was meant to be. And for each, the reward is the same: The creation itself evokes the "ooohs" and "aaahs," while the preparer smiles behind the door.

The Editor as Seed Crystal

LOGO•PHILE

On the theory that editors are just as narcissistic as the general population, and that we enjoy talking about ourselves just as much as failed actors and newly engaged couples, this LOGO*PHILE holds up the mirror to our sacred profession. The question is, what do we actually do?

First, since the glass doesn't lie, let's admit the truth. Despite the justifiable pride we may take in our craft, the living of an editor, like that of a book reviewer, is basically derivative. If it weren't for writers, most of us would be slinging hash instead of ink. Nonetheless, our profession does have standing of its own. There is some comfort, for example, in learning that—in English, at least—the verb *edit* did not come first, followed by the noun *editor*, as one might think. The *Oxford English Dictionary (OED)* reveals that *edit* is a back-formation from *editor*. (The *OED*'s first usage citation for *edit* is dated 1793; the first citation for *editor* is dated 1648.) This chronology does not necessarily mean that who we are takes precedence over what we do. It only revalidates the eternal truth that the ways of language are mysterious and there is no accounting for how some things get started.

A New Profession

Which brings us to point number two: Compared to a number of other professions, editing hasn't really been around all that long. It is only since the early eighteenth century that editors have been understood as persons who prepare the literary work of others for publication by a process of selection and revision. For about 150 years before that, *editor* was synonymous with *publisher*. Apparently, the assumption was that authors didn't need any help with their writing, only with the less savory task of getting it before the public. Thus, from the beginning, we editors have been in the mercantile mire. Knowledge of one's origins is a great antidote for professional hubris.

But like any useful new idea, the notion of an editor has caught on and gone from strength to strength. Like engineering, medicine, law, and theology, editing has proliferated specializations, continually rejustifying its precarious existence on the fringes of literature. There are acquisitions editors, line editors, copyeditors, photo editors, technical editors, abstract editors, style editors, story editors, general editors, and to supervise them all, editors-in-chief. Thus, editors have become like doctors; you don't know without asking what any of them really does.

Dinner with the Queen

What most editors mostly do (we're talking here about the ones who do *not* get to take authors to lunch at Elaine's or the Four Seasons) is to read manuscripts with pencil in hand, correcting the errors of organization and presentation that may confuse a reader, offend the canons of standard English usage and grammar, or aggravate the ulcer of a printer.

If that sounds like a piece of cake, you either do not understand editing at all or have not been doing it very long. The main problem with our profession, as William Bridgewater, former editor-in-chief of Columbia University Press has pointed out, is that it is a task without thoroughly set limits. In other words, in editing, as in dressing to go to dinner with the Queen, it's hard to know when you're "ready." And, truth to tell, more than anything else, what defines "ready" is that your manuscript, like your person at the palace, has a time beyond which, if it doesn't show up, it embarrasses everyone connected with the enterprise. You most of all.

Message and Medium

My own view of editing is a little more exciting than that, however. For me, editing is an immersion in the endlessly fascinating chemistry of the English language. I have yet to meet the editor who is really as self-absorbed as my tongue-in-cheek introduction to this column makes out. In truth, there is nothing editors care about so much as the endless possibilities for combination and recombination in language, and finding the right set of combinations for a particular manuscript. This passion is usually put in terms of the editor's responsibility to the author; what we really *must* care about is creating that arrangement of the author's words that best expresses the author's intention. What we seek is a kind of harmony, a crystallization in which message and medium merge.

When we do our jobs right, editors are like seed crystals. In chemistry, crystals are regular forms that seem to arise spontaneously and then replicate themselves in a stable manner. What sets this process off is a "seed crystal," which, when inserted into an assortment of molecules, brings those molecules together in a unique formation. Once the seed crystal is inserted, the molecules buzz around until, almost miraculously, they find the perfect arrangement to express exactly what they are. The result is maximum order and stability, in which all the molecules are organized in a way that leads to their continued existence. That's a job description for an editor if I ever heard one.

 (#118, 6/85)

The Editor's Art

Expert editors work in a triangle of happy relationships—with words, with people, and with the publication process. It takes a lot of effort and knowhow to work all three angles. (We never promised you a prose garden.)

The best of books won't substitute for experience, but some books go a long way toward distilling the knowhow. Two especially good books cover two of the three points of the triangle:

Getting the Words Right: How to Revise, Edit & Rewrite, by Theodore A. Rees Cheney (Cincinnati: Writer's Digest Books, 1983, 215 pp.) and *The Elements of Editing: A Modern Guide for Editors and Journalists*, by Arthur Plotnik (New York: Macmillan, 1982, 156 pp.).

The Words

Cheney presents an effective approach to getting every word in a manuscript right. He recommends a sequence of revision to follow "until you just naturally do it all simultaneously" and guides readers through the details of the three main steps.

Step 1: Reduction:

- Stand back from the manuscript and look objectively at the major chunks. Do they all belong?
- Move in a little closer. Are there paragraphs or sentences the manuscript could live without?
- Lean over the pages still closer. Are there idle, cluttering phrases or words?
- Finally, get out your magnifying glass. Could shorter words express the thought as clearly; could some words be shortened, even by a letter; and would contractions here and there be appropriate to the tone?

Step 2: The chapter on rethinking and rearranging clearly explains how to achieve unity, coherence, and emphasis. A small but telling point on emphasis:

Ironically, most cases of de-emphasis occur in a misguided attempt to gain extra emphasis. The de-emphasizers include

- the exclamation point
- the passive voice
- abstractions
- euphemisms
- intensives
- worn words
- hyperbole

Step 3: Rewording shows writers how to ensure good style and how to find their own. For example, "Scrutinize the verbs," Cheney says, making this point: "Is it a form of the verb "to be" (is, am, was, were, are, will be, etc.)? If it is, try to eliminate it."

I'm continually impressed by how my sentences are improved by dropping these weak-kneed forms of "to be." I used to hear my professors talk about them; I've read over and again how I must minimize them. Some time ago I decided to discipline myself in this regard. It's not easy. I find I can't get rid of them all. You can drive yourself crazy trying to rid your writing of every single form of "to be," but you should make a firm effort to do so.

The point, of course, is that finding a substitute verb, especially an active one, perks up the entire sentence. You may have to turn the sentence around or inside out, but it comes out stronger.

The Publication Process

Plotnik devotes few pages to "the agony and the agony" of the craft of line editing—the material Cheney covers so thoroughly. *The Elements of Editing* addresses the range of practical problems confronting a new editor—"enough guidance to let new staff get on with their work and learn by doing."

With humor and common sense, Plotnik provides "handy, practical, wide-ranging and short-winded advice" on such matters as the steps in processing a manuscript, copyright, the basics of graphics and photography, and trouble-shooting for libel or invasion of privacy. One sample of his advice is Plotnik's definition of editorial perception.

> *Perception* for editors means hearing what the author is trying to say while keeping an ear tuned to the sensibilities of the readers. Listening to the author requires empathy and a suppression of ego.

Plotnik knows well that deadlines often prevent the complete treatment presented in Cheney's book:

> The most common failing of inexperienced copy editors is inconsistency in the depth of their work on a given project. They approach a fat manuscript in an attack mode, full of fighting spirit, and completely rewrite the first three pages, carefully checking the accuracy of every revised statement and bringing the prose up to a biblical level. Then, exhausted and short on time, they scan the remaining pages for nothing more than omitted commas and throw the script on the boss's desk with a "Whew!"

He discusses the kind of editing a manuscript needs (some "require more attention to fact than to beauty") and the level of editing needed. His description of planning for a 6,000-word manuscript about a tennis player:

> I plan my level of editing according to the time I have available for the job. Perhaps something like this:
> *One day:* Correct spelling and the worst grammatical errors; style according to house rules of punctuation, numbers, capitalization, etc.; resolve inconsistencies; check any statements that seem absurd or actionable.
> *Two days:* In addition to the above, rework some of the prose to make it more active and concrete; cut or shift a few paragraphs to create a powerful opening and logical development. Spot-check one or two sources (the brat himself, if possible) to be sure they are being quoted accurately.
> *Three days:* In addition, rewrite some of the weakest passages, establishing a momentum that keeps the reader going; carefully cut any passages interfering with this momentum and provide the necessary transition; check as many facts as possible with resources at hand or nearby. Thoroughly reread the revised manuscript and judge it against the author's original tone and intent, conferring with the author if there are serious differences and with an attorney if legal questions remain.

Plotnik describes the "editorial personality" in terms of good and bad compulsiveness. The signs of dysfunctional (editor-related) compulsiveness include

- holding to favorite rules of usage, whatever the effect on communication,
- musing for 15 minutes on whether to use a hairline or one-point rule, and
- changing every passive construction to an active one.

The signs of functional (reader-oriented) compulsiveness include

- following up (Plotnik's mantra: Nothing happens when it's supposed to happen without well-timed reminders),
- rewriting every headline that fails to motivate readership,
- quadruple-checking page proofs,
- staring at the type specifications you've written a full 10 seconds (to be sure they're right),
- reading every word in its final context, and
- insisting that work begin on the next issue as soon as the last one is put to bed.

Who Can Use These Books?

- Subject experts who can't write well

Back in 1979 (Issue 32), a reader of *The Eye* asked if anyone had guidelines to help authors who know their subject but don't know how to write well. At last we have an answer: Insist that such writers read every word of *Getting the Words Right*—because, of course, improving writing always involves expert revision.

- Experienced editors

Editors of other people's writing (professional revisers) will enjoy reading Cheney as they would enjoy listening to a respected colleague who may confirm their convictions, offer new ideas on how to go about their wordwork, or both.

Editors who would "rather proofread five-point type than train new staff" can refer new staff to Plotnik's book, which fully meets its purpose—"to lighten the basic-training load of busy editors or at least mitigate their guilt over doing nothing."

- New editors

Plotnik has written a good primer for new editorial staff. A cover blurb calls it "the perfect companion to *The Elements of Style*." Not so. Strunk and

White's classic belongs on every editor's bookshelf, but it is neither so thorough nor so easily assimilated as Plotnik's book.

I recommend Cheney as Plotnik's companion for training. Beginning editors who absorb the two books will be well on their way to mastery of the craft and the art of editing.

—Peggy Smith (#107, 8/84)

Commandments for Copyeditors

1. Thou shalt not change the author's meaning.
2. Thou shalt not introduce new errors; especially shalt thou not change something correct to something incorrect.
3. Thou shalt change nothing except to improve it.
4. Thou shalt hearken to thy instructions and do precisely what is expected of thee.
5. Thou shalt honor and obey those in charge over thee.
6. Thou shalt mark clearly and write legibly in a color that photocopies well.
7. Thou shalt protect the manuscript from rain, hail, wind, coffee, children, pets, and all things damaging.
8. Thou shalt meet thy deadlines.
9. Thou shalt assume nothing but shalt seek answers to all things doubtful or unspecified.
10. Thou shalt read and study the English language continually.

(#36, 12/79)

Editing Standards: Department of Defense

Continuing our effort to publish editorial standards and policies from a variety of organizations, we present excerpts from the Department of Defense *Technical Writing Style Guide.*

Desirable Editor Attitudes

Be reader conscious. Think usability. All writing problems must be solved with maximum provision for the needs of the user. At all times ensure maximum readability and comprehensibility as a basic requirement for whoever your readers may be.

Be skeptical. Take nothing for granted. Don't be unduly impressed with apparent authenticity of either source material supplied or the manuscript. Be alert for discrepancies; clear up all questionable items.

Be objective. Have a substantial reason or authority for every change you suggest. Do not make changes on the basis of merely personal preference or on the basis of what you may think is "conventional" practice. Because it has been done this way for umpteen years does not necessarily mean it is better than the writer's input—unless it is inconsistent with other parts of the manual or other manuals and may cause confusion. An editor's preferences may be not better than those of the original writer and changing only results in waste of time.

Be accurate and consistent. Avoid substituting a new set of mistakes or inconsistencies for those originally present.

Be well informed. An editor should be an expert in the following areas:

- Good grammar
- Style-guide rules
- Standard editing marks
- Security regulations and contractual requirements
- Applicable specifications and deviations
- Technical aspects of equipment or system involved

Editors who are not expert in all these subjects should take steps to become so.

How a Writer Can Facilitate Editing

In addition to technically accurate and complete manuscript content, there are some simple precautions which the writer can take to greatly facilitate the mechanics of editing. Some of these are

Avoid overcrowding a page. Double- or triple-space between lines. Double-double space between paragraphs. Leave wide margins. Leave at least a 1-inch margin on left side so that no information can get lost in punching holes or binding pages.

Write legibly. Form letters and numbers or symbols recognizably. Use adequate pressure on writing tool. Place date in position it is intended to be. Use standard edit marks as necessary; rewrite if necessary.

Number pages in sequence.

Use one side of page only.

Use same size sheets for all entries ($8\frac{1}{2} \times 11''$). Small notepaper may get lost; flaps which need to be lifted on larger sheets become tattered and illegible and may be overlooked in typing.

By comparison of cost to writer's or editor's time, paper is cheap. Adequate blank space on a page can save time and help ensure understandability of the editing. An already overcrowded page which needs a heavy edit is a potential source of errors and misunderstandings.

Suggestions to the Editor

Never blank out or erase original input so that it can no longer be referred to. If you have second thoughts about your edit and wish to unedit it, the use of correction tape on edit is acceptable. However, DO NOT use non-transparent correction tape on manuscript original input. Also, if you have totally rewritten a page, DO NOT throw away the original page. There is always a chance that you may have misunderstood the writer's reason for his version and it may be necessary to go back to it. If it is destroyed that becomes impossible.

Edit in a different color or a different line weight of writing tool from the original manuscript. The editing should stand out conspicuously from the manuscript for clarity and easy recheck by the original writer. The color and intensity of changes or corrections should be capable of producing legible copies on copying machines available. Yellow wax pencil is helpful for identifying areas checked on schematics or diagrams.

Don't overcrowd editing so that it is difficult to understand what goes where. It saves time and errors in the end to rewrite a line or a sentence with the desired changes. (This is particularly pertinent where the manuscript has been single-spaced.) Be liberal with rewriting your desired version as an insert on an additional page, placed before the page to which it applies. On the manuscript page use a caret to show where the insert belongs.

(#5, 4/78)

From Section 19, pp. 19/1, 19/2, and 19/3. Approved manual for use by all departments and agencies of the Department of Defense, MIL-HDBK-63038-2 (TM) 1 May 1977.

Editorial Style: Consistency Is the Aim

"Knowledge of editorial style is what distinguishes the copyeditor from the English teacher," said Laura Horowitz when she taught copyediting at George Washington University.

The aim of a set of style rules is to eliminate inconsistencies that would distract the reader and reduce a publication's quality. Style rules provide guidance on abbreviation, capitalization, compounding, punctuation, numbers, spelling, and word division. Editorial style may also dictate word choice (memoranda, memorandums; toward, towards) and the treatment of foreign words, book titles, quotations, footnotes, and bibliographic data.

. . . . . .

Many organizations codify their own "house" style. Some widely used style guides are published by the American Psychological Association, the Council of Biology Editors, the American Medical Association, the Modern Language Association, United Press International, the Associated Press, *The New York Times,* and *The Washington Post,* as well as by GPO and the

University of Chicago Press. *Words into Type* (Prentice-Hall) is a standard reference in many organizations.

The chart shows a few examples of differences in editorial style according to the GPO *Style Manual*, *A Manual of Style* (The University of Chicago Press), and *The Associated Press Stylebook*.

Category	**GPO Style**	**Chicago Style**	**AP Style**
■ Abbreviations			
– Eastern standard time	e.s.t.	EST	EST
– ships	the U.S.S. *Iowa*	the U.S.S. *Iowa*	the U.S.S. Iowa
■ Capitalization	The Star-Spangled Banner Lake Erie, Lakes Erie and Ontario Washington State, the State of Washington	The Star-spangled Banner Lake Erie, Lakes Erie and Ontario Washington State, the state of Washington	The Star-Spangled Banner Lake Erie, lakes Erie and Ontario Washington state, the state of Washington
■ Compounding	a well-worn book, the book is well worn	a well-worn book, the book is well worn	a well-worn book, the book is well-worn, the book looks well worn
■ Punctuation			
– serial comma	a, b, and c	a, b, and c	a, b and c
– apostrophe	the 1920's	the 1920s	the 1920s
■ Numbers	They had many animals: 10 dogs, 6 cats, and 97 hamsters.	They had many animals: ten dogs, six cats, and ninety-seven hamsters.	They had many animals: 10 dogs, six cats and 97 hamsters.
■ Word division	ad-verb-i-al pe-ren-ni-al	ad-ver-bi-al pe-ren-ni-al	ad-ver-bi-al per-en-ni-al

(#48, 10/80)

The Conscientious Copyeditor at Work

. . . ~~whose~~ *the* broad stripes and bright sta~~rs~~ *of which* through the perilous fight . . .

—*Francis Scott Key*

The wages of sin ~~is~~ *are* death.
For thine ~~is~~ *are* the kingdom~~,~~ and the power~~,~~ and the glory.

—*King James Bible*

The tumult and the shouting die~~s~~.

—*Rudyard Kipling*

To be~~,~~ or not to be: ~~that is~~ *those are* the question*s*. . . . And damn'd be ~~him that~~ *he who* first cries, "Hold, enough!"

—*William Shakespeare*

These are the times that try men's *and women's* souls.

—*Thomas Paine*

~~Four score and~~ *Eighty-*seven years ago . . .

—*Abraham Lincoln*

When ~~in the course of human events it becomes necessary for~~ one people *need* to dissolve the political bands ~~which~~ *that* have connected them . . .

—*Thomas Jefferson*

(#51, 11/80)

What Is Technical Editing?

Although the tools and techniques used in technical editing have changed considerably over . . . 15 years, a number of problems—including defining the job and devising the best training for it—remain no closer to solution now than in 1967, according to participants in a workshop led by three veterans in the field.

Mary Fran Buehler, Alberta Cox, and Lola Zook, who shared a platform at the International Technical Communications Conference (ITCC) in 1967 and then again in May 1982, reviewed some of the major changes in technical editing that have taken place in the intervening years.

The major change most participants mentioned is the considerable increase in the sophistication of the technical editing process. Controlled efforts to apply different levels of editing to different types of material and to modify materials to fit the specific interests and literacy levels of an audience were among the examples cited to illustrate the greater skills and flexibility technical editors are now expected to have.

The potential benefits and limitations of "computer editing," now in the developmental stage, also were vehemently debated. Participants agreed, however, that computer-assisted routines are already useful in copyediting and formatting.

Lingering Problems

Whatever the changes, a wide range of opinions about the nature of technical editing was still evident in the conference discussions. Some participants tended to define *technical* narrowly, in some cases limiting it to fields related to engineering. Others used the term broadly, suggesting that *technical* could cover specialized content in almost any art, trade, profession, or discipline.

Some people said that *technical editors* should be trained in communication skills and then learn the particular technical content on the job. Others suggested that prospective editors should first receive scientific training and then be taught publishing skills on the job. The same argument was being waged in 1967. During the interval, however, technical communications programs at universities and colleges have expanded from perhaps 5 in 1967 to more than 30 now, a development that indicates wider recognition that special qualifications are needed for competent work in this field.

The problem of identifying audience characteristics clearly continues to plague technical editors and managers. The most difficult assignment, editors agreed, is the manuscript that has several important but conflicting audiences—technical peers and nontechnical decision makers, for example. Participants who had experience in tailoring technical material to specific purposes offered various editorial approaches to organization and language for such material.

(#73, 5/82)

Black Eyes

Today, as many as 70 million Americans suffer from [headaches] on a regular basis, and because of them patients make about 18 million visits to a doctor.

—No wonder we can't get an appointment.

—*The Cincinnati Post*
April 6, 1984

His activities today are "almost a 360 degree turn" from the life he knew in the Ukraine, Walter said in a rare interview.

—Right back where he started from.

—*The Cincinnati Post*
April 9, 1984

Thanks to Marion Curry, Cincinnati, Ohio

(#107, 8/84)

Test Yourself

Editor's Maze

The following maze, by Ruth D. Hill, is reprinted from *Editor & Publisher* (Sept 6, 1980).

The 52 words most often misspelled by editors, writers, and college graduates, listed on page 4, are hidden—correctly spelled—in the maze below.

You can refer to the list or you can try to work the puzzle without the list.

Draw a ring around the words, which may appear horizontally (left to right or right to left), vertically (up or down), and diagonally (up or down). We show you three words already ringed. Note that letters of words may overlap.

Nine letters will be left. Put them together to spell out what you can do to improve your mind and your spelling. Caution: Work neatly or you may not be able to spot the leftover letters.

One word is misspelled in the maze. It is also misspelled elsewhere in this issue.

D	E	M	A	G	O	G	U	E	T	A	L	I	H	I	N	N	A
E	I	I	T	S	Y	L	A	T	A	C	A	M	P	A	I	G	N
T	N	S	M	U	I	N	N	E	L	L	I	M	S	I	E	V	E
A	N	C	S	P	H	L	E	G	M	A	C	H	I	E	V	E	O
D	O	E	U	I	S	U	D	C	E	M	E	T	E	R	Y	N	P
I	C	L	P	N	P	S	C	R	O	A	K	A	L	F	Y	G	B
P	U	L	E	O	I	A	D	U	E	L	N	O	I	R	N	E	U
A	O	A	R	C	G	G	T	T	A	G	O	L	S	I	N	A	S
L	U	N	S	U	O	E	E	E	E	A	W	G	S	C	A	N	I
I	S	E	E	L	T	L	Z	G	D	E	L	E	I	A	R	C	T
D	B	O	D	A	H	N	A	E	E	O	E	T	M	S	Y	E	I
Y	R	U	E	T	M	L	T	I	E	T	D	E	D	S	T	S	L
C	O	S	A	E	E	T	R	E	C	A	G	L	A	E	W	N	L
A	C	P	D	S	I	I	Z	L	X	R	E	E	U	E	H	E	I
T	C	N	U	M	A	I	A	W	E	I	R	D	Z	Z	O	C	S
S	O	F	O	R	E	I	G	N	Y	F	E	U	Q	I	L	I	N
C	L	L	P	S	H	E	R	I	F	F	A	C	I	A	L	L	O
E	I	Z	E	P	H	Y	R	A	S	P	B	E	R	R	Y	E	T

Answers

The nine leftover letters spell "DO A PUZZLE." The misspelling in the maze is *ecstacy*, also misspelled in Black Eyes; its correct spelling is *ecstasy*.

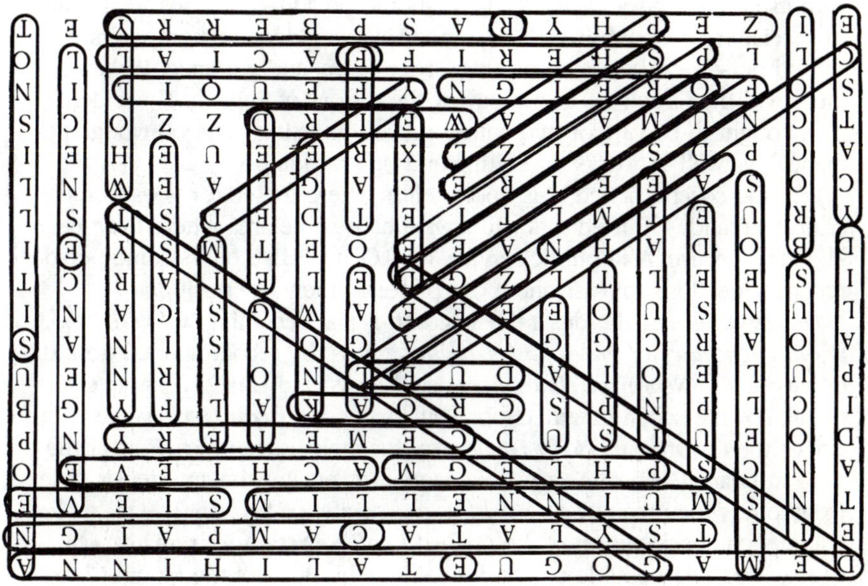

(#58, 5/81)

■ Depth at Every Position

LOGO•PHILE

Editors are like coaches. The lives of both are dominated by next week's game, and both continually fiddle with "the lineup" in search of the elusive combination of elements that will produce a winner. Coaches characteristically seek the answer to this problem in "depth at every position." They know that without a strong bench, the team can't play well consistently.

The editor's bench is the bookshelf. Here, too, the name of the game is depth at every position. Editors need two or three general dictionaries, each with its singular advantages. To these should be added dictionaries peculiar to special areas of publishing, e.g., medicine, engineering, computers. There should be several books on writing, style, usage, and grammar. Perhaps there will be a book on etymology or the history of English. There definitely ought to be one or two collections of quotations, a good typography manual, as well as works on editing and proofreading.

Like the coach's bench, this bookshelf is where the editor goes to meet critical situations. But editors will always have some area where they feel slightly insecure. As a public service, the LOGO*PHILE offers some personal recommendations for just one more player at a few key positions.

Dictionaries. For the desk, the standard is fast becoming *Webster's New World Dictionary of the English Language*. It is the recommended desk dictionary at *The New York Times,* Associated Press, and United Press International. For the second team, choose either the *American Heritage Dictionary* or the *Oxford American Dictionary* for their usage notes. But for the pure in heart, *Webster's Second International* remains the apotheosis of lexicography, which many *New World* users specify for backup. The two-volume, compact edition of the *Oxford English Dictionary* remains, of course, the best possible reason for joining the Book of the Month Club (although you don't get the supplements).

Usage. Here, happily, the depth problem can be solved readily. Most editors know and use several standard works, but Roy Copperud's *American Usage and Style: The Consensus* (Van Nostrand Reinhold, 1980) compares books by nine major usage authorities (Bernstein, Bryant, Copperud, Evans and Evans, Flesch, Follett, Fowler/Gowers, Mager and Mager, and Morris and Morris) and summarizes their views. It is the most helpful book on usage in print.

Style. The equivalent to Copperud in the area of style is *Words Into Type* (Prentice-Hall, 1974) by Marjorie Skillin and Robert Gay. In addition to their comprehensive treatment of style, Skillin and Gay provide a large grammar section, as well as chapters on such topics as preparing manuscripts for publication, copyright, reading copy, typography, and commonly confused words. They also include a thorough discussion of printing technology and an exhaustive glossary of printing and typesetting terms.

Grammar. Most editors will have a copy of George Kittredge and Frank Farley's *Advanced English Grammar* (Folcroft, 1973), unfortunately out of print, or for quick reference a student handbook like the *Harbrace College Handbook* (Harcourt Brace Jovanovich, 1984) by John C. Hodges and Mary E. Whitten. But for real depth you can't beat George O. Curme's *A Grammar of the English Language* (Verbatim edition, 1980). Finding one's way around the two volumes (*Parts of Speech* and *Syntax*) takes getting used to, as does Curme's occasionally recondite style (here the depth threatens to become bottomless), but if you are looking for a discussion of the optative subjunctive, you will find it here. Examples are superabundant.

Thesaurus. Here I would favor putting Roget on the bench to provide the depth and putting another, less well known work in the starting lineup. The best English thesaurus in print is *The Synonym Finder* by J.I. Rodale, as completely revised by Laurence Urdang (Rodale Press, 1978). It contains more than a million synonyms arranged alphabetically; thus, unlike Roget, Rodale doesn't make you look up everything twice.

Book of Quotations. The main entry sections of the standard works are arranged chronologically (*Bartlett's Familiar Quotations*) and alphabetically by author (*The Oxford Dictionary of Quotations*). Either is fine for checking quotations, but topically arranged volumes are more useful when looking for an apt line to spice up a piece of writing. Here again, depth comes from two seldom-mentioned works. *Webster's Treasury of Relevant Quotations* (Merriam Webster, 1978) by Edward F. Murphy provides access to many quotable writers who do not appear in other collections. The *Dictionary of Quotations* (Delacorte, 1968, out of print), edited by Bergen Evans, arranges quotations chronologically within topics. The book also provides many subcategories—under "Love," for example, there are 26; under "God," 9.

General Knowledge and Fact Checking. As is well known, *The Encyclopaedia Britannica* is not a handy desk reference. The *New Columbia Encyclopedia* is an excellent one-volume reference book—in my view the best. To acquire depth, however, editors should have a copy of *The Harper Dictionary of Modern Thought* (Harper, 1977), edited by Alan Bullock and Oliver Stallybrass, which contains thumbnail descriptions of many topics Columbia doesn't deal with, such as *multivariate analysis*, *fiscal policy*, and *social Darwinism*. For checking facts, it's still hard to beat *The World Almanac and Book of Facts*, or the *Information Please Almanac*, both published annually. Many editors simply buy them in alternate years. Where else can you find out the cost of sending an 8-ounce package via air parcel post to Malawi ($6.50) without making a phone call? That, fellow coaches, is depth.

 (#106, 7/84)

Are Writers and Editors Obsolescent?

Is Quality Writing Obsolescent?

Printed media may be almost extinct by the year 2000, if the prophecies of a panel of six professional communicators are accurate. The panelists spoke at a symposium of the World Future Society in Washington in July 1982 on the impact of technological change on the communications industry. Among their topics were the bleak prospects for printed books and the people who write and edit them, the erosion of language subtleties by "computerese," and the obsolescence of sophisticated editorial skills.

Demise of Printed Books and Their Authors

By the end of the century, books as we know them will be rare, expensive, beautifully produced artifacts, predicted Joseph Foote, president, Joseph Foote Associates. While technological advances are enhancing the speed and economy of print production, electronic media are swiftly taking over the information and entertainment functions of newspapers, magazines, and books. Foote believes that this process will continue until printed books serve chiefly as collectors' items.

Bernard Asbell, investigative reporter and biographer, believes he is part of a vanishing species. Citing statistics showing that only 11 percent of the American population bought a book last year and only 25 percent read a book, Asbell said he can foresee no way for writers to live by writing books. They may, of course, write for the various electronic media that are supplanting books, but will devote less time and care to writing. Asbell believes that writing will become the province of the wealthy, of academicians, and of part-time authors who support themselves by other work.

Availability of Data for Research

Roger Bezdek, an economics writer with the Treasury Department, discussed the availability of data for research, noting that the U.S. government remains an extremely rich and often ignored source of free information for writers.

Several commercial firms, he said, have prospered by repackaging and selling such information. In the future, the government may charge a fee for use of its information, and private enterprise will probably play a greater role in its dissemination. He predicted that computer terminals will replace books as the chief research medium.

Effects of "Computerese" on Language

Marvin Grosswirth, a freelance journalist, examined the effects of "computerese" on language. He said that the subtlety of the language is threatened by the need for standardized language that can be interpreted by computers and can be used for quick, simple communication. Grosswirth stressed that just as a personal interview provides a richer quality of information than a telephone interview, exploring a library of books offers a richer experience than scanning information on a computer terminal. Writers must guard against loss of subtlety and precision in their use of language, and preserve its riches for their readers.

Obsolescence of Editing Skills

Mellen Candage, president of Grammarians, Inc., described today's editing skills as obsolescent. Audio and visual images are replacing written text. Quality editing takes more time than the information industry will be willing to spend, because the primary need will be to pass information on to consumers as quickly as possible. Moreover, educated readers who demand well-crafted prose are disappearing. She predicted that editors will either become "word mechanics," involved in all production steps, or will move from editing to writing.

Copyright Dilemma

The future of copyright and royalties is cloudy, according to Flora Davis, a contributor to *Mademoiselle* magazine. Use of copying machines already makes copyright violation of printed materials an everyday occurrence. Audio and visual materials and even computer programs are readily pirated. In the United States, library users contribute no royalties to the authors whose books they read.

Of the solutions to the copyright dilemma now being considered, none is ideal. It is possible to equip copying machines with recorders so that authors can be compensated for copies of their work, but these recorders could be circumvented. Current efforts to encode electronic media to prevent unauthorized duplication are repeatedly foiled by ingenious pirates. Charging users of computer terminals for access to information endangers the users' privacy.

Governments in England and the Scandinavian countries administer a library lending fee that helps compensate authors for use of their works. Some writers want a similar system for this country, but librarians fear the burden of recordkeeping that would be involved.

Royalties might simply be abolished, said Davis. Like screenwriters, authors could sell all rights to their works for a flat fee. Davis, like most of the writers in the audience, found this idea abhorrent because she thinks it would remove much of the incentive and pride that spurs writers to create.

Audience Reaction

When moderator Shirley Rosenberg, president of SSR, Inc., invited the audience to discuss the panelists' ideas, many people expressed dismay over the fate of printed media that the speakers predicted. Writers did not dislike the idea of writing for electronic or computerized media so much as they decried the idea of abandoning reading the printed page. For the futurists at this symposium, printed books and newspapers are still the friendliest medium, and libraries filled with books and helpful human beings still the best tools of their trade.

—Lee Mickle (#77, 8/82)

II. SPECIAL EDITORIAL PROBLEMS
NEUTRAL LANGUAGE

Check Out Your Sexism

Jean Ward, a former staff writer for *The Minneapolis Tribune* who now teaches journalism at the University of Minnesota, has compiled a guide to sexist presumptions from examples in the print media. She invites readers to match the excerpts from news accounts to the sexist presumptions they reflect. In some cases, more than one presumption may apply.

A Journalist's Guide to Sexist Presumptions

A. All people are male unless proven female.
B. A woman's relationship to a man (or men) is her defining identity.
C. A woman's appearance always requires comment, whether she defies or exemplifies a popular stereotype.
D. A woman can safely be identified as "his wife"; it is unnecessary to identify her by name.
E. Although stylebooks prohibit words with grafted feminine endings and such designations as "coed," ignore the rule if that suits you.
F. After marriage, a man remains a man and a woman becomes a wife.
G. Homemaking and parenting are not work.
H. It is newsworthy when a church member, parent, and neighbor is successful in business or the professions, provided the successful person is a woman.
I. Status as housewife takes precedence over all other kinds of status.
J. Events in a woman's life must be identified as A.M. (Ante Marriage) or P.M. (Post Marriage).

Test Yourself

On Sexist Presumptions

Match the examples below to the preceding sexist presumptions.

______ 1. The "documentary" delightfully explores the rivalries between different orchestral sections, as well as some of the personal ones, like the feud between a woman cellist who takes nips from a whiskey bottle and a violinist she accuses of molesting little girls.

—*The Minneapolis Tribune* 11/14/79

______ 2. An Illinois man and wife were charged here Tuesday with illegal possession and intent to sell about 12 pounds of hashish worth about $30,000.

—Associated Press 10/11/79

______ 3. At 38, she is still a stunner, with a robust sense of humor, a throaty, husky laugh and green eyes that sparkle like gemstones.

—Associated Press 10/10/79

______ 4. To her neighbors in the Baltimore suburb of Towson, Md., Jean M. Kirk is simply a pleasant, church-going, working housewife and mother of four. But then there's the T. Rowe Price Associates Inc. business card that carries the title of assistant vice president.

—*The Wall Street Journal* 11/13/79

______ 5. The death penalty will be sought against a 24-year-old South Side man who pleaded guilty Tuesday to kidnapping, raping and murdering a doctor's wife last year, prosecutors said.

—*The Chicago Tribune* 10/10/79

______ 6. San Francisco inducted its first group of homosexuals into the Police Department Tuesday. Nine women and 16 minority race recruits also were in the class of 50 cadets.

—UPI 11/14/79

______ 7. For most farmers, a wife is an immense asset as a livestock feeder, errand-runner and extra tractor-driver. But Mr. Nelson's wife, Leona, is more than that; she ran the farm single-handedly 5 days a week for 20 years.

—*The Wall Street Journal* 5/22/79

______ 8. In fact, though no one ever talks about it very much, booze has played as big a part in the lives of modern American writers as talent, money, women, and the longing to be top dog.

—*Commentary* 3/76

______ 9. *Headline:* REENTERING COLLEGE: OLDER WOMEN BATTLE TO BECOME COEDS AGAIN

—*The Los Angeles Times* 9/9/79

______ 10. The Etelsons were married in 1950, and for the first years of their marriage, Mrs. Etelson operated a cafeteria in an industrial plant. She stopped working between 1958 and 1961 to care for her two young daughters.

—*The Wall Street Journal* 5/4/78

______ 11. Thatcher—"Maggie" to her friends and to Fleet Street, "Mrs. T" to politicians outside her inner circle, and "the Blessed Margaret" to the Conservatives' resident wit, Norman St. John-Stevas—is a small, fine-boned woman, with pale blue eyes, the kind of complexion the English always liken to a rose. . . .

—*The New York Times* 4/29/79

______ 12. Mundal, Norway—On a summer's day in 1856, a farmer named Fredrik Mundal, his wife and their 6-year-old son, Ole, set out on a long and perilous journey from this remote village of 400 people, nestled beneath the mighty Jostedalsbre glacier along the spectacular Fjaerlands Fjord.

—*The New York Times* 4/16/79

______ 13. *Headline:* WOMAN PHOTOGRAPHER WINS SMITH SABBATICAL

—*The Minneapolis Tribune* 5/9/79

______ 14. Anne Millard doesn't fit most people's idea of a farmer. She stands just over 5 feet tall and, in her work clothes, weighs somewhere around 110 pounds. But she owns 800 acres in Cottonwood County, farms 480 of those herself and raises chickens, hogs and cattle. Not bad for a 60-year-old widow.

—*The Minneapolis Tribune* 12/5/76

Answers

1. A
2. F
3. C
4. G, H
5. B
6. A
7. A, I
8. A
9. E
10. G, J
11. C
12. D
13. A
14. B, C

—Excerpted from the *Columbia Journalism Review,* May/June 1980 (#73, 5/82)

Avoiding Sexism in Language, DOL Style

Does He or She or S/He or Do They or Does One?

Because so much sexism in language occurs in discussions of work, *The Editorial Eye* thought the following Labor Department guidelines on sexist language would be useful as an authoritative reference.

These guidelines appeared in a request for proposals issued by the Employment and Training Administration.

All written materials issued by a contractor or grantee shall conform to the following guidelines for eliminating sexist language and artwork:

1. *Avoid the use of sex references in job titles.* Titles should conform to the Census Bureau's occupational classification system and the 1976 edition of the *Dictionary of Occupational Titles.*

   —Longshore workers instead of longshoremen.

2. *Avoid the use of male and female gender word forms.*

   —Aviator to include men and women pilots, not aviatrix.

3. *Include both sexes by using terms that refer to people as a whole.*

   —Human beings or people instead of mankind.

4. *Avoid the use of masculine and feminine pronouns or adjectives in referring to a hypothetical person or people in general.* Change sentences such as: The average American worker spends 20 years of *his* life in the workforce.

   —By rewording to eliminate unnecessary gender pronouns and adjectives. (The average American worker spends 20 years in the workforce.)

   —By recasting into the plural. (Most Americans spend 20 years of their lives. . .)

   —By replacing the masculine or feminine pronoun or adjective with "one," "you," "he or she," "her or him," or "his or her." (An average American spends 20 years of his or her life in the workforce.)

5. *Refer to both men and women in such generic terms* as economist, doctor, or lawyer. Identify sex through the use of pronouns.

   —The lawyer made her final summation.

6. *Avoid the use of stereotyped terms or expressions such as "man-sized" job.*

   —Employee-years and employee-hours (or staff-hours) instead of man-years and man-hours.

7. The use of *artwork in publications* should conform to the following guidelines:
   a. Strive to use racially and sexually balanced designs.
   b. Depict both men and women in artwork on general subject matters.
   c. Show men and women in a variety of roles in photographs, illustrations, and drawings.
   d. Show women and men as managers and skilled laborers.

(#6, 5/78)

He or She: Author Objects to Editors' Changes

I have been writing a lot of medical articles for an encyclopedia over the past couple of years, and now the galley proofs are starting to arrive. The gratuitous insertion of "or she" whenever I use generic "he" bugs me, so I wrote the enclosed letter to the managing editor. The issue of "sexism" in language seems to be a perennial one in *The Editorial Eye*, so I thought you might want to reprint my letter. (The letter follows:)

> I have changed "he or she" and "his or her" back to the generic, perfectly correct, and noncumbersome "he" and "his" in a couple of enclosed galley proofs. I don't think the medical care system will fail to come to the

aid of a woman in a coma, for example, if the words "or she" and "or her" are left out of my description of that condition. Nor do I think that leaving them out will cause anyone intelligent enough to read an encyclopedia to conclude that only males become comatose.

I like to think that your encyclopedia will outlast all this trendy messing around with the language to make political points whose impact on real social problems is zero. I simply don't believe that bludgeoning the reader with the obvious fact that both men and women can sink into a coma is going to fling open the doors of opportunity for women, ease the plight of middle-age housewives who have been abandoned by their husbands, guarantee the uninterrupted flow of alimony and child support payments, and abolish wife abuse and rape.

My practice is to use potentially jarring phrases like "he or she" and "his or her" sparingly, when it is vital to stress that someone may be of either sex, and then only when referring to a specific individual. For example: The murderer left few clues at the scene of the crime, but investigators suspect that he or she was known by the victim.

The irony is that while my articles were zealously purged of nonexistent "sexism" they were replete with serious typesetting errors.

—Peter Petrakis (#33, 10/79)

II. SPECIAL EDITORIAL PROBLEMS
QUOTES

How to Convert Direct Quotation to Indirect

An indispensable skill in reporting and editing is the deft conversion of direct speech into indirect speech. This operation often can transmute the confused verbatim record of a stormy meeting into a clear, fluent, even elegant summary.

Formulas for this editorial alchemy may be found in the United Nations' guidelines on indirect speech. For writers of minutes, briefing or interview summaries, or meeting reports, here are some of the U.N. techniques:

1. To change direct or quoted speech to indirect or reported speech, add a principal clause containing a verb in the past tense of *say*, *think*, *report*, etc. (He said that . . . , she reported that. . .). Although not repeated in every sentence, this clause governs the tenses of all the verbs.

2. Even if the statement in the subordinate "that" clause is obviously still valid at the time of reporting, make the verb in the subordinate clause agree with the past tense of the verb in the main clause. (He said that the sun was 93 million miles from the earth.)

3. Change future tenses (shall, will, will be doing, shall have done, will have done) to the corresponding secondary future tenses (should, would, would be doing, should have done, would have done).

4. Generally, use the auxiliary "must" where it was used in direct speech. (She warned that steps must be taken.)

5. Use infinitive phrases to avoid awkward repetition of "that." (Change "It has been shown that the population is falling" to "He pointed out that the population had been shown to be falling.")

6. Change personal pronouns and possessive adjectives in the first and second persons to the third person. (Change "I must stress that you cannot have your cake and eat it" to "She stressed that they could not have their

cake and eat it" or "She stressed that it was impossible to have one's cake and eat it.")

7. Change adverbs, adverbial phrases, and adjectives denoting time and place to more indirect forms. (Change *here* to *there*, *now* to *then* or *at that time* or *currently*, *present* to *current* or *existing*, *today* to *that day*, *yesterday* to *the day before*, *tomorrow* to *the day after*, *ago* to *before* or *earlier*.)

   (An omnibus—if ponderous—example: Change "In keeping with the position I took yesterday, I ask that the present tax rate be reduced here and now to its level of a year ago" to "In keeping with the position he had taken the day before, he asked that the existing tax rate be reduced there and then to its level of a year earlier.")

8. Change the words *this* and *these* to *that* and *those*. In cases of ambiguity, change *this* and *these* to *the*. (Change "The aim of this conference is to stimulate debate" to "The aim of the conference was to stimulate debate.")

(#42, 4/80)

■ Is It Wrong to Tamper with a Quotation?

"This journalist, like most, feels it's a cardinal sin to tamper with a quote, even if the effect is to turn it into correct English," Bob Levey, columnist for *The Washington Post,* recently wrote. "Honesty is my policy—because it's the best policy."

Levey was justifying his use of uncorrected quotations from a letter writer who had written about "the confusion of my mother and I" and from a telephone caller who had referred to women as "girls."

Is Levey's kind of honesty the best policy for all circumstances? The answer often depends on whether the quotation is from a written source or a spoken source. And the answer can vary with different authorities, publications, and quoters.

What May You Correct in Quoting from a Written Source?

Responsible writers and editors know they must be sure that quotations repeat an original written source nearly word for word and letter for letter (with omissions and interpolations clearly indicated).

Different authorities specify different style rules on what and how changes can be made. The principle behind any codified style, however, is the same: to be clear and grammatical within the context while being fair to the source.

Some style guides more than others assume that the reader understands that certain small changes may be made without notice. Such changes include capitalizing or lowercasing an initial letter to fit the context.

Few style guides, however, permit correction of errors. Chicago style permits correction of obvious typos without notice in quoting from a modern document but calls for retention of "any idiosyncrasy of spelling" in quoting from an older work. Other style guides specify that either the suggested correction or the word *sic* be put in brackets after an error.

But style rules are not the same as the courtesy rules that apply to letters to the editor. Some publications post notice; for example, *Time* magazine says, "Letters may be edited for purposes of clarity or space." *The Washington Post* warns, "Because of space limitations, [letters] published are subject to abridgment."

Some publications routinely correct blatant errors without notice but check with the letter writer before making extensive changes. *New York Times* policy, for example, is to correct misspellings and grammatical errors in letters to the editor, and to make small cuts and changes to fit a letter into the allotted space. If any change of substance is involved, the letter writer is asked to make the cuts.

And *Writer's Digest* usually corrects misspellings and grammatical errors in letters to the editor, unless the errors are intentional (for example, to make fun of something the magazine has done). If time allows, a letter edited for clarity or space is sent to the writer in typeset form before publication.

What May You Correct in Quoting from a Speaker?

On repairing the redundancy, vagueness, jargon, and clichés in interviews, Mel Mandell, editor of *Computer Decisions,* writes (in *Editors Only,* March 1983), "My remedy and the one I train my editors to apply is heavy editing of quotes. . . . We never get any complaints."

Lyle L. Erb writes the following on newspaper reporting (in *in black and white)*:

> A direct quote should be the speaker's own words. But don't quote illiteracies except where color is needed. It may subject the speaker to ridicule. The speaker will insist it's a misquotation. Correct the grammar and other errors.

According to the Associated Press and United Press International style guides, in writing the news, a reporter should correct errors that "would go unnoticed in speaking, but are embarrassing in print." *The Official Reporter* for the House of Representatives follows the same practice.

In fact, Bob Levey mentioned that once when he quoted a fire chief as saying "I ain't never seen," Levey received 30 phone calls from outraged readers. Many firemen protested that if the chief had, in fact, said "ain't," Levey "should have 'mended' the quote so [the chief] didn't look bad."

Editing Transcripts

A thorough treatment of the matter of editing transcripts appears in a handbook, *English for the Shorthand Reporter,* put out by the National Shorthand Reporters Association (NSRA). The first two chapters explain why transcripts should be edited; the rest of the book tells how to do the work.

What happens to a transcript, of course, depends on what the client or employer prescribes; the result can range from a verbatim record to a heavily edited one.

When the reporter has a choice or when editing is specified, the NSRA book recommends that speeches be edited deftly and inconspicuously to correct "gross errors of English, inexact quotations from standard and accessible sources, endless sentences, false starts, immaterial asides, and other crudities," all done "so naturally as to escape the observation of the speaker himself."

In court reporting, the book strongly cautions against editorial changes that would in any way affect the testimony of witnesses or the substance of judges' charges and rulings.

Conclusion

Clearly, many people in the business of quoting believe that certain situations call for "tampering" with quotations ("editing quotations" is a kinder phrase). The motive may be consideration for the speaker or original writer and for the reader. Or the motive may be self-defense, to avoid being thought an illiterate, inaccurate, or insensitive reporter.

The NSRA book illustrates what can happen if editing isn't done. "Young man," said the statesman to the reporter who insisted that the record of the statesman's speech was accurate, "I don't *doubt* your accuracy; I *dread* it."

—Peggy Smith (#89, 6/83)

Editor's Note: The Eye follows a "don't embarrass your contributors" approach and routinely (without seeking permission) corrects typos, misspellings, and errors in punctuation or grammar in letters we print. Black Eyes, of course, are a different matter, but when identifying the source would embarrass someone, we usually omit the author's name. In interviews, we improve the language, but only if we check the change with the person being interviewed. If the person cannot be reached, we edit out ungrammatical or convoluted remarks.

Test Yourself

On Quotations

All of the following are misquoted or misleading because incomplete. What are the correct quotations?

1. I Timothy: Money is the root of all evil.
2. Emerson: Consistency is the hobgoblin of little minds.
3. Coleridge: Water, water, everywhere, and not a drop to drink.
4. Pope: A little knowledge is a dangerous thing.
5. Proverbs: Pride goeth before a fall.
6. Shakespeare: . . .to gild the lily.
7. Lincoln: . . .that government of the people, for the people, by the people shall not perish from the earth.
8. Nathan Hale: I regret that I have but one life to give to my country.
9. Ben Franklin: Never put off till tomorrow what you can do today.
10. Sir Edward Coke (1552-1634): A man's home is his castle.
11. John Heywood (1497-1580) *Proverbs:*
    Beggars can't be choosers.
    One good turn deserves another.
    Little pitchers have big ears.

(#28, 6/79)

Answers

1. The love of money is the root of all evil.—I Timothy 6:10
2. A foolish consistency is the hobgoblin of little minds.—Emerson, *Self-Reliance*
3. Water, water, everywhere, nor any drop to drink.—Coleridge, *The Rime of the Ancient Mariner*
4. A little learning is a dangerous thing.—Pope, *Essay on Criticism*
5. Pride goeth before destruction.—Proverbs 16:18
6. . . . to paint the lily—Shakespeare, *King John*
7. . . . that government of the people, by the people, for the people shall not perish from the earth.—Lincoln, *Gettysburg Address*
8. I only regret that I have but one life to lose for my country.—Nathan Hale
9. Never leave that till to-morrow which you can do to-day.—Franklin, *Poor Richard's Almanac*
10. A man's house is his castle.—Sir Edward Coke *First Institute* (Bartlett's *Quotations*)
11. Beggars should be no choosers.
    One good turne asketh another.
    Small pitchers have wyde eares.—John Heywood, *Proverbs*

(#29, 6/79)

■ "And You Can Quote Me on That" LOGO•PHILE

Now that the quadrennial silly season (i.e., the elections) is well behind us, I can hardly help noticing that quoting is back out of vogue. As a rule politicians like to pepper their speeches with quotes, especially those electoral hopefuls toiling at the long uphill climb from politico to statesman ("Politicians quote statesmen; statesmen quote their gardeners"—Peter Sellers). But politicians seem to be the only quoters around; and alas, the fondest desire of most of them remains not so much to quote as to be quoted.

Quotability comes as second nature to some, but seems to lie totally beyond the reach of others ("I never thought my speeches were too long; I've always enjoyed them"—Hubert Humphrey). Still others remain quotable no matter what ("Now when I bore people at parties, they think it's their fault"—Henry Kissinger).

Politicians aside ("I remain just one thing . . . a clown, and that places me on a higher plane than any politician"—Charlie Chaplin), you can still run into someone who quotes now and again if you hang out with college presidents, literary critics, or burned-out high-school Latin teachers. A favorite of mine was "*Ignis aurum probat, miseria fortes viros*" ("Fire tests gold, misery brave men"—Seneca). But I've had few opportunities to use it since 1956, the year I endured the misery of Latin II.

And that's the problem. What quoting gets you is mostly rolled eyeballs. I mean, besides George Will and William F. Buckley, who actually quotes in general conversation these days? Lots of people used to. It was a sort of conversational salt that teased out the flavor of tasty ideas ("I often quote myself; I find it adds spice to the conversation"—George Bernard Shaw). My Scotland-born grandfather spouted Bobby Burns whenever he could create the opportunity. The average churchgoer used to be able to punctuate any half-way interesting conversation with a verse of Scripture or an apt biblical metaphor, which, I may add, did not have to be explained to everyone in the room under 30 ("You can learn more about human nature by reading the Bible than by living in New York"—William Lyon Phelps).

But these days there seems to be a definite preference for Emerson's view ("Don't recite other people's opinions. Tell me what you know") over Montaigne's ("I quote others the better to express myself"). I am not sure where this aversion to other people's words comes from. Part of it, surely, is that people aren't nearly so well read as they used to be ("Since television, the well-read are being overtaken by the well-watched"—Mortimer Adler). Add to this the fact that much of what does get read doesn't bear repeating ("Jacqueline Susann is quite possibly the least quotable author of our era"—Tazewell Pflaum), and the beginnings of an explanation begin to take shape.

Still, I can't help wondering if we aren't the worse for letting our recapped recollections go flat. A quotation is, after all, a very versatile device. You can use one to be modest ("There's no trick to being a humorist when you have the whole government working for you"—Will Rogers), or to brag about the company you keep ("West Virginians have always had five friends—God Almighty, Sears Roebuck, Montgomery Ward, Carter's Little Liver Pills, and Robert C. Byrd"—Sen. Robert C. Byrd). You can quote to deliver an off-the-wall compliment ("There are a lot of mediocre judges and people and lawyers, and they are entitled to a little representation"—Sen. Roman Hruska, on the nomination of G. Harold Carswell to the Supreme Court), or an insult ("He looks like a female llama who has just been surprised in her bath"—Winston Churchill, on Charles deGaulle).

The payoffs of quoting are subtle, but for those willing to invest in *Bartlett's Familiar Quotations* or Laurence J. Peter's *Quotations for Our Time*, there are treasures indeed. At their best, quotations provide a serious talker with a triple whammy: authority ("Nothing overshadows truth so completely as authority"— Alberti); aptness ("A turn of phrase is as good as the turn of the screw"—H. James); and economy ("The Moral Majority is neither"—B. Sticker).

So, whether at the office ("Work is the refuge of people who have nothing better to do"—Oscar Wilde) or at play ("Golf is a good walk spoiled"—Mark Twain), let's start quoting again. But as we do, we need to recall the words of John Mason Brown: "A good conversationalist is not one who remembers what was said, but says what someone wants to remember."

 (#120, 8/85)

(The author admits he sometimes makes up things people should have said and attributes the remarks to them.)

II. SPECIAL EDITORIAL PROBLEMS MISCELLANY

How to Proceed with Proceedings

If you plan to publish the proceedings of conferences, workshops, or symposia, here are some ideas to help simplify the process and lower costs.

Verbatim Transcript

Few people want to read a verbatim transcript replete with every golden "yeah" and "okay." Therefore don't promise that any such document will be available. A 2-day conference can easily generate 1,000 to 1,500 pages of typescript—too many for readers to handle easily, let alone search through for a particular point.

If your organization really wants or has to provide a verbatim transcript, just print the copy you get from the transcriber, with a disclaimer that no editing has been done. (To save on printing and postage costs, arrange to get transcripts single spaced rather than with the traditional double spacing.) You'll save the thousands of dollars you would spend on editing, reviewing, and retyping the transcript, proofing the new transcript against the old, sending copies to participants for approval, and incorporating their changes.

In addition, you won't get blamed for the errors that are bound to remain, however Herculean the efforts of the editors.

You could also, with the speakers' permission, prepare and distribute tapes of the sessions.

If you are committed to an editing and review process, you can cut costs by typing the transcript directly on word processing equipment. . . . The transcript can then be revised without total rekeyboarding.

Summary of Proceedings

Most participants and other interested parties will be happiest with a summary publication, provided it is done well. Here are three common kinds.

1. A *summary proceeding* can be just a boiled-down transcript, with or without an "executive summary" overview of the main points of the formal presentations and the panel sessions.

In this approach, the editor makes the record coherent and the speakers say what they intended to say—when their meaning can be discerned. Among the transcript's record of stuttering starts and "Can we hold on a few more minutes before coffee?" may well be some vital information.

The editor must emphasize what is important; smooth the language; cut repetition; delete irrelevant interruptions; standardize the editorial style; correct spelling and punctuation; correct subject-verb disagreements; clear up double negatives; clarify pronoun antecedents; trim fillers such as "kind of," "sort of," and "you know"; and do anything else necessary to create a readable, well-organized document.

In this approach, no real summarizing is done, but the bulk is reduced by about one-third. Because such an edited transcript will still be long, an introductory executive summary will be useful.

2. A *variation* on this type of summary proceeding is a volume in which formal speeches are included substantially as presented, but the editor may be asked to condense panel discussions. Discussion reports may identify the main points discussed and present the arguments without identifying speakers by name.

   It takes longer to prepare this type of summary than simply to edit the colloquy, but the result is often more satisfying.

   What is to be done when the speaker fails to deliver the address on the program, but rambles on about perhaps a very different subject? In such cases, it may be advisable to ignore the transcript and substitute the prepared address. Such a substitution will require careful handling of any ensuing discussion, but the speaker and most readers will be grateful.

3. The *executive summary volume* may consist of (a) an introduction telling what the conference was supposed to or did accomplish and who came; (b) an overview, with synopses of all formal speeches and discussions; and (c) longer summaries of each speech and panel discussion, covering all main points and arguments.

   This approach is probably the best, even though it requires considerable effort by editors, writers, and staff members who attended the sessions to report accurately what took place. A strong effort is needed, particularly if the subject is technical or jargon-laden.

Work with the Editor-Writers

Ideally, of course, the editor-writers should attend the conference; in practice, organizations tend to call on them for help after the conference is over.

If before the conference you hire professionals with journalism experience and brief them well on your reporting requirements (length, degree of detail, organization, style, identification of speakers), you can often avoid the entire transcript process and its costs.

If you call for help after the conference, tell the editorial project manager as much as you can about the proceedings, including which speakers and panels kept to the assigned subjects and which did not.

Then assign people in your organization who attended the conference sessions to be advisers to help the editor-writers. Advice will be needed about what to emphasize or play down; queries will need answers.

Getting the Draft Reviewed

Advisers might also review drafts of the summaries before final versions are prepared. In that way, the nuances of a technical or controversial presentation can be checked before the work is finished.

If possible, submit the final edited copy to each speaker for review. Give the speakers a firm deadline for submitting changes, noting specifically that you will interpret failure to return comments by the deadline as approval of the draft as submitted.

Advance Camera-Ready Copy

Some organizations compile a book of proceedings made up of copy that contributors furnish before the conference.

Different contributors will use different typewriter styles (some may provide graphics and typeset copy), and the finished volume may be 2 inches thick. Still, the product can be attractive, useful, and, above all, timely.

For such a book, give contributors firm specifications for manuscript length, page size, margins, headings, and bylines. Set a deadline that gives you time to add page numbers and a table of contents, and to get the book printed and bound.

Specify if contributors should provide complete texts or abstracts of their speeches or workshop presentations.

Some Other Hints

- Ask speakers to provide advance texts or summaries, or both, of their presentations.

- Get to work right after the conference, while memories of events and discussions are fresh.
- If you use your own people as reporters, require them to submit their notes or write-ups promptly (ideally before leaving the conference site).
- Add heads and subheads to text.
- Give the writers and editors copies of previous proceedings especially if you want the same style and format.
- Index the proceedings.

A Note of Caution

A summary cannot rise much above its source. If the quality of the conference sessions was uneven, the summary probably will be uneven. Editors can rarely make scintillating reading of a dull discussion. By judicious selection, however, they can make the most of what happened and provide a valuable meeting record.

—Priscilla Taylor (#34, 10/79)

Coping with Statistics

If you are a nontechnical editor confronted with statistical text, the manuscript will undoubtedly look like Greek to you. Much of it may, in fact, be Greek. Don't despair! Greek letters and other symbols, numbers, and nonwords usually can be conquered with patience and caution.

Let the Author Help

Many of your questions and doubts about statistical text can be resolved in advance by getting from the author a list of key words and symbols. This list is particularly important if the author wrote Greek letters in longhand. If possible, discourage an author from using unconventional notation; unusual symbols may have to be hand set, often at considerable cost.

Editors at the American Statistical Association (ASA), who deal daily with statistical symbols, give authors a notation checklist to fill out to guide the editor. An adaptation of this list points up some potential symbol problems to resolve before plunging into a manuscript.

Words to Watch

Technical terms may be harder than symbols to pin down in advance, even with the author's help. Words that seem technical to you may not seem so to the author. Worse, words that may *not* seem technical to you may be sacred in Statisticsland. Treat with respect such seemingly innocent words as these:

universe	validity	random
population	tail	variable
deviate	student	integrate
dependent, independent	significance	mode
differentiate	space	reliability
constant	global	tweak
regress	sample	bushy mess
mean	distribution	confidence

As with any technical text, make liberal use of queries to the author. Don't assume that an author is given to contorted usage and thus carelessly alter terms whose technical meaning may have escaped you. You cannot take the attitude that you don't know much about statistics, but you know what you like in writing.

Acronyms

Statistical text is well laced with acronyms. Some of the acronyms are so familiar to readers of technical matter that authors don't bother spelling them out initially (actually, the only way to spell an acronym is initially, right?). Some short forms, however, vary among style guides and need defining.

A particular hazard in statistics is not distinguishing between acronyms or other abbreviations and letter symbols. The difference is important to an editor because letter symbols should be italicized and abbreviations should not. In ordinary text, capital letters flag the possible presence of an acronym, but in statistics, acronyms can be either uppercase or lowercase and so can letter symbols. If you see the letters "df," for example, does the author mean the derivative of some variable "f" (*df*) or degrees of freedom (df)?

The ASA editors work from a reference list of about 90 statistical abbreviations. Those they meet most often follow (other styles may differ):

ANOVA — analysis of variance
cdf — cumulative distribution function
cf — continuous function
df — degrees of freedom
exp — exponential
iid — identically and independently distributed
iff — if and only if
LIML — limited-information maximum likelihood
ln — natural logarithm
log — logarithm
max — maximum
min — minimum
MLE — maximum likelihood estimator
MSE — mean squared error
OLS — ordinary least squares
pdf — probability density function
plim — probability at the limit
RMSE — root mean square error
rhs — righthand side
2SLS — two-stage least squares
UMP — uniform most powerful
var — variance
$\overline{X}$ — sample mean of X

The ASA statistical editors may introduce their own temporary acronyms for frequently used technical terms. For example, if an author refers 50 times to a "Durbin-Watson statistic," the editors may substitute DWS 49 times.

Hyphenation

Statisticians are willy-nilly hyphenators. Even though a rare author may follow the statistical conventions, these conventions are not particularly consistent. Consider, for example, the mysterious compounding in the guide the ASA editors use:

chi-square test, chi-squared variate, mean squared error
t-test, *F*-test, *s* method, *M*-dimensional, random walk, student *t*, student-*t* distribution
goodness-of-fit, lack-of-fit, log-linear, log-likelihood, least-squares (used as adjectives)
two-stage least squares, one-way situation
real world discussion
maximum likelihood estimator, minimum quadratic loss
Monte Carlo study
error-free probabilities
autoregressive moving average

Where to Turn for Help

An author's advice, although essential on substantive questions, may be of little help on matters of style. The following may be rescue sources:

Basic statistics text: Freedman, Pisami, and Purvis. *Statistics*. New York: W. W. Norton, 1978.
Helpful encyclopedia: Kruskal and Tanur (eds.). *International Encyclopedia of Statistics*. New York: Free Press, 1978.
An index to articles in statistical journals: *Current Index to Statistics*. (Published by ASA and Institute of Mathematical Statistics.)
Style guides:

- Ellen Swanson. *Mathematics Into Type* (1971) and *A Manual for Authors of Mathematical Papers* (1970). Providence, RI: American Mathematical Society.
- *Mathematics in Type*. Richmond, VA: William Byrd Press, 1954.
- Also check the University of Chicago Press's *A Manual of Style* and Marjorie Skillin et al., *Words Into Type*.

—Charlene Semer (#30, 7/79)

(With many thanks to Maureen Stotland and Mary Courtney of the ASA editorial staff and Vita Pariente of Blue Pencil Group.)

AUTHOR'S CHECKLIST FOR STATISTICAL TEXT
(adapted from the American Statistical Association's checklist)

1. CIRCLE ALL GREEK LETTERS to be used in the manuscript:

	l.c.	CAP		l.c.	CAP		l.c.	CAP
Alpha	α	A	Iota	ι	I	Rho	ρ	P
Beta	β	B	Kappa	κ	K	Sigma*	σ	Σ
Gamma	γ	Γ	Lambda	λ	Λ	Tau	τ	T
Delta	δ	Δ	Mu	μ	M	Upsilon	υ	T
Round Delta	∂		Nu	ν	N	Phi	φ	Φ
Epsilon	ε	E	Xi	ξ	Ξ	Chi	χ	X
Zeta	ζ	Z	Omicron	o	O	Psi	ψ	Ψ
Eta	η	H	Pi	π	Π	Omega	ω	Ω
Theta	θ	Θ						

2. CIRCLE OTHER SPECIAL LETTERS AND NOTATIONS to be used in the text:

Factorial	!	Kronecker product	x
Infinity	∞	Lowercase script "el"	*l*
Integral	∫	Multiplication	×
Product	Π	Natural log	1n
Summation	Σ	Proportionality	∝
Element of	ε	Vertical bar	|

3. INDICATE OTHER CHARACTERS USED (e.g., German and English *script* letters; variations of standard Greek characters; handwritten symbols, etc.)

*Circle cap sigmas in text or they will be set as summations.

(#30, 7/79)

From Messy Text to a Readable Table

Technical reports often contain text that is too detailed to be easily assimilated; sometimes such information is more appropriately presented in a table. It is important to recognize when you can convert messy text into a neat table, highlighting the important information and deleting unnecessary detail.

Here is a page from a technical paper that describes a special kind of warship in such detail that the main message is unclear. In the top half of the page, the editor has underscored important material to be pulled from the text for a table.

CHARACTERISTICS

- **SPEED** – a sustained sea speed at full load displacement of 22 knots is required. A flank speed of 25 knots is desired. This emergency overload condition must be sustainable for two hours.

  Rationale: *The specialist fire support ship must have a sufficient speed margin to maneuver around an amphibious group sustaining 18 to 20 knots.*
- **DRAFT** – The full load draft must not exceed 20 feet.

  Rationale: *The specialist fire support ship will have to operate inshore during several phases of amphibious operations.*
- **RANGE** – A range of 8,000 n.mi. at 20 knots is required.

  Rationale: *This range will allow transit between most advanced bases and the Area of Operation without refueling.*
- **AVIATION FACILITIES** – A flight deck and control facilities capable of operating the following aircraft:

  (1) One CH53E, or
  (2) Two CH46F, or
  (3) One AV-8B, or
  (4) Two AH-1J

  The aviation facility should be capable of rapidly refueling and rearming the aircraft and should provide for rapid removal of cargo from the flight deck by mechanized means (yellow gear).

  If possible a covered hanger for one aircraft should be provided (note: an aircraft elevator and below deck hanger is an admissible solution).

NARRATIVE

Table 1 shows how the side headings—speed, draft, and range—from the original text can be used as rows for the table. The other important words are presented as subordinate information, with the dimensions listed at the right.

Table 1
Characteristics of Fire Support Ship

Characteristics	
Speed (full load displacement, knots)	
Sustained	22
Flank	25[a]
Draft (feet)	20
Range (n.mi.)	8,000

[a] Sustainable for 2 hours.

None of the information in the bottom half of the page shown in the original text was used in the table. Instead the editor condensed the material into two sentences and restored them to the text.

(#74, 6/82)

This article was adapted from a presentation by Renee K. Barnow at the International Technical Communications Conference in Boston in May 1982.

How to Be Sure Editing Changes Are Improvements

A cardinal principle of editing is to avoid making unnecessary or wrong changes. It is particularly inexcusable for an editor to change something that is correct as it stands and thus make it wrong. The best way to ensure that the changes you make are improvements is to give careful thought to them. Don't base a change on only a superficial analysis, especially if you are not sure what the author is trying to say. Instead, ponder the passage a while; read what comes before and after it; consult reference books. If after due deliberation you still cannot be sure, at least you should be in a position to see several possible intended meanings, and you will have a basis for asking the author intelligent questions.

—*Guide for Beginning Technical Editors,*
Wallace Clements and Robert G. Waite,
Lawrence Livermore Laboratory

(#50, 11/80)

Black Eyes

Campus net passes test

Runs first year without major gliche

They must have some real men in charge.
—Submitted by Mike Willoughby, Wichita, KS

DIVORCE MEDITATION
Cooperate, don't litigate. Male/Female. Social Worker/Counselor at Law. Call Ann Riley, LCSW at Divorce Resource Center 345-7474.

We'll have to think about it.
—Submitted by Ann Thompson Cook, Washington, DC

(#99, 2/84)

Editing Legalese

"Our lawyers are their own editors," says a partner in one of Washington's largest and most prestigious law firms. "A lawyer who can't write wouldn't last 20 minutes in this firm."

Beneath that statement lurk some of the reasons editors have difficulty working with lawyer-authors. Good lawyers must write precisely or with calculated imprecision to cover all contingencies. Their definition of good writing is writing that avoids creating legal problems. No wonder lawyers are reluctant to have their carefully crafted language edited by nonlawyers.

The Uses and Abuses of Legal Language

A number of lawyers are indeed outstanding writers, but for every Auchincloss there are hundreds of habitual obfuscators. How much of their obfuscation is really necessary? George D. Gopen, in *Writing from a Legal Perspective* (St. Paul: West Publishing Co., 1981), claims that legal writing serves four purposes: (1) the need for precision and deliberate imprecision to cover unforeseen circumstances, (2) the need to articulate steps and connections in a logical argument, (3) the need to recognize that people differ in their responses to words or arguments, and (4) the need to maintain clarity of expression. Any language that does not directly serve these needs, says Gopen, is merely legalese.

James C. Raymond, an English professor who has conducted a number of seminars for legal organizations, goes even further. He claims the traditional language of law becomes an obstruction of justice when lay people cannot understand the legal documents that control them and when "lawyers themselves cannot agree on the meaning of what they have written" ("Legal Writing: An Obstruction to Justice," *Alabama Law Review*, vol. 30, no. 1, Fall 1978).

The "plain English" movement is an embodiment of Raymond's point. The lawyers who create public documents are learning, reluctantly in many cases, either to identify and excise their own legalese or to work with editors who can help them do so. Lawyers for some insurance companies and other industries that use standard contracts are trying to simplify those contracts. Many major law schools now require first-year students to take a course in legal writing, and several legal organizations sponsor seminars and workshops in writing for established lawyers.

Unfortunately, few private attorneys have hopped on the plain English bandwagon. An informal survey of some large Washington law firms failed to discover any that have in-house editors or that regularly contract for editorial services.

The Editor's Role

How could editors help these firms? First, by simple copyediting. A lawyer-editor who regularly works with legal writing claims that elementary grammatical errors abound among his lawyer clients. Gopen cites passive constructions and weak verbs as particular ogres in legal writing.

A large legal publishing company in Virginia uses copyeditors to correct spelling, grammar, and syntax; to check citations; to sort out footnotes; and to make sure the style is consistent with "The Blue Book"—Harvard Law Review Association's *A Uniform System of Citation* (a widely used legal style guide, but not the only one—any internally consistent style of citation is generally acceptable). Lawyers, mainly concerned with substance, might be delighted to have an editor attend to these routine problems.

Skillful, experienced editors also could help lawyers write for nonlawyers—including their own clients. Jeffrey Davis, of Rutgers University Law School, designed a survey to discover how legal documents could be made more comprehensible to the general public ("Protecting Consumers from Overdisclosure and Gobbledegook," *Virginia Law Review*, vol. 63, no. 6, Oct. 1977). His survey instrument was based upon a finding by social scientists that the degree to which people understand written information depends upon the information load (the number of facts presented in one source), readability, and conceptual difficulty. The last factor depends partly on the reader's prior knowledge, of course, so the writer should be aware of the audience.

Davis asked two sets of shoppers to read different contracts. One was a typical, complicated installment contract; the other was simplified to eliminate government-required disclosures, to reduce unnecessary seller clauses, and to improve readability. Davis used a combination of readability formulas to judge readability. He then asked both groups to answer 15 questions about important contract provisions. The shoppers with the simplified contract averaged 26 percent more correct answers than the other group.

Although an editor is trained to improve readability, lawyers may be justifiably suspicious of a lay editor's ability to decide which information is superfluous. Some editors are also lawyers, of course. The legal publishing company mentioned above, for example, employs lawyers who have journalism or English undergraduate majors. These specialists help the firm's "service" (substantive) editors and copyeditors resolve substantive inconsistencies and spot technical errors. The lawyer-editors generally go back to original sources if they suspect an author has an incorrect citation or has misinterpreted those sources. Paralegal training or on-the-job experience also might provide an editor with enough technical expertise to handle such work.

Lawyer-Editor Relations

Short of legal training or experience, diplomacy may be the most important noneditorial skill for working with lawyers. An experienced legal editor in Washington emphasizes the importance of establishing in advance which words or constructions are essential to the lawyer's purpose and of agreeing on the types of changes the editor will be making.

The substantive editor's first task then is to define clearly and mutually with the lawyer-author what constitutes legalese—excess legal baggage for a particular purpose and for a particular audience. That definition may be quite different for a book intended for lawyers from what it is for a divorce agreement or a magazine article. Editors who dismiss all legal language as legalese deserve the paranoid reaction they receive from lawyers, but lawyers who dismiss readability as nonprofessional do their clients and their public a disservice.

Some Shining Examples

Alan Siegel, a leading Plain English consultant, has considerable experience in making contracts understandable without sacrificing legal effectiveness. The following examples are from Siegel's article in *Across the Board,* The Conference Board magazine ("The Plain English Revolution," Feb. 1981):

Massachusetts Savings Bank Life Insurance Policy

BEFORE

IN CONSIDERATION OF THE APPLICATION for this policy (copy attained hereto) which is the basis of and a part of this contract and of the payment of an annual premium as hereinafter specified for the basic policy as of the Date of Issue as specified herein and on the anniversary of such date in each year during the continuance of this contract until premiums have been paid for the number of years . . .

AFTER

Please take the time to read your SBLI policy carefully. Your SBLI representative will be glad to answer any questions. You may return this policy within ten days after receiving it. Deliver it to any SBLI agency. We'll promptly refund all premiums paid for it.

BEFORE

The Bank Hereby Agrees upon Surrender of this Policy to Pay the Face Amount Specified Above, less any indebtedness on or secured hereunder . . . upon receipt of due proof of the Insured's death to the beneficiary named in the Application herefor or to such other beneficiary as may be entitled thereto under the provisions hereof, or if no such beneficiary survives the Insured, then to the Owner or to the estate of the Owner.

AFTER

We will pay the face amount when we receive proof of the Insured's death. We will pay the named Beneficiary. If no Beneficiary survives the Insured, we'll pay the Owner of this policy, or the Owner's estate.

Any amount owed to us under this policy will be deducted. We'll refund any premiums paid beyond the month of death.

St. Paul Fire and Marine Insurance Co. Policy

BEFORE

a. Automobile and Watercraft Liability:

1. any Relative with respect to (i) an Automobile owned by the Named Insured or a Relative, or (ii) a Non-owned Automobile, provided his actual operation or (if he is not operating) the other actual use thereof is with the permission of the owner and is within the scope of such permission, or

2. any person while using an Automobile or Watercraft, owned by, loaned or hired for use in behalf of the Named Insured and any person or organization legally responsible for the use thereof is within the scope of such permission.

AFTER

We'll also cover any person or organization legally responsible for the use of a car, if it's used by you or with your permission. But again, the use has to be for the intended purpose.

You loan your station wagon to a teacher to drive a group of children to the zoo. She and the school are covered by this policy if she actually drives to the zoo, but not if she lets the children off at the zoo and drives to her parents' farm 30 miles away.

Sanford C. Bernstein & Co. Investment Agreement

BEFORE

It is the express intention of the undersigned to create an estate or account as joint tenants with rights of survivorship and not as tenants in common. In the event of the death of either of the undersigned, the entire interest in the joint account shall be vested in the survivor or survivors on the same terms and conditions as theretofore held, without in any manner releasing the decedent's estate from the liability provided for in the next preceding paragraph.

AFTER

Other signers share your interest equally. If one of you dies, the account will continue and the other people who've signed the agreement will own the entire interest in it.

(Examples reprinted with permission of Alan Siegel—copyright permission granted by The Conference Board)

(#63, 9/81)

On Readability Formulas

Editor's Note: In Issues 83 and 86, *The Eye* presented the views of two writers who pointed up some shortcomings of readability formulas. Here we present a brief review of the subject by Jefferson Bates, from his highly successful *Writing With Precision* (Washington, DC: Acropolis Books, 3rd ed., 1980), plus letters from two readers who support the use of readability formulas.

Rudolph Flesch, Robert Gunning, Edgar Dale, John McElroy. . . . These are among the best known of the many writers, psychologists, linguists, and other scholars who have turned their attention to the many problems of making writing more "readable." (There is a difference between "readable" and "effective," although the two usually go together.). . .

Flesch was the . . . first to popularize the subject of readability: first with his book *The Art of Plain Talk* (1946), then with *The Art of Readable Writing* (1949). . . . Flesch, unlike some others in the field, is quite good at practicing what he preaches.

Robert Gunning is another real "pro." . . . Gunning's approach to measuring readability—called the "Fog Index"—has been widely used by both government and industry in recent years. In truth, Gunning's "Fog Index" and Flesch's "Readability Scale" are not all that different. Both are concerned primarily with two factors: (1) the average length of sentences, and (2) the percentage of "difficult" words—that is, words having three or more syllables.

To use the Flesch system, one must employ a chart or—a less well-known but more accurate word—a nomograph. By making a couple of simple counts involving average sentence length and number of syllables per hundred words, you can easily come up with a "reading ease" score. You simply place a ruler or straight-edge on the appropriate numbers on the two outside columns of his nomograph and observe where they cross a center line labeled the "Reading Ease" score. That score can range from zero (for extremely difficult material) to 100 (for very easy material).

Because I am really terrible at arithmetic, I like the Flesch formula, which requires little effort on my part. The trouble is, you must have the . . . nomograph on hand. And, of course, many times when you need it you simply won't have it available.

Doubtless that explains why Gunning's Fog Index has achieved somewhat wider usage. It is easy to commit the formula to memory, and then you can work out a score any time, anywhere. (If you're good at math!)

. . . With both [the] Flesch and Gunning methods, your first step is to pick a 100-word sample and figure the average sentence length.* Next, you count the number of "difficult" words (that is, words having three syllables or more) in the sample. You then add the average number of words per sentence to the number of "difficult" words per hundred. Then, in the Gunning version, you multiply the result by 0.4. The result, rounded to the nearest whole number, gives you the Fog Index, which Gunning has cleverly designed to be roughly equivalent to the grade level a reader must have completed in order to understand the material. (The Fog Index of that last sentence would be appalling—but remember, you don't go on the basis of single sentences. You go by the average. And that is why I now hasten to throw in some short sentences.)

If all this does not seem clear, perhaps an example will help: Suppose that you find the average length of sentence is 15 words. Then you determine that the percentage of "difficult" words is 13. Add the 15 and the 13, and you come up with 28. Multiply the 28 by 0.4, and you get a Fog Index of 11.2, which you round off to 11 even. That means a person with an 11th grade education should be able to understand the material. (A score of 6 would mean a 6th grader could handle it. . . . And so on.)

What Readability Formulas Can and Can't Do

Nobody can learn to be a writer by using a mathematical formula. Indeed, I have seen many would-be writers mess themselves up by trying to apply the formula while they were actually writing. . . . They would lose their flow of words, forget their thought patterns, and end up with nothing worth saving.

The formulas work just fine after the fact, but not before or during. Get the first draft down as fast as possible; don't worry in the least about long sentences and difficult words. You have time enough, when the draft is finished, to check with the formula. Then you can edit, rewrite, or whatever else you need to do to bring the score within a desirable range.

Also remember this. A piece of writing with a bad score is almost undoubtedly unclear, unless the writer was or is a true master of the language.

On the other hand, a good score on the formula does not necessarily guarantee that writing is either good or clear. The formula cannot evaluate the content or information of a message; also, it cannot evaluate the style.

With these provisos in mind, I believe you can use readability scores to excellent advantage, after the fact. . . . If you are arguing with a colleague about the readability of a particular item, when all else fails, trot out the formula. You may snatch victory from the jaws of defeat. Of course, if you try this on your boss, the converse could well be true.

The Famous Simple-Minded Bates Formula

. . . Rudolph Flesch's famous nomograph tells us that "standard" reading ease (a numerical score of 60 to 70) could theoretically be achieved with an average sentence length of 30 words. To do this, however, you would have to use almost nothing but one-syllable words, and that's not too easy.

To get the desired score with much less trouble, the trick is to cut down to an average sentence length of about 20 words. That way, you can use more long words.

Now let's bring Robert Gunning's Fog Index into the computations. We'll assume a Fog Index of 12 is about equivalent to Flesch's "standard" reading ease. You can obtain this index by averaging 20 words per sentence with, say, about 10 percent "long" words—three syllables or more.

Actually, a Fog Index of 12 may be too high these days, since reading skills have been deteriorating sharply for more than a decade. A Fog Index of 10 would probably be a better goal to shoot for.

Well, here's my simple-minded formula. Any time you can knock two words out of a sentence, you'll reduce the Fog Index by roughly one point. OR, if you can shorten two "long" words, you'll get the same effect. If you can eliminate two long words, you'll bring that score down by two whole points—a consummation devoutly to be wished.

So, first of all, keep that average sentence length at 20 or under—if possible, well under. Then, if you find you have sentences that are too long, counterbalance them with some sentences that are very short. And, if that doesn't do the trick, go through cutting out excess verbiage until the score comes down.

—Quoted with the permission of the author. Jefferson Bates heads his own consulting firm, Hampton Bates & Associates, Inc., in Fairfax, VA. His most recent book, written with James R. Jeffries, is *The Executive's Guide to Conferences, Meetings, and Audiovisual Presentations* (New York: McGraw-Hill, 1983).

(#89, 6/83)

*To use Gunning's Fog Index, you must know exactly how he defines a sentence and counts syllables in compound words. See Robert Gunning, *The Technique of Clear Writing* (New York: McGraw-Hill, 1968).

Letters to the Editor: Readability Formulas

Are Readability Formulas Useful?

I was pleased to note that someone besides me believes that readability formulas are essentially useless, or at least misleading.

We recently evaluated a particularly difficult manuscript that had been submitted for publication using two different scales, and the differences were striking. On the scale that counts the number of short words (and then subtracts to arrive at the number of long words), the manuscript scored 11th-grade reading level. On the one that considers sentence length, it scored fifth-grade level. The reason for this difference was that the writer had omitted most of the articles (as military writers so often do). This made it extremely hard to follow, but without all those pesky little words it did have short sentences! (Because of this and lots of other problems, even 11th-grade reading ability was not enough. Nobody, no matter how much education, could have understood it without considerable effort and guesswork.)

Readability has a lot more to do with such things as the logical organization of ideas, transitions between sentences and paragraphs, word choice, and parallelism than it has to do with either sentence length or word length. And, as Mr. Sides points out, the familiarity of the words counts too. Yet many people still swear by these scales and use them religiously in their attempts to lower the reading level of all kinds of instructional materials.

We all enjoy your publication and find it useful.

—Marie B. Edgerton, Fort Benning, GA (#86, 3/83)

In Defense of Readability Formulas

. . . Certainly Marie Edgerton (Issue 86) is right when she says that *readability* includes far more than can be measured by a readability formula, but I cannot agree with her when she says the formulas "are essentially useless."

Her position, I suspect, arises from misunderstanding (1) the kinds of readability formulas available and (2) how best to use them. This misunderstanding leads to the kinds of abuses of formulas she alludes to, and to severe reactions to those abuses—reactions like hers.

Readability formulas are not all created equal. Of the hundreds available, some are clearly better than others. Perhaps Ms. Edgerton's opinions about readability formulas could be improved by trying out formulas that are more sophisticated—and accurate—than the ones she cites in her letter.

True, a formula that measures only sentence length is likely to give results quite different from results of a formula that measures only vocabulary difficulty (long words). But readability formulas that measure *either* of those two sentence features to the exclusion of the other are not, in my experience, very reliable anyway.

I suggest that Ms. Edgerton try a readability formula that measures *both* sentence length and vocabulary difficulty. The Dale-Chall, Fry, and Flesch formulas, mainstays of readability testing over many years, are examples of this kind of formula.

Even the better readability formulas are limited. But then, so are thermometers, those time-honored medical tools physicians use to diagnose disease. Thermometers measure only temperature, one symptom of disease.

But few doctors would do without them. Readability formulas measure only one or two things about sentences. But, when used properly, they are excellent tools for predicting the relative difficulty that different readers are likely to have with certain passages of text.

I suggest also that we not try to equate the factors measured by readability formulas with the cures that need to be effected. Would any doctor simply conclude that because the thermometer registers an above average temperature, the solution is to drop the temperature, say, by plunging the patient into a tub of ice until the thermometer registered an acceptable temperature? Of course not. [The doctor] would take other diagnostic steps to determine precisely the causes of the temperature and treat those causes, measuring the one predictive factor—temperature—from time to time with the thermometer.

Readability formulas are our thermometers. They simply measure some of the symptoms or characteristics that make writing difficult—sentence length and vocabulary difficulty—and tell us just how pronounced they are (in terms of grade level). But to prune out difficult words and shorten sentences *only* is akin to "curing" a fevered patient by immersing him in ice water.

Readability formulas can give us useful information, but those who abuse them—either by overrelying on them or by dismissing them out of hand—do themselves a disservice.

—A. Gregory Brown, Salt Lake City, UT (#89, 6/83)

Readability for Military Writers and Editors

Please let me say a kind word for the much-maligned "fog indices" and readability formulas.

Many of us who use RGL [reading grade level] formulas—Air Force, Gunning, Flesch, or any of the other numerous ones available—are aware that they are not perfect, precise, exact, or infallible. We use them simply to gain an *indication* of the difficulty level a slug of prose presents. The formulas are especially useful as a quick illustration to writers who have never considered their audiences.

I direct technical report writing workshops for government employees. Believe me, thousands of writers have never been taught to consider the reading skills (or time limitations) of their readers. Such a notion comes as a brilliant flash of illumination to them. In such instances, perhaps in a 3-day workshop where a consultant's time is extremely limited, introduction of an

RGL formula is a quick, dramatic means of showing workshop participants how far on- or off-target they may have been.

. . . A really fine article [is] "The New Readability Requirements for Military Technical Manuals," by J.D. Kniffin, published in *Technical Communication* (Third Quarter, 1979). Research showed serious mismatches between training material RGL's and reading skills of our volunteer military forces. Whatever can close that gap between reader and writer is desperately needed. Military readability and comprehensibility regulations are a step in the right direction. Not a *big* step, but a step. . . .

[Amateur] writers won't begin to improve their prose until they're convinced a problem exists. Only *after* an RGL formula shocks them into attention will they try to learn something about organization, transition, parallelism . . . the whole 9 yards.

. . . If a teaching technique works, I'll use it. When it stops working, I'll drop it. In the meanwhile, here's to more and better use of RGL formulas. . . .

—Martha Eckman, El Paso, TX (#89, 6/83)

How to Get Along with Authors

How can you—an editor both competent and courteous—get along with a writer who mistrusts editors?

This problem and others in establishing and keeping a good relationship with authors were addressed at a workshop of the National Association of Government Communicators' (NAGC) conference in Washington, DC, in Dec. 1980.

The panel members—Debbie Massey (U.S. Department of Agriculture), Janet Redish (Document Design Center), and Priscilla Taylor (EEI)—offered the following advice:

Make a Strong Beginning

To start from a sound position, know the range of your skills, the degree of support you can expect from your boss, and your working environment.

In your initial meeting with the author, (1) mutually define the goals of your project; (2) emphasize your mutual interest in achieving the author's goals; (3) explain the publication process; (4) discuss your roles in the process; (5) ask the right questions to understand the audience, tone, and purpose of the manuscript; and (6) set realistic deadlines.

Use a detailed checklist for instructions. A checklist can (1) assure the author that you will do certain tasks (correcting spelling, punctuation, grammar, etc.); (2) remind you to get the author's judgment on certain kinds of changes (whether, for example, the first person is to be deleted everywhere except the preface); and (3) spell out the degree of substantive rewriting and reorganizing expected.

Also at the first meeting, find out (1) if you are expected to incorporate author or agency changes as the work progresses and (2) how many review cycles are planned. To avoid major last-minute changes, try to get the top person to approve your approach before you progress very far. Try to impose a "Doctrine of No Surprises" on the job.

Be Accessible; Don't Be Intrusive

Be accessible to authors but don't telephone them too often. Most authors expect an editor to use judgment and imagination—and to list questionable decisions instead of reaching for the phone. Unclear passages and unexplained acronyms often clear themselves up in later pages.

Back Up Your Changes

It is important to impose agreed-upon editorial style, but avoid imposing personal prejudices that do not relate to precision and cannot be justified by an authority. If you are reduced to explaining a change with "I just don't like dashes (or colons, or parentheses, or the word *such*)" you will lose influence in more significant editorial recommendations.

Explain Your Changes

Explain your changes succinctly in the margin, where practical. Long queries and suggestions belong in a separate memo or a general list of notes to be attached to the manuscript (along with a list of style decisions about words, numbers, etc., that could be treated differently) when the package is returned to the author.

Meet with the author after you have completed the editing and the author has reviewed your work. Be prepared to explain all recommendations—and know which are negotiable. If a writer denigrates your editing in general, ask him or her to detail specific problems and objections. Back away from a power struggle; instead present your problems with the manuscript from the standpoint of a representative member of the intended audience.

Other Helpful Tips

Ask for two copies of every manuscript (1) to facilitate checking on the original arrangement of material once you have begun shifting sections around or (2) to enable you to expedite the work if necessary by sharing the editing with other workers.

Take care to write legibly in dark black pencil on a manuscript or on a photocopy and to retype heavily revised paragraphs. Type major revisions on separate sheets of paper as inserts, not "flopovers," because the material under flopovers does not appear in a photocopy, and edited manuscripts are often photocopied for review by several people at a time.

—Priscilla Taylor (#53, 1/81)

Examples of Questions for Editors to Ask Writers

1. *Audience:* (Answer first for the primary audience, then for other audiences.) Sex, occupation, income level, ethnic group, age, geographic breakdown (urban/rural), size, education level, current knowledge of subject, other?
2. *Purpose:* What is the general purpose of this publication? List in order of importance (a) the specific things you want the audience to learn from this publication and (b) the specific things you want the audience to do as a result of reading this publication.
3. *Use:* Is the audience intended to read and discard this publication or to keep it as a reference? Will the audience use the publication at work, at home, at a desk, in the field, or elsewhere? Will the audience use this publication along with other materials? If so, which ones? Will the material in this publication be explained or reinforced in training sessions or elsewhere? If so, how? How do you plan for the audience to get this publication?

—Adapted from a list by Debbie Massey,
Food and Nutrition Service, U.S. Dept. of Agriculture (#53, 1/81)

■ Editing the Prima Donna

Nancy Davidson has learned what it takes to edit temperamental academics successfully. She is an associate editor at the Brookings Institution, a public policy think-tank in Washington, DC, where many of today's (and tomorrow's) top-level issues are analyzed by some of the brightest people in the world. They don't necessarily take kindly to editing, and that's the point at which Davidson's skills amount to more than the ability to sift out the dangling participles and comma splices.

Ask her to describe her job and she'll tell you it's part editorial skill, part tact, and part teaching ability, with the emphasis decidedly on the latter two. She confesses, "During my interview for the position at Brookings, they were as concerned about my ability to deal with academics as they were with my editing qualifications."

In her editorial career, both as a freelancer and as a staff member at Brookings, Davidson has developed a successful method for working with difficult authors—from the starry-eyed newcomers who believe their every word is a pearl to the full professor who has been known to intimidate a senator or cabinet member. Davidson shared some of her accumulated wisdom during a recent interview with *The Eye*.

Getting to Know You

At the outset, Davidson says, it's important to get to know the author. She tries to have a face-to-face conversation with each writer to determine if he or she views the editing process as a necessary nuisance or as a valuable step in making the book or article better. Is the author ready to turn the work over and let her handle every detail? Does the writer want only periodic consultations or full control over every semicolon?

Davidson believes the editor should not be overawed by the author's credentials or reputation. It is important to let the author know (subtly) that the editor, too, is a professional who commands expertise.

Once Davidson has learned as much as possible about the author, she next learns what she can about the context for the author's work. What stage is it in? Is the author still excited about the project, bored with it, or ready to pitch it out the nearest window? Has the piece been through several revisions already? Will more be required?

If she has already glanced through the manuscript, Davidson talks briefly with the author about the "little" points she has noticed: the length of chapters, the way tables have been deployed, the number of footnotes in each chapter, the appearance of the figures. Experience has taught her that a casual conversation on minor points will often elicit remarks from the author that can help her determine how to handle the editing.

Next, Davidson edits a sample chapter or section. She usually chooses something from the middle of the work that is fairly representative of the job as a whole. During this phase, she does a thorough editing job. She will suggest moving a paragraph here, deleting another there, or changing the wording somewhere else. Once again, a talk with the author is appropriate to assess the reaction to the sample edit.

On to the Query Sheet

Once one chapter has been successfully edited, the task of editing the entire manuscript is eased by a tactfully written query sheet, which explains the changes she prefers and how those changes will improve the final product. A query sheet, Davidson advises, stands a much better chance of eliciting a favorable response from the author than a list of peremptory demands or the return of an entire manuscript awash in blue pencil.

At this point, Davidson says, it is surprising how many authors want to argue grammatical issues with her. The author may have a Ph.D. in economics, but chances are he or she knows little about grammar, except, of course, what some eighth-grade English teacher said. Often, about all the author remembers is "never split an infinitive" and "never begin a sentence with the word *and*." But those points are remembered as gospel!

Here Davidson begins a little inservice education of her own, with the aid of books such as Theodore Bernstein's *Miss Thistlebottom's Hobgoblins,* which Davidson calls a "marvelous" usage book that tells writers everything their eighth-grade teachers should have told them. Davidson's pupils soon find out when it's acceptable (indeed, preferable) to split an infinitive, or when what seems to be a dangling participle is actually an absolute construction. Davidson frequently copies a page from *Miss Thistlebottom's Hobgoblins* and sends it along to an author to buttress a point.

What Happens When the Author Balks?

Sometimes, despite the diplomacy, authors still dig in their heels. What then? Says Davidson, it's time for another conversation. She asks her authors, "Please tell me in your own words exactly what you are trying to say." Davidson says it's amazing how a light bulb often will go on in the editor's brain, illuminating clearly the author's intention *and* a solution.

But sometimes this tactic doesn't work. Tact and a fresh look at the material don't work. Even a page from *Miss Thistlebottom* does not budge the author. No more quibbling about commas; now is the time for serious compromise. At this point the trade-off becomes the editor's most potent ally; here is where it becomes advisable to give ground on a nonparallel construction, for example, in return for a more substantive change.

Davidson has also devised a strategy for persuading authors to use less opaque language. She reminds them that eliminating jargon or changing phraseology will make the book or article more accessible to a wider audience, thus helping to ensure larger sales. Many authors find the argument appealing.

Court of the Last Resort

When all else fails, Davidson's fallback position is to invoke the house style guide, pointing out that it says NOT to capitalize the names of government programs like social security. She points out that another effective strategy can be kicking the problem upstairs: A managing editor or director of publications can be most helpful to staff editors. But, she admits ruefully, even Brookings has had to give in to a few unyielding authors; even the house style guide can be overridden.

Although few disputes go beyond author and editor, there is a final precept for the editor to remember when dealing with a prima donna: When the last battle over a misplaced modifier has been lost, when all of your efforts toward clarification have been in vain, remember that the work really does belong to the author.

—Connie Moy (#120, 8/85)

Test Yourself

On Spelling

The 52 words most misspelled by editors, writers, and college graduates, according to *Reader's Digest Almanac*, are listed below. Can you find the six we have intentionally misspelled?

1. Achieve
2. Algae
3. Annihilate
4. Athlete
5. Broccoli
6. Campaign
7. Catalyst
8. Cemetery
9. Condemn
10. Croak
11. Demagogue
12. Delete
13. Dilapidated
14. Dissipated
15. Duel
16. Ecstasy
17. Excede
18. Facial
19. Foreign
20. Fricassee
21. Fuselage
22. Gloat
23. Gynecologist
24. Innocuous
25. Innoculate
26. Knowledge
27. Licence
28. Liquify
29. Millennium
30. Miscellaneous
31. Missile
32. Omitted
33. Phial
34. Phlegm
35. Prairie
36. Raspberry
37. Sieze
38. Sheriff
39. Sieve
40. Spigot
41. Subpoena
42. Supercede
43. Tariff
44. Tonsillitis
45. Tyranny
46. Usage
47. Vengeance
48. Weird
49. Wholly
50. Yield
51. Zeal
52. Zephyr

Answers

Here are the correct spellings for the six misspelled words:

17. Exceed
25. Inoculate
27. License
28. Liquefy
37. Seize
42. Supersede

(#58, 5/81)

Developing a Writer's Voice

Education writer Joseph Featherstone once characterized the writing of John Dewey as having "the monotonous consistency of peanut butter." Whether or not they agree about Dewey's writing, most editors agree that writers who work hard at it develop styles of their own (creative writing teachers call it "finding your own voice"). Sometimes style achieves the level of self-portraiture, to the point that the writer cannot be mistaken for anyone else: Joyce and Hemingway are good examples. Obviously, this does not happen often, but when it does, writer and editor are entitled to apply for a joint appointment to *The New Yorker*.

Many editors can nevertheless help the writers they supervise to develop their own styles. By attending to a few simple precepts, editors can guide new writers in the right direction.

Presumption

The first lesson the editor must teach is that style is not simply "the dress of thoughts." Lord Chesterfield was wrong when he defined style this way, because his idea presumes that language and thought can somehow be separated. They cannot. The purpose of style is not to take an idea and dress it up, but to put an idea before the reader in the form that comes naturally to the writer and goes just as naturally to the mind of the reader. Here, the medium truly becomes the message. An idea is not a department store window to be trimmed but an opening into the world.

It follows that style is not a form of exhibitionism, a parade of long words the writer knows or of verbal pyrotechnics, à la Spiro Agnew's "nattering nabobs of negativism." Style is, in the words of Swift, "proper words in proper places."

A Lesson from Milton

The next task of the editor is to make sure the writer works at mastering the writing craft. I remember reading once about a class on Milton taught by W. H. Auden at the University of Michigan. He required that each of his charges look up every single word of Milton's *Lycidas* (228 lines!) in the *Oxford English Dictionary*. The poem begins,

> Yet once more, O ye laurels, and once more,
> Ye myrtles brown, with ivy never sere . . .

The students discovered that although the entries for words like *laurels* were rather long, the entries for words like *yet* were even longer.

Editors interested in developing new writers should encourage them to take a piece of submitted or assigned work and do Auden's *OED* exercise with it. This forced immersion in the sea of language can have two effects, both of them healthy. First, rubbing the writer's nose in every word tends to point up the defects of overblown prose. Whatever its other effects, the tedium produced by such an exercise certainly gives a new writer a generous regard for economy of expression. Second, and far more important, time spent perusing the dictionary creates a new respect for the power of mundane words, such as Milton's *once*, *more*, *and*, *with*, and *never*. Familiar words are the workhorses of good writing, and the more deeply writers understand them, the better their writing will be.

Analysis, Writing, Rewriting

New writers should also be encouraged to become thoroughly familiar with their own writing. Here are some questions they should ask themselves:

- What kinds of sentences do I write (compound, complex, compound-complex)? What kinds do I avoid?
- What is the ratio of transitive to intransitive verbs in my writing? Active to passive constructions? Adjectives to nouns? Adverbs to verbs?
- How orthodox are my grammar and syntax? Are my reasons for breaking rules good (they serve the piece) or not so good (showing off)?
- Am I partial to particular figures of speech (metaphors, similes) or constructions (not only . . . but also; either . . . or; both . . . and; on the one hand . . . on the other hand)?
- How many of the expressions in my writing are really clichés?

Editors prospecting for and nurturing writing talent should also instruct new writers in the art of writing with cadence. (Technical writing is an exception.) A style without cadence is a parade without a drummer; let it go on for long and its feet get tangled. Speech writing is a particularly good training ground for developing this most neglected stylistic tool. A particularly fine lesson in cadences is on pp. 107-108 of James J. Kilpatrick's *The*

Writer's Art (Kansas City: Andrews, McMeel & Parker, Inc., 1984), where Kilpatrick walks readers through the construction of one of his columns.

But the best way for new writers to acquire a style, better than analyzing their own prose, is to produce it. Writing forces the writer to make choices, and exercising the muscles of selection and rejection turns a novice into a real writer. (Editors have a self-interest in these gymnastics because the more ruthlessly writers edit their own writing, the easier the editor's job.)

Even better than writing, of course, is rewriting and, in this vein, a thoughtful gift for a promising writer is a framed motto from Dr. Johnson: "Read over your composition, and when you meet with a passage that you think particularly fine, strike it out."

—Bruce O. Boston (#109, 10/84)

III. LEVELS OF EDIT

The JPL Approach

As every editor knows, different manuscripts require different degrees of editing, depending on the manuscript's condition, purpose, intended readership, budget, and deadline. The more finely tuned the editing is to each manuscript's needs, the more economical and better the editing will be.

Probably the finest tuning so far has been developed at the Jet Propulsion Laboratory (JPL), California Institute of Technology. In their booklet, *The Levels of Edit*, Robert Van Buren and Mary Fran Buehler, two JPL senior technical editors, describe five levels of edit using nine "types" of edit.

Here is their list, which starts with the lowest level and adds tasks cumulatively at each higher level.

Level 5

- *Coordination Edit*—includes planning and estimating, maintaining records, scheduling, monitoring, coordinating production, and maintaining contact with authors to discuss changes and ensure that deadlines are met.
- *Policy Edit*—verifies that the publication conforms to house policy; for example, in cover and title page, credit statement, table of contents, abstract, references, and endorsement of any company's products or services.

Level 4

- *Integrity Edit*—ensures, among other things, agreement of table of contents with headings, figure captions, table titles, and page numbers; callout (citation in the text) for each table, figure, reference, footnote, and appendix; existence of text elements cited in cross-references in earlier volumes.
- *Screening Edit*—checks spelling, subject-verb agreement, completeness of sentences, clarification of incomprehensible statements, and reproducibility of figures intended as camera-ready copy.

Level 3

- *Copy Clarification*—entails clarifying unreadable copy and, in general, giving clear instructions to typists, typesetters, keyboarders, and graphic artists.
- *Format Edit*—refers to instructions on typography: typeface, column width, justification, form and position of headings, and layout (for example, instructions for new pages, positions of illustrations).

Level 2

- *Mechanical Style Edit*—ensures appropriate and consistent style in capitalization, spelling, compounding, numerals, italic or other special fonts, and acronyms and abbreviations.
- *Language Edit*—includes work that may be done separately, without other types of edit. It covers preferred spellings according to the dictionary of choice; grammar and syntax; punctuation according to the specified style guide; usage according to the designated authority; fluency; parallel construction; conciseness; and proper use of description, exposition, narrative, and argument and their effect on verb tenses.

Level 1

- *Substantive Edit*—deals with the meaningful content of the publication, restoring, for instance, the coherence of individual parts, eliminating gaps and redundancies, resolving apparent discrepancies in meaning in different parts of the report, deleting inappropriate material, and ensuring that emphasis placed on various elements is appropriate to their significance.

(#54, 2/81)

The EEI Approach

EEI (Editorial Experts, Inc.) divides editing into two broad categories—copyediting and substantive editing. For every job, a checklist is filled out, specifying tasks needed in each category, and a second editor "reads behind" the first to maintain quality.

Copyediting

EEI copyediting includes reviewing a "finished" manuscript for spelling, grammar, punctuation, and consistency. Copyediting can include checking completeness, accuracy, and format of tables, bibliographies, and footnotes. It does not include rewriting or reorganizing.

Substantive Editing

EEI substantive editing includes copyediting, rewriting, reorganizing, writing transitions, writing chapter or section summaries, eliminating wordiness, reviewing content for accuracy and logic, and ensuring the proper tone and approach for the intended audience. Substantive editing can also include helping plan and outline publications and consulting with authors and publishers.

Teamwork

On certain jobs, a substantive editor and a copyeditor work together to increase speed and reduce overall project costs. The substantive editor works on the bulk of the text; the copyeditor works on tables, bibliographies, lists, and footnotes. Ideally, each editor should have a complete copy of the manuscript.

The Checklist

To avoid confusion among clients and editors on just what is meant by a "light copyedit" or a "really substantive edit," EEI uses a checklist for each job.

Item by item, the checklist first details the minimum tasks for each job, including correction of spelling, grammar, and punctuation errors. A minimum edit also includes correction of inconsistencies, particularly in number style, capitalization, compound words, abbreviations, uses of italics, lists, and alphabetical or numerical sequences.

The checklist specifies that editors retype hard-to-read passages, make sure all pages are numbered in sequence, and write a cover memo outlining what they did and did not do and listing their editorial style decisions and queries.

The checklist then itemizes additional copyediting tasks that a client may specify, including making a table of contents and a list of tables, making elements in a series parallel, clarifying pronoun antecedents, changing passive voice to active, eliminating the first person and sexist language, checking answers to questions in textbooks, and explaining unfamiliar acronyms and abbreviations at first mention.

The final section of the checklist covers heavier, more substantive editing, rewriting, and related tasks, including reorganizing significant amounts of material; rewriting awkward, turgid, or confusing sections; reviewing a manuscript for portions that can be cut; and checking accuracy of content.

Editing Distinguished from Proofreading and Writing

EEI carefully separates editing from proofreading and writing.

Proofreading is defined as comparing a later stage of copy to an earlier stage, looking for typographical errors, poor type quality, and deviations from typing or typesetting instructions. Proofreading includes queries on blatant errors and inconsistencies. "Editorial" proofreading includes extra attention to style matters and can include extensive queries.

To EEI, writing means starting almost from scratch, with no manuscript or with only notes, an outline, or a point of view from which to work. Writing can include research, interviews, publication planning, outline and draft preparation, summaries, and consultations.

—Priscilla Taylor (#56, 3/81)

Two More Approaches

"All it needs is a copyedit." Sound familiar? Too many times editors receive a manuscript with instructions to copyedit only and gear up for that level of time and effort, only to find the manuscript is poorly organized, full of redundancies, and written in language only the fond author can understand. Perhaps the author has worked 6 months on his opus and can't believe it needs more than a comma here and a hyphen there.

Or perhaps the author doesn't know the difference between copyediting and substantive editing. Many authors don't, according to Shirley Rosenberg, president of SSR, Inc. In a workshop address at the May 1981 Washington Edpress conference, Rosenberg pointed out that editing, at present, is ill defined. Even if copyediting and substantive editing were well defined and their definitions well known, the two often overlap in practice.

Rosenberg reported that the . . . Association of Editorial Businesses, composed of 25 member companies, is attempting to develop standard definitions of all editorial procedures, including copyediting and substantive editing. The definitions under discussion are

Copyedit—Review manuscript for correct spelling and grammar, check cross references, make style consistent. Beyond this definition, Rosenberg suggests, a copyedit could include preparation of a style sheet, checking facts and the accuracy of tables, charts, bibliographies, and footnotes.

Substantive edit—Review and revise tone, logic, and accuracy of manuscript; may involve reorganization of manuscript, writing transitions and summaries, rewriting portions of text, and working with the client to clarify text and to incorporate reviewers' suggestions.

Another distinction between substantive editing and copyediting, Rosenberg said, is their order in the sequence of editorial tasks. Substantive editing starts the sequence (after writing), while copyediting ends it. A manuscript edited for substance should go back to the client to make sure that the editor, in improving the author's presentation, hasn't distorted the author's meaning. When a client brings in a manuscript for copyediting, the author should already have signed off on it, except for style.

Theoretically, a copyedited manuscript should be ready to go directly to the printer. But often—and this is one of the many instances in which the distinction between copyediting and substantive editing blurs—the copyeditor will have questions only the author can answer. At this late stage of the game, however, authors are loath to rewrite. Further, the copyeditor may not have the technical background in the author's subject that a substantive editor should have. So, copyeditors should query as lightly as possible.

Agreement with the client about style should help eliminate the need for postediting conferences. Does the client want GPO? Chicago? Some hybrid? A house style? What about specialized terms in this manuscript that are not covered in the general style manuals?

If the manuscript has had a substantive edit, that editor may have developed a style sheet showing unusual hyphenation, capitalization, spelling, and other elements of style that will apply to this manuscript. If no style sheet exists, the copyeditor should develop one as the work progresses, consulting the client as necessary to determine appropriate style for technical or unfamiliar terms.

The ARINC Approach

The ARINC Research Corporation distinguishes two levels of editing—thorough editing and cursory editing—and suggests a sequence of procedures for each.

In thorough editing the editor should—

1. Read the entire draft carefully, to get the best possible understanding of its content and organization.
2. If reorganization seems necessary, discuss the proposed revision with the author and get . . . approval before proceeding. Other questions that arise during the reading can also be taken up at this time.
3. Proceed with the editing, including any necessary reorganization of the report, with the purpose of achieving the style objectives set forth [below].
4. Consult with the author as required to clear up questions arising during the editing, but keep the number of such consultations to a minimum in the interest of saving both the author's and the editor's time. Accumulate groups of questions and list them in writing, with appropriate references to the relevant passages in the draft, as a means of avoiding oversights and loss of time.

In cursory or "minimum" editing, the editor should—

1. If time permits, read the entire report once and discuss any serious organization problem with the author.
2. Proceed with editing, stressing [style objectives 1-4; work on objectives 5-12] to the extent that time allows.

The ARINC *Publications Style Manual* lists these 12 elements of effective report-writing style as editorial objectives:

1. Scientific objectivity
2. Clarity of meaning
3. Sentence structure based on good English usage
4. Approved spelling
5. Conciseness
6. Directness—the active voice whenever possible
7. First-person and third-person styles—use them interchangeably (ARINC prefers the first-person style on grounds that it is more direct and more informal than third-person style.)
8. Avoidance of fad words, coined words, and overuse of words
9. Logical sequence of thought
10. Fluidity of sentence and paragraph structure
11. Conformity to ARINC research style for specialized expressions, and consistency in such expressions throughout the report
12. Consistency in technical terminology.

ARINC's priority order of editorial objectives precludes making a distinction between copyediting and substantive editing. For example, items 11 and 12 would be considered copyediting tasks; yet they might not be included in a cursory edit. Checking for objectivity and clarity, normally part of a substantive edit, is a "must" in all ARINC's editing.

(#59, 6/81)

NCHS Approach

The following breakdown of levels of editorial effort appeared in a recent request for proposals from the National Center for Health Statistics (NCHS) of the Department of Health and Human Services:

- Level 1, *production editing,* includes reviewing the manuscript for completeness and correct spelling, grammar, and punctuation; checking references to tables and figures; and ensuring consistency of style.
- Level 2, *copyediting,* includes all of the above as well as reorganizing up to one-third of the manuscript for clarity, checking for agreement between the data in the text and those in the tables and charts, styling references and verifying references to NCHS publications, deciding on the best setup and arrangement of charts and tables, and working with the author(s) to clarify text and to incorporate suggestions.
- Level 3, *substantive editing,* includes all of levels 1 and 2 and reviewing; revising the tone, logic, and accuracy of the manuscript; writing transitions and summaries; and rewriting large portions of text.

(#72, 5/82)

Minimal Editing: How Much Is Too Much?

How should an editor handle a bylined article by a well-known author? Use "minimal editing," says the U.S. Census Bureau's Gerald A. Mann. Mann gave these suggestions for such editing at the 1980 International Technical Communications Conference of the Society of Technical Communication:

- Correct mechanical errors, but don't change the author's style unless it interferes with readability.
- Review the entire manuscript for proper reader "framing" and focus, usually through a good introduction and appropriate writing style.
- Check for a clear plan of organization, with good transition from section to section.
- Try to ensure that no questions will be unanswered in the reader's mind.
- Make only those changes that can be justified in terms of the reader's needs: Don't allow your personal preferences to intrude on the author's style.

An example of minimal editing is shown in the box below. Mann comments,

The edited version retains the style and tone of the original, but includes some minor rephrasing to clarify the meaning. Nothing that remains in the edited version of this passage is incorrect; it is simply more ornate than many of us are accustomed to.

An inexperienced editor might have practically rewritten the entire passage with an eye to achieving a low fog count, but in doing so he or she would have completely eliminated the author's distinctive style. Not only would this be presumptuous and unfair to the author, it would be unjustified in terms of the reader's needs. The typical reader interested in this kind of subject matter will also probably appreciate this kind of style.

To represent in painting the joining of the two worlds in forms which are, as it were, true to nature, is necessarily one of the most difficult and challenging tasks of art. It involves a paradox: the artist has to represent the invisibility of the gods, or their transition from invisibility to epiphany, in a visual medium and yet he has to make it look—as, indeed, must be the case when it happens in nature—as if this transition were one of the most natural occurrences that connect heaven and earth. The gods in the woods and fields are the spirits of the landscape and, as such, have a life and will of their own, but they are also the landscape itself, or its real sense, and must therefore, if adequately rendered, in all of their manifestations be recognizable in the duplicity of their uniqueness.

To represent in painting the joining of the two worlds, in a form which is true to the nature of each, is necessarily one of the most difficult and challenging tasks of art. It involves a paradox: The artist must represent the invisibility of the gods, or their transition from invisibility to epiphany, in a visual medium, and he also has to make it look as if this transition were one of the most natural occurrences that connect heaven and earth. The gods in the woods and fields are the spirits of the landscape with a life and will of their own, but they are also the landscape itself, or its real sense; their adequate rendition, therefore, must clearly represent this unique double nature.

—Priscilla Taylor (#49, 10/80)

■ Crash Editing: One Way to Do It

One person's interesting—and controversial—opinions on how to edit a manuscript quickly to meet a short deadline are outlined in "Coping With Crash Editing" by Brian Jarman (*27th ITCC Proceedings*, 1980).

A typical crash editing job, says Jarman, consists of three main steps: psyching up for the job, attacking the manuscript, and deciding how to compromise quality to meet the deadline. Here is how to use Jarman's methods to do a crash editing job:

Psyching Up

In the first step, psyching up, you develop the right attitude to do the job.

Some of the psychological tricks Jarman uses: Cultivate a low, calm voice and relaxed manner. Establish your control over the job by taking the manuscript from the author as soon as possible. Give an up-tight author your full attention. Hold the manuscript in your hands. Flip through the pages, and ask the author five crucial questions:

- What is the manuscript supposed to sell; what is its purpose?
- Who will read it?
- Is there anything special to be done; for example, are there points to emphasize or to play down?
- How far along are the illustrations?
- What is the deadline?

If the author does not give a definite answer to the last question, get the information you need to figure out the deadline yourself. (For example, will the manuscript be reviewed? If so, when? How many typists will be available to incorporate editing changes?) Then estimate the time available for editing; do not, at this time, estimate how long it will take you to edit the manuscript.

Attacking the Manuscript

Never tell an author the extent or depth of the editing you will do (one of Jarman's controversial statements). Do not read the manuscript; instead, begin to edit (another controversial statement). Determine the level of editing you can do in the time available: time yourself as you do a full, indepth editing job at your best speed on the first two pages of text; apply the resulting average rate of speed per page to calculate the time needed for the whole manuscript. Then, if you find you cannot meet the deadline with an indepth job, edit to a lower level.

As you work, you will set a rhythm. To avoid breaking the rhythm, work as long as you can at a stretch. Edit the text, figures, and tables separately, each to its own rhythm. Go back and read the text to check the descriptions of the figures after you finish editing the figures. Do the same for the tables.

Take a few minutes' break to clear your mind. Then read the manuscript, but do not rewrite or edit again; just look for inconsistencies you can correct in a hurry.

Compromising on the Quality of Editing

Following Jarman's assignment of priorities to five levels of editing (as shown in the chart below), edit to the highest priority the available time allows. (The assignment of priorities is another point of controversy; some editors would change priority 5 to priority 1.)

Priority	Editing Level (Cumulative)
1	Correct errors in punctuation, grammar, and spelling
2	Make sentences more effective
3	Correct improper word usage
4	Make formatting changes
5	Reorganize contents

—Peggy Smith (#50, 11/80)

IV. STYLE MANUALS

Preparing Your Own Style Guide

Preparing a style guide involves a lot of time, effort, and hard work, but can pay off, according to Bonnie Baron. At a 1978 Washington Edpress miniworkshop, Baron, an editor with the Association for Childhood Education International, discussed side benefits of an inhouse style guide. Such a guide can—

- *Save time* by providing quick answers,
- *Save money* by avoiding correction costs (when you realize at galley stage that one word is spelled two ways throughout!), and
- *Develop professionalism.* In writing and maintaining a style guide, not only can staff members share expertise and knowledge, but you can improve your group's image.

Necessary Steps

In getting started—the hardest part—first *decide who will use the guide*. If you are the only user, then the guide can be informal. But if others will use it, you must consider who they are (typists, designers, etc.), what information they need, and how to organize the material to meet their needs.

Second, *decide if your guide should apply to more than one publication* or type of report. Sometimes a specialized guide is more useful than a general guide.

Third, if you will need to update the guide from time to time, *consider using a looseleaf binder* instead of a printed book, the cost of which cannot often be justified.

Fourth, *consider adopting as your primary source a standard style manual*, such as the Government Printing Office *Style Manual* or the University of Chicago Press *A Manual of Style*. Let your guide cover only what is unique and preferred in your publication.

Fifth, *involve all potential users* during the development and revision stages to obtain the decisions and to ensure guide use.

Baron gave other useful suggestions—

- *Use an existing style guide as a starting point* to develop topics and format.

- *Divide among the staff the responsibilities* for writing sections of the guide.
- *Illustrate* specific examples of style wherever possible (table format, heads, captions, etc.).
- *Provide a table of contents*; use tabbed section dividers if necessary.
- *Give each page a number and a date* to facilitate revision.
- *Make one person responsible for receiving new ideas and carrying out revisions.*
- *Distribute revised pages to the staff*, and call attention to changes or additions.

—Andrea De La Garza (#6, 5/78)

New Chicago Manual Is Published

After 7 years in the making, the 13th edition of *The Chicago Manual of Style*—at 738 pages—has finally been published. Experienced users will find little news in terms of editorial style: the rules for spelling, capitalization, word division, compounding, and the myriad points of style have not changed appreciably from the 12th edition. But the manual has undergone a metamorphosis. No longer is it simply a collection of rules for editors; it is now a clear blueprint for even the most inexperienced editor to follow in editing and producing a book or article.

The major change concerns technological advances in the publishing industry that were in their infancy when the 12th edition was published in 1969. The opening sections, particularly chapter 2, "Manuscript Preparation and Copyediting," take account of word processing techniques in manuscript production, including the techniques of editing OCR scanner copy. In keeping with the editors' stated purpose of making the manual more accessible to inexperienced editors, a new section in that chapter explains, with illustrations in the typeset line, how to make editorial marks. The discussion of how to write a cover letter to the author, to accompany an edited manuscript (on pp. 70 and 71), is beautifully simple.

Removal of Sexism

The manual has been rigorously edited to remove the generic "he"; comparison of the new edition with the old provides a textbook example of clean, unobtrusive editing to remove sexist references. For example, compare these two passages on the author as indexer:

> The author most nearly approaches the ideal as indexer. Certainly, he knows better than anyone else both the scope and limitations of his work; and certainly, he knows the audience to which he has addressed himself. At the same time, he can be so subjective about his own work that he may be tempted to include in his index even references to milieu-establishing, peripheral statements. . . .
>
> —12th ed., par. 18.14, p. 404

> The author most nearly approaches the ideal as indexer. Certainly, the author knows better than anyone else both the scope and the limitations of the work, and the audience to which it is addressed. At the same time, authors are sometimes so subjective about their own work that they are tempted to include in an index even references to milieu-establishing, peripheral statements. . . .
>
> —13th ed., par. 18.20, p. 518

Rule for Possessives

On the question of denoting the possessive of proper names ending in *s*, Chicago comes down forthrightly in favor of adding *'s*. Although this has always been Chicago's preference, the new edition outlines the reasoning for it. Sections 6.21 through 6.23 set forth a cogently reasoned argument which, the manual says, "is essentially a restatement of William Strunk's 'Rule no. 1' in the famous *Elements of Style.*" Rejecting the rule that only the apostrophe should be added to words of more than one syllable ending in a sibilant, the manual notes that adherence to that rule would produce such absurdities as "Parrish' cartoons," *sh* qualifying as a sibilant. This choice of style is widely at variance with other commonly used style guides, particularly those of newspapers and wire services.

Tables

A new section on constructing tables from raw data illustrates the steps involved in building usable, comparable statistical tables. From presenting the data in their simplest terms, the discussion progresses through successively elaborate stages of presentation. The section is profusely illustrated with sample tables that are far easier to read and understand than those in the 12th edition. Another new section explains how to estimate the size of a table and how to correct odd-shaped tables. Samples of differing table styles are at the end of the chapter.

References, Notes, and Bibliographies

The new edition of the manual contains three exhaustive chapters on documentation, whereas the old had two. The new edition begins with a general discussion in chapter 15, "Documentation: References, Notes, and Bibliographies," which describes four methods of documenting texts: author-date, long popular in the natural sciences and gaining currency in the social sciences and humanities; endnotes; traditional footnotes; and unnumbered notes or notes keyed to a line or page number.

Chicago strongly encourages the use of the author-date system for all its books in the natural sciences, most books in the social sciences, and any book whose author is willing to cooperate. The reason: this system saves the most space, time, and money. It allows addition of names and titles to the reference list up to the last minute because it does not involve complex renumbering of notes; it is less distracting for readers; and it may save some readers the effort of turning to the notes to understand the citation.

But this preference does not diminish the importance or clarity given to all the forms of documentation—not only how they should look and what information they should contain, but the editorial and design considerations involved in choosing among forms. Matters of reference style are still fully explained and illustrated, and there is a good selection of sample bibliographies at the end of chapter 15. Chapter 16 concentrates on bibliographic style, including a new section, "Nonbook Materials," that covers citation of such works as computer programs and video-recordings. Chapter 17, titled "Note Forms," presents the familiar reference style guide.

Indexing

The indexing chapter alone is worth the price of the book. A beginner could learn to make a useful index just from a careful reading of this chapter. The discussion in the new edition concentrates more fully on the philosophical considerations involved in choosing entries, as well as on simpler and clearer explanations of the terms and mechanics of the indexing process.

Alternative methods for more experienced indexers are also discussed. Even the tedium of some indexing methods—and the extra work they involve—is explained and justified: there are few short cuts in manual indexing. Also included are helpful tips on verifying page numbers, keeping cards in order, deciding what to put on a card, and eliminating what should not be indexed. A new section discusses the problems of editing an index compiled by someone other than yourself, including what to do if the index is a disaster. This section also contains a good checklist for reading behind an indexer.

Design and Typography

Chapter 19, "Design and Typography," contains a new section on photomechanical and electronic composition as they affect choice of typeface, cautioning that even familiar faces look different when produced by the new methods. Gone are the lush sample pages of typefaces, set in Mono- and Linotype and produced by letterpress, that graced previous editions, victims of the publishing exigencies of the modern age: scarcity of skilled labor, expense of hand operations, and lack of time.

Composition, Printing, and Binding

The final chapter, "Composition, Printing, and Binding," gives a short history of printing and typesetting processes—both hand and machine—well illustrated with halftones and line cuts to show handsetting, assembled galleys, and pages locked in a frame or chase—as well as printing processes, imposition, papermaking, and binding. The heart of this chapter, however, is a concise discussion of the impact of recent technological advances in production. This edition of the manual itself was set by computer, using the Penta system. The section on 20th-century composition and makeup covers several generations of typesetting equipment: strike-on, photocomposition, CRT composition, and electronic typesetting systems driven by computers.

This chapter may well be the most significant aspect of the new manual, recognizing (as it does in an oblique way) that editors nowadays seldom have the luxury of being purely manuscript editors. More often than not, today's editor is also designer, paste-up artist, and production coordinator. Other technical manuals cover production processes in considerable depth, and are, of course, indispensable to editors who must be responsible for production; but with the addition of this interesting and informative chapter, along with the expanded treatment of indexing, constructing tables, and making editorial marks, *The Chicago Manual of Style* becomes, for both novice and veteran editors, a definitive guide to all phases of the publication process.

—Mara Adams (#79, 9/82)

Test Yourself

On Chicago Style Manual

The Chicago style manual lists the following abbreviations for the various parts of a book. Fill in the blanks with answers to these questions: What do the abbreviations stand for? What are their plural forms? (Hint: All but seven add *s*).

1. app.	______________	______	14. n.	______________	______
2. art.	______________	______	15. no.	______________	______
3. bk.	______________	______	16. p.	______________	______
4. chap.	______________	______	17. par.	______________	______
5. col.	______________	______	18. pl.	______________	______
6. div.	______________	______	19. pt.	______________	______
7. eq.	______________	______	20. sc.	______________	______
8. ex.	______________	______	21. sec.	______________	______
9. f.	______________	______	22. ser.	______________	______
10. fasc.	______________	______	23. st.	______________	______
11. fig.	______________	______	24. supp.	______________	______
12. fol.	______________	______	25. v.	______________	______
13. l.	______________	______	26. vol.	______________	______

Answers

1. appendix	apps.	14. note, footnote	nn.
2. article	arts.	15. number	nos.
3. book	bks.	16. page	pp.
4. chapter	chaps.	17. paragraph	pars.
5. column	cols.	18. plate	pls.
6. division	divs.	19. part	pts.
7. equation	eqq.	20. scenes	scs.
8. example	exx.	21. section	secs.
9. and following	ff.	22. series	sers.
10. fascicle	fascs.	23. stanza	sts.
11. figure	figs.	24. supplement	supps.
12. folio	fols.	25. verse	vv.
13. line	ll.	26. volume	vols.

(#47, 9/80)

New GPO Manual Goes Straight: No More 'Aline' or 'Subpena'

The new GPO style manual is just out (as of June, notwithstanding the March 1984 date on its cover) and despite all the typos (*1st Calvary*, p. 168) and inconsistencies, it will be welcomed by everybody who hated *aline* (now it's *align*), *gage* (now *gauge*), *marihuana* (*marijuana*), *subpena* (*subpoena*), and *sirup* (*syrup*). The new manual even restores the distinction between *insure* (protect) and *ensure* (guarantee), and, bowing to pressure from programmers nationwide, has abandoned *programed*, *-er*, and *-ing*. Although the preface of the new manual repeats verbatim the statement in the 1973 edition that it "attempts to keep abreast of and sometimes anticipate changes in orthography, grammar, and type production," obviously GPO has had second thoughts about some previously anticipated changes.

Some of the other welcome changes are marred by the editors' failure to implement the agreed-upon changes throughout the book. This problem particularly plagues the guidance on capitalization. *Social Security* has at last been capitalized (at least on p. 56), but the change didn't get made under the guidance on *amendment* (p. 36) or in a list of compounds that do not require hyphenation (p. 75). Similarly, users will doubtless be mystified by *free world* (p. 47) and *World: New, Old, Third*; but *Free world* (p. 61).

These and other inconsistencies tend to undercut the statement in the front of the book: "For the purposes of this Manual, printed examples throughout are to be considered the same as the printed rules" (p. vi). Using the manual becomes a challenge: Which listing truly reflects what the GPO Style Board intended?

The Pressures for Change

Robert McArtor, chairman of the GPO Style Board, has mixed emotions about his product, deploring the typos, inconsistencies, and "perfect" binding (my copy fell apart in the course of a telephone interview), while explaining the pressures under which the manual is produced. His job, in essence, is to standardize everything that can be standardized while trying to accommodate the demands of members of Congress, cartographers, lawyers, librarians, and assorted other groups nationwide—not to mention the demands imposed by technological changes in the publishing industry.

Those technological advances (the old edition was set in hot metal) were responsible for the Style Board's decision to review all material in the manual—and for the subsequent 2-year delay in publication. Computerization of the publishing industry also was responsible for some style decisions. For example, because computers don't know that they should avoid a line break between the parts of abbreviations and the initials of a personal name, the space has been eliminated: *Texas A&M*, *R&D*, *A.B. Secrest* (p. 135), and *S&L's* (p. 149).

McArtor is justly proud of the new general instruction section of the manual (pp. 8ff.), which includes guidelines of the American National Standards Institute for standardizing title page information in publications. GPO was responding to pressures from librarians and others who deal with standardized bibliographic information. Another useful section is the enlarged list of government publications available to authors and editors, including technical and scientific guides, manuals on correspondence style, and legal writing aids (pp. 2–4).

Although McArtor describes himself as opposed to unnecessary capitalization, the new manual reflects congressional pressures to retain *State* and *Nation*; in fact, GPO has added caps for *Program* "if part of name" (*Social Security Program*, p. 54).

Geographic Style

Deferring to people who felt passionately about the matter, the manual has changed the name it gave natives of Utah to *Utahn*, but in a footnote retains *Utahan* as the adjectival form (p. 72).

Despite complaints from Marylanders in Prince George's, Queen Anne's, and St. Mary's counties, among other people, the manual continues to drop the apostrophes but has added this explanation: "Following the practice of modern-day geographers and cartographers (i.e., the U.S. Board of Geographic Names) the genitive apostrophe is not used in county names" (p. 245). Cartographers' concerns that map readers might confuse an apostrophe with a prime mark overrode citizen complaints. (It doesn't seem to have occurred to GPO's style makers that perhaps they could lay down one rule for mapmakers and another for the rest of the printing world.) Nonetheless, one geographic location with enough political clout did retain its apostrophe: *Martha's Vineyard* (p. 117).

And speaking of geography, the new manual has adopted the Postal Service system of two-letter abbreviations (as the American Psychological Association manual did last year). Although McArtor confesses he has trouble remembering whether MI refers to Michigan, Minnesota, Missouri, or Mississippi, he says the GPO adopted the new system because it permits consistent abbreviation of all state names.

Advice on Using the Manual

McArtor emphasizes first that the rules in the new manual are more important than the listings because they show the reasons for style decisions. For example, he points to an excellent new section that explains the formula for achieving uniform treatment in the formation of coined words and symbols (p. 142):

> **Coined words and symbols**
>
> **9.48.** To obtain uniform treatment in the formation of coined words and symbols, the following formula, which conforms to current usage, should be applied:

When only first letter of each word or selected words is used to make up symbol, use all caps:

APPR (Army package power reactor)
MAG (Military Advisory Group)
* MIRV (multiple independently targetable reentry vehicle)
SALT (strategic arms limitation talks)
* STEP (supplemental training and employment program)

Where first letters of prefixes and/or suffixes are utilized as part of established expressions, use all caps:

CPR (cardio*p*ulmonary *r*esuscitation)
* ESP (*e*xtra*s*ensory *p*erception)
* FLIR (*f*orward-*l*ooking *i*nfra*r*ed)

Where an acronym or abbreviated form is copyrighted or established by law, copy must be followed:

ACTION (agency of Government; not an acronym)
MarAd (*Mar*itime *Ad*ministration)
NACo (*N*ational *A*ssociation of *Co*unties)
* MEDLARS (*Med*ical *L*iterature *A*nalysis and *R*etrieval *S*ystem)

When proper names are used in shortened form any word of which uses more than first letter of each word, use caps and lowercase:

Conrail (Consolidated Rail Corporation)
* Vepco (Virginia Electric Power Co.)
* Inco (International Nickel Co.)
* Aramco (Arabian-American Oil Co.)

In common-noun combinations made up of more than first letter of lowercased words, use lowercase:

loran (*lo*ng-*ra*nge *n*avigation)
sonar (*so*und *na*vigation *r*anging)
secant (*se*paration *c*ontrol of *a*ircraft by *n*onsynchronous *t*echniques)

The manual's producers must count on users' remembering all these examples, because those that have asterisks do not appear in the long list of standard word abbreviations that follows (pp. 146ff.).

Curiously, the new manual contains another list of coined words and symbols (pp. 308–310) apparently intended only for use in printing the *Congressional Record*, although it's unclear why this list could not have been integrated with the long list of standard word abbreviations on pp. 146ff., since the two lists overlap considerably. The new list's description of CBS as referring to *Columbia Broadcasting Co.* seems an odd lapse; the name of the company used to be Columbia Broadcasting System but is now CBS Inc. But not to worry—it seems unlikely that many people will discover the new list; like so many other handy things in the manual, it cannot be found in the index.

McArtor's second piece of advice to manual users is to read the introductions to lists carefully. For example, lists of words in the guide to compounding can be misleading to someone who has not read the small print in the introduction, which says, "note that two-word forms in the adjective position use a hyphen, except as laid down in rules 6.16, 6.21, and 6.24" (p. 82).

An Overall Assessment

The new GPO manual offers some welcome changes, but the level of the proofreading errors and inconsistencies is unacceptable in a style manual. The errata list, which must inevitably follow, will be long. Nevertheless, the GPO manual remains one of the most useful resources in the editorial arsenal, whether the user ever edits for the government or not. It's reassuring to know that when time hangs heavy one can study how to treat particles in personal names (*Du Pont* or *du Pont*? *De Kalb* or *DeKalb*? pp. 25 and 46), or check out difficult plurals (*italic*, *Kansas Citys*, p. 69), or learn what GPO considers completely anglicized words that no longer require diacritical marks: *auto(s)-da-fe*, *cause celebre*, *coup d'etat*, *table d'hote*, *tete-a-tete*, and *vis-a-vis*, among others (p. 67).

Users of the old manual will welcome the updating of the useful list of derivatives of proper names (*brazil nut*, *herculean task*, pp. 43–44) and the list of trade names and trademarks (*Airwick*, *Ping-Pong*, pp. 58–59) and the addition of a list of company names (*A–C Spark Plug Co.*, *Procter & Gamble Co.*, p. 46).

But don't plan to use the new manual as a model for the graceful removal of sexism:

> 2.83. If the proofreader detects inconsistent and erroneous statements, it is his or her duty to query them.
>
> 2.84. If the grammatical construction of a sentence or clause is questioned by a reader and it seems desirable to change the form, he must indicate the proposed correction, add a query mark, and enclose all in a ring. (p. 15)

The *U.S. Government Printing Office Style Manual* can be ordered from the Superintendent of Documents, U.S. Government Printing Office, Washington, DC 20402.

—Priscilla Taylor (#105, 7/84)

Test Yourself

Which Is Correct and Why?

Harry S. Truman
or
Harry S Truman

(#4, 4/78)

Answers

(#5, 4/78)

Harry S./S Truman

From Robert C. McArtor, Chairman, GPO Style Board:

I fear the wisdom of Solomon will not suffice to satisfy those purists who still insist on removing the period from Mr. Truman's battered initial. Mr. Truman had no middle name, thus for much of his life his middle initial carried no period. So much confusion resulted from constant resetting of his name that he, by memorandum, instructed the period be used. His Presidential papers and his own autobiography include the troublesome point.

■ All the Style that's Fit to Print

The foreword to the 1962 edition of *The New York Times Style Book for Writers and Editors* suggested that style rules could be summarized in this way: "The rule of common sense will prevail at all times."

The 1977 edition, *The New York Times Manual of Style and Usage,* has added many entries that concern language usage rather than printing style—hence the adjustment in the book's title—but the philosophy remains the same.

The *Times*'s identity is, of course, conservative. The manual comes out strongly against *chairwoman* and *chairperson,* which, it says, "should not be used; *chairman* (like *foreman, spokesman* and some similar terms) suffices for both sexes. In the case of a mixed group whose members have similar titles—Councilman and Councilwoman, for example—the best solution in plural references is *Council members* or some equivalent."

The *Times* also adheres to *Mr., Mrs.,* and *Miss* in news stories, reserving *Ms.* only for quoted matter, letters to the editor, and news articles discussing the term itself.

A sampling of style and usage entries follows:

- *alphabetizing names.* When dealing with *Mc* or *Mac, alphabetize* by the second letter: *Mabley, MacAdam, Maynard, McNeil. . . .*
- *comprise* means to include or contain; the whole comprises the parts. *The system comprises 35 formerly independent rail and bus lines.* Not: *Thirty-five lines comprise the system.* And not *comprised of.*
- *co-* co-author (n.; never a verb), co-chairman, co-defendant, coed, coeducation, coequal, coexist, coexistence, co-op, cooperate, cooperation, cooperative (n., adj.), coordinate, coordination, co-owner, co-partner, co-pilot, co-star, co-worker.
- *couple* (n.). In the sense of two associated persons, the word should be construed as a plural: *The couple were married in 1952. The couple separated in 1960. The couple argued constantly; in fact, they* (not *it) never let up.* An exception: *Each couple was asked to give $10.*

- *dilemma* does not mean simply a problem; it involves a choice between two alternatives, both unattractive.
- *due to* is properly used in the sense of *caused by* or *resulting from* when *due* is an adjective modifying a noun: *His dismissal was due to that single escapade.* (The modified noun is *dismissal.)* But *due to* should not be used when there is no modified noun: *He was dismissed due to that single escapade.* In this instance, *because of* solves the problem.
- *fused participles.* They should be defused. For example: *The police tried to prevent him jumping* should be changed to *prevent him from jumping* or *prevent his jumping.*
- *Hobson's choice* means that one must accept what is offered or receive nothing at all; there is really no choice.
- *lectern, podium.* One stands *behind* a lectern and *on* a podium.
- *Lloyd's* (insurance), *Lloyds* (bankers).
- *Lloyd's Register* (shipping).
- *mean, median.* In statistics, a *mean* is an average; a *median* is a figure that ranks midway in a list of numbers arranged in ascending or descending order. For example, in a discussion of the varying wages of 51 workers, the mean is the total of their pay divided by 51. The median is the wage in the middle—higher than 25 of the wages and lower than the remaining 25. If the total of items listed is an even number—50, say, instead of 51—the median is the average of the two numbers in the middle of the listing. In other words, if the 25th number in a listing of 50 is 200 and the 26th is 220, the median is 210.
- *ongoing.* An overworked adjective that should be replaced when possible by one of its many synonyms: *continuing, progressing, underway,* etc.
- *oral, verbal.* Use *oral* to convey the idea of words that are spoken. *Verbal* is less precise; its chief meaning is words used in any manner—spoken, written, or printed.
- *people, persons.* In general, use *people* for round numbers and groups (the larger the group, the better *people* sounds), and *persons* for precise or quite small numbers. *One million people were notified. He notified 1,316 persons. He said 30 people had been asked to volunteer. Only two persons showed up. Seventeen persons were injured.* The important thing is to avoid the ridiculous: *As we all know, persons are funny.*
- *rack, wrack. Rack* means to stretch, strain, torture; *wrack* means to wreck, ruin, destroy. Thus *nerve-racking* describes something that strains or tortures the nerves. As for *wrack,* its work is better done by *wreck, ruin, destroy,* or the like.

- *University* is often misplaced in names. It is not, for instance, *the University of Indiana;* it is *Indiana University.* It is not *Notre Dame University;* it is the *University of Notre Dame.* If you don't know, check. Do not, however, capitalize *the* in names like *the University of Chicago,* even though the university may follow that style.

—Priscilla Taylor (#79, 9/82)

Book Review: CBE Manual

CBE STYLE MANUAL: A Guide for Authors, Editors, and Publishers in the Biological Sciences, by the CBE Style Manual Committee. 5th ed., revised and expanded. Bethesda, MD: Council of Biology Editors, Inc., 1983, 326 pp.

This style manual serves its constituency exceedingly well. It addresses international as well as U.S. usage; for example, it lists British proofreading marks. It presents a clear exposition of general style conventions, the generally accepted rules for nomenclature in special fields such as microbiology and biochemistry, and some of the problems of style disagreement among professional organizations. A list of abbreviations and symbols, for example, shows the term "volume" as "*V*," "vol," or "vol."—depending on which style guide is used.

A good part of the *CBE Style Manual* is useful, or at least interesting, to any editors who want to exercise and strengthen their editorial eyesight. Chapter 1, "Ethical conduct in authorship and publication," for example, points out two principles that should govern us all:

> (1) All scientists have an unwritten contract with their contemporaries and those whose work will follow to provide observations honestly obtained, recorded, and published. . . . (2) A scientist's observations and conclusions are his or her property until the scientist presents them to the scientific community in a published paper.

A tip about a minor concern—the prevalence of *that*—suggests replacing *that*-phrases with participles. An example:

> Many biological journals, especially those that regularly publish new scientific names. . . .
> The revision: Many biological journals, especially those regularly publishing new scientific names. . . .

But, useful as this tip is, a yellow-light principle applies: Not every *that*-phrase is eligible. For example, with a *that* quite properly used, the manual gives us an axiom to remember: "Changes that shorten a sentence may also put its elements into a clearer sequence."

This is a valuable book, especially for those who work with scientific and technical material.

—Peggy Smith (#119, 7/85)

(Ordering Information: Council of Biology Editors, 9560 Rockville Pike, Bethesda, MD 20814.)

■ Book Review: APA Style Manual

A 2-year effort to revise and enlarge the *Publication Manual of The American Psychological Association* (APA) was completed with the publication of the third edition on April 30 [1983].* A major goal has been to make the book—already a standard style guide for psychologists, educators, and students—easier to use. Among the principal changes are these:

- A simplified (consolidated) approach to reference lists
- A greatly expanded (and very useful) section on preparing tables and figures
- More detailed metric tables
- A new section on writing abstracts
- A new section on avoiding common grammatical errors
- An improved, more detailed index.

The new book is considerably thicker than the old one, and its many varieties of black type and black lines that divide everything (from paragraphs and sections to single lines in the table of contents) provide quite a busy contrast to the rather bland second edition. Still, the new format is practical, and scholarly authors and editors seeking guidance on technical and scientific material will find the new book a valuable addition to their reference shelves.

"Everybody asked for more examples," said Leslie Cameron, the APA staffer who coordinated the revision process, so examples were added throughout, particularly in the reference section. In fact, the reference section has been revamped through the elimination of reference "notes." All references except personal communications are to be in one alphabetical list; personal communications are to be mentioned only in the text.

Reference Citations

"Authors found it difficult to distinguish between reference 'notes' and the reference 'list,' " Cameron said. Since moving an item between categories involved changing numbers, the authors of the style guide decided to eliminate this source of possible errors.

The manual also now specifies that the year of publication is to come immediately after the author's name in the reference list. This change makes it easier for readers to correlate the intext citation with the reference list citation and, according to Cameron, "conforms with the style that publishers are increasingly using."

Along with supplying expanded tables of metric measurements, the style guide requires authors who made their measurements on nonmetric equipment to supply the metric equivalents of measurements cited.

Grammar and Usage

The new edition has an informative section demonstrating the grammar and usage problems that occur frequently in manuscripts submitted to APA journals (misplaced modifiers, nonparallel constructions, unclear pronoun references, subject-verb disagreement). The guide comes out firmly in favor of data *are*, and illustrates the distinction between *that* and *which* this way:

> *That* clauses (called restrictive) are essential to the meaning of the sentence: The animals that performed well in the first experiment were

used in the second experiment. *Which* clauses (called nonrestrictive) merely add further information: The animals, which performed well in the first experiment, were not proficient in the second experiment.

The new edition also has incorporated (and improved) the guidelines for nonsexist language first developed by APA in 1977 as a supplement to the second edition. Again the manual provides numerous illustrations to help readers gracefully avoid language that could be construed as sexist. (*Man-machine interface* becomes *user-system interface* or *person-system interface*; *manpower* becomes *work force*, *personnel*, *workers*, or *human resources*; *coed* becomes *student* or *female student*.)

The new book also has several notable minor changes:

- Two-letter U.S. Postal Service abbreviations are specified for the names of states (VA, DC).
- Authors who refer to articles or chapters in books are required to add inclusive page numbers.
- Typists are not permitted to break words at the end of a typed line.

Revision Procedure

The revision of the APA manual was carried out by a number of APA staff members plus a volunteer task force consisting of the same four psychologists who had worked on the second edition in 1974. Early in the process, the APA circulated a questionnaire to discover which sections of the old manual users had found confusing and which helpful and solicited suggestions for improvements. Questionnaire recipients included authors of articles in press in APA journals, graduate departments of psychology (for distribution to faculty and graduate students), and editors of APA and non-APA journals. The first mailing of 700 questionnaires had a 30 percent response rate. A second mailing was sent to other known users of the second edition.

—Priscilla Taylor (#88, 5/83)

*Copies are available from APA, 1200 17th St., NW, Washington, DC 20036.

WRITING

I. TOOLS FOR WRITERS

The writer is the editor's bane and blessing, a source of frustration as well as satisfaction. In the midst of manuscript revision, it is well to remember that without writers, editors would have no reason for being; we, like critics, populate an entirely derivative profession.

Editors are interested in writing not only because it is their daily bread, but because we, like writers, believe in the power of the written word to transform. But precisely because what passes through our corner of the world so often needs transforming, most of us do a fair amount of writing ourselves. True, few among us aspire to the elevated ranks of literature; we are not the field marshals of prose. We are the noncommissioned officers, the corporals and sergeants who keep the vast army of communicators marching, sometimes in step, usually in the same general direction—toward the City of Greater Clarity.

Which means that "writing" is probably an overstatement of what we do; what we mostly do is rewrite. It falls to us to keep the paragraphs, sentences, and clauses from tripping over one another in the author's headlong rush to make the point. The author relies on us to sort out the rats' nests of usage, administer the trivia of capitalization and punctuation, and make the written word look good on the page. We are the guardians of that holy of holies, what the writer "meant to say." We write—and rewrite—because the most significant difference in the world is the one between "good" and "better."

On the "if you're so smart, why aren't you rich" model, the cynical view of the writing part of editing has it that if the editor really could write, he or she would spend time creating copy, not correcting it. But writing at its best, after all, is never just the flock of words that circle 'round a meaning, beating at the fog to find a thought to land on. Sometimes, someone must turn on the runway lights that will guide ideas home through the haze. A good editor knows where to find the switch.

In the end, then, the editor writes the better to edit, and edits the better to write. And with luck, the landing is a safe one.

What You Should Know Before You Start Writing or Editing

If you want a realistic estimate of the time and cost involved in a writing or an editing job, you need certain basic information about the project.

In "How to Buy Writing and Editing Services" published in *Governmental Purchasing* magazine in 1975, EEI president Laura Horowitz and writer David Aiken listed what writers and editors should know before undertaking a job:

What Writers Need to Know

1. What will the final product be? A book, a speech, a brochure, a handbook, a script?
2. Who is the primary audience? The general public, interested organizations, experts in the field?
3. What purpose will the document serve? What will the audience use it for? Why is it needed?
4. Roughly how long should the finished product be?
5. Has anyone already done any work on the project? If so, what shape are things in? Is there already a rough draft, or is there only a collection of raw material to work with? If someone's previous draft was rejected, what was wrong with it?
6. Is there an outline that shows exactly what topics will be covered, or is that something the writer will be expected to produce?
7. If the contractor must do interviews or gather raw material and background information, who must be interviewed and where is the material? Who can answer the contractor's questions about needed information?
8. If the contractor must attend conferences or meetings, how much time is likely to be required? Do the other people involved in the meetings have particular times they will or will not be available?
9. If tape recordings are to be provided as part of the background material, will they be transcribed or not?

10. Who will review the writer's drafts? One person, a committee, outside readers?
11. How many cycles of review and revision are expected?
12. Is there a firm deadline for the final product?

What Editors Need to Know

In addition to such basics as the purpose and audience of the final product, editors need to know the following:

1. How many pages are in the existing manuscript? Are they single spaced or double spaced? (or, heaven forbid, handwritten?) Is the manuscript expected to be significantly shorter in its final form?
2. Does the manuscript contain tables, footnotes, equations, bibliography, charts, graphs, or other nontext material? If so, roughly how much such material is there?
3. Can the editor arrange to look at the manuscript to see what work will be needed? Some manuscripts are fairly well written and need only a relatively light editing for grammar, spelling, and consistency; others need many changes—almost a total rewrite—to be readable. Most editors will want to see for themselves how much and what kind of work will be required.
4. Exactly what tasks will be required? Will the editor be responsible for marking typefaces and sizes for the typesetter? Will the editor be expected to check math in tables? To verify all bibliographic entries at the library?
5. Has a graphic designer already been chosen to design the document and prepare any charts, cover art, and illustrations? Will the editor be expected to find someone to perform those tasks?
6. If photos or other illustrations will be used, who will provide and select them?
7. Does the agency have a preference for a particular style on such matters as capitalization, punctuation, and hyphenation (e.g., Vice-Chairman or vice chairman)?
8. Will the original author review the editor's changes? If so, will the editor need to meet with the author?
9. Who . . . will review the editor's work?
10. Will there be more than one cycle of review and revision?
11. Will the project director . . . or the author be available to answer questions as the editing progresses?

12. Is there a firm outline that the manuscript should follow, or can the editor move sections around if a transfer seems to help the flow?
13. What are the chances that the author or the agency will want to make changes midway in the editing process—for example, dropping or adding sections?
14. In what condition should the manuscript be returned? Marked up with changes on the original, or retyped?
15. What is the condition of any illustrations that will accompany the manuscript? Finished art, rough sketches, suggestions?

(#16, 11/78)

The Ax, the Pruning Hook, the Exacto Knife, and the Metronome

LOGO•PHILE

"Writing is easy. All you have to do is cross out the wrong words."

—Mark Twain

Peter Drucker, the management consultant, has a reputation for calling them the way he sees them. Writers can learn something from Drucker, who refers to his first draft as "the zero draft." His reasoning is that he is entitled to start counting only after he gets something down on paper.

Everyone who writes seriously knows that the real work begins only after there is something to work on. Beginners think to themselves, "If I come up with a great idea, it can carry me." Wrong. Even the noblest of ideas, the most absorbing of themes, can be twisted out of shape in the hands of a careless craftsman; but, in the loving hands of a master like Annie Dillard, even so prosaic a thing as the description of an anthill or a leaf can dazzle.

Good writing is mostly rewriting. Anthony Burgess says he might revise a page as many as 20 times. Short story writer Roald Dahl states that by the time he nears the end of a story, the first part will have been reread and corrected as many as 150 times. If memory serves, Hemingway claimed to have rewritten the final chapter of *A Farewell to Arms* 39 times.

There is nothing particularly praiseworthy in this; it is simply a fact of life for people who care about language, or more to the point, about getting things right. If you want to be a pianist, you practice. If you want to be a runner, you train. If you want to write, you rewrite. But editing yourself is hard to do, mostly because writers are easily seduced by their own prose. The editorial act must therefore be a deliberate infliction of pain, a conscious and vigorous assent to the proposition well expressed by magazine writer Bil Gilbert: "Writing is essentially weeding out your own stupidity."

A Set of Tools

But there are tools that writers can use to improve their work. The first is the ax. It should be laid to the root of entire paragraphs—those that don't belong, that belabor the obvious, or that add just enough detail to distract the reader instead of providing essential information. I often find, on rewriting, that an entire paragraph can be distilled into a phrase, or sometimes even a word, which can be added to a preceding or following paragraph. The result is a piece that becomes more taut, and taut is better than slack.

Second is the pruning hook. This is the tool that inflicts the most pain, because the pruning hook is best applied to the turns of phrase we most admire. Disagreeable as it is, writers would do well to follow the advice of novelist Nancy Hale, who counsels excising the language they believe most clever, most apt, most apposite. Her perfectly sound reasoning is that they wouldn't admire their own words so much if they weren't protecting them. (No mother believes her baby is ugly!)

Pruning writing is the same as pruning apple trees: The point is not so much to get rid of the dead branches (which are easy enough to spot) as it is to shape the tree to produce the best possible fruit. This can involve cutting off live limbs, which may be beautiful in themselves, but bad for the whole tree in light of its purpose. An unpruned article, like an unpruned tree, wastes its natural energy.

Third is the exacto knife, a tool as essential to self-editing as it is to doing paste-up. Use it to attack the manuscript phrase by phrase and word by word: Is this verb the best possible one? Does this analogy work? Is this metaphor the right one? Isn't that phrase really too threadbare to use? As a precision instrument, the exacto knife is well designed for the surgical removal of such minute blemishes as the misplaced comma and the superfluous adverb.

Finally, one of the tools of self-editing most often neglected by even the most careful writers is the metronome. Its job is to measure out the cadence of the writer's words. James J. Kilpatrick recommends (in *The Writer's Art*, Andrews, McMeel & Parker, 1984) that writers who wish to master cadence write verse. I concur. This does not mean writing free verse—which Robert Frost once likened to playing tennis with the net down—but verse with rhyme schemes and meter: sonnets, rondeaux, villanelles, haiku. The poetry doesn't have to be good; it just has to be workmanlike. Sound out the sentences. Unless writers want their words to march across the page with all the discipline of the Keystone Cops, they need to pay attention to cadence.

When to Quit?

When does this process end, if at all? Any good piece of writing can be ruined with too much tinkering. But, as Tolstoy observed, "I scarcely ever read my published writings, but if by chance I come across a page, it always strikes me: All this must be rewritten; this is how I should have written it." The real writer is never satisfied because every piece, if it is done right, is still full of potential the moment it is finished.

So, the short answer is that the process never ends; the clock merely runs out, and the time comes to tear the paper from the typewriter and press it into the hands of the next editor. Each piece must be sent off the way the girl back home sends her young soldier off to war, with a heart that longs for just one more day, hour, minute.

 (#116, 4/85)

Trees: A New Tool for Writers

Can't see the forest for the trees? Don't believe it. You can use trees not only to see the forest but to find your way through it as well.

The Tree Form

Constructing a tree, or "treeing," is a way of structuring ideas into a cohesive system. A tree is a visual representation of the reasoning process. It is a hierarchical array of information elements and subelements (nodes) connected according to their interrelationships (branches). The result resembles a Christmas tree:

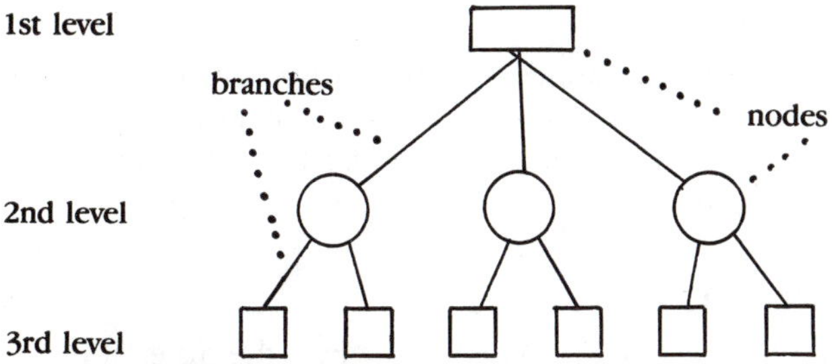

The treelike nature of intellectual processes is not a new concept, and several species of trees have been developed—decision trees, issue trees, fault trees, and relevance trees. New tree applications sprout constantly and survive if they prove useful. Particularly intriguing is the . . . application of issue treeing to expository writing.

In 1973 David Wojick developed the issue tree at Carnegie-Mellon University. He has used issue trees to analyze policies and regulations, to plan procedures, to guide meetings and conferences, and to synthesize the discussion. Wojick's manual, *Issue Analysis* (1975), explains the technique of treeing writing materials.

Tree vs. Outlines

A tree substitutes for an outline in expository writing. In fact, trees and outlines have much in common; the different levels of nodes on a tree correspond to the heads and subheads of an outline. But in several ways an issue tree is a more versatile tool.

- It provides a comprehensive, visual impression of the structure of an article—like a builder's blueprint.
- It separates the problem of structuring the ideas from the problem of articulating them, whereas an outline dictates the order of presentation.
- It makes explicit the logical connections among ideas.
- It can be used—along with other criteria—to evaluate alternative structures and presentations of ideas.

The Treeing Process

How would a writer or an editor use an issue tree? Consider, for example, the process used to write the present article.

Constructing the Tree

The first step was to decide what pieces of information the article should include and how these pieces were related. These decisions about structure were colored by the nature of the information, the audience, the medium, and the purpose of the article.

Evaluating the Structure

Now, look at what the tree can tell you about the way the material is structured:

- Depth—Two of the three branches have only three levels: somewhat superficial, but all right considering space, medium, and purpose.
- Thoroughness—The first level branches three times and the second level averages fewer than four: a relatively thorough treatment, given space constraints.
- Balance—The "How use?" branch has more levels and more branching than the others: might indicate faulty structure but judged acceptable for "how-to" emphasis of article. (Note, however, that the imbalance results in unevenly spaced heads and in subheads on the "heavy" branch only.)
  —There are no undeveloped, "dead-end" branches (which should be pruned if they occur).

—There is no unnecessary repetition of nodes among the branches (which, again, might suggest restructuring or pruning).

Writing the Article

We have decided to go with this structure. Now, how do we traverse the tree or make our way from point to point? A journalistic treatment would move horizontally from one node to the next; a scholarly treatment would follow each branch to the end before beginning the next:

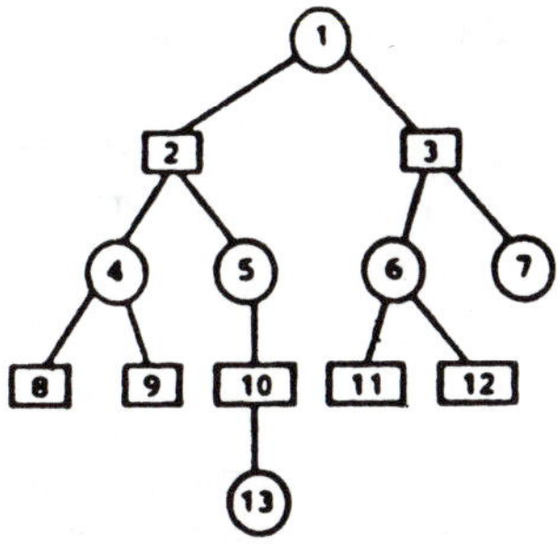

Newspaper

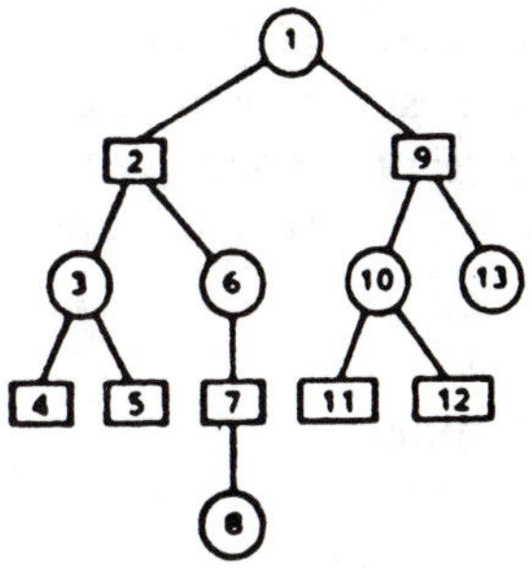

Scholarly Journal

Scholarly writing often seems repetitious because its linear path involves backtracking to an earlier level to pick up the logical juncture with the next branch. But it involves fewer nonlogical connections than the journalistic path, whose jumps sometimes make newspaper articles hard to follow.

The scholarly path generally is more suitable for complex information and ideas. For news items, which are usually limited in scope and complexity, the shortcut path is acceptable and necessary, given space considerations. Most exposition—like this article—follows a path somewhere between these extremes. The logical structure does not dictate how information will be conveyed. The path you follow is a matter of choice. You can even start in the middle of the tree if it suits your style or purpose to do so.

The Value of Issue Trees

Obviously, issue trees can supplement, but not supplant, a writer's skill and experience. Each step in the treeing process requires subjective decisions. The tree makes these choices explicit rather than intuitive.

—Charlene Semer (#29, 6/79)

The Researcher's Writing Guide

The key question to answer before attempting to write a technical paper is *What do I know now*? Forget all the mistakes, incorrect preconceived notions, and bad experiments. Try to pretend that all the results are freshly discovered—just delivered to your desk that day. How should you best put them together?

Guidelines for preparing each section of a technical paper are discussed here, with the objective of setting out the basics of sound reporting procedures.*

The Summary

The summary is a separate mini-report—a distillation of the most important aspects of your full paper. And because the summary must be concise and complete, it is often the most difficult section to write. Writing it becomes especially difficult if you have nothing to summarize, so always write the summary last.

The summary should briefly introduce the subject, outline the objectives and rationale of the research (including perhaps a line or two of relevant background), identify the experimental approach, highlight the results, and state the main conclusions. Brevity is the key. In citing results, do not dwell on methods, false leads, or details; hit the results. Also, when writing this section, keep its function in mind. The summary is not the place to present any material that is not in the main body of the text; it is simply a synopsis of what follows.

The Introduction

The introduction should do what the name implies: introduce the material to the reader. It isn't the same as the summary, and it doesn't contain results. The introduction generally identifies the objective of the research and discusses the rationale behind it. Thus, you should use the introduction to tell what you did, why you did it, what led up to it, and how the work fits into the overall scheme of things. It should provide your reader with the "big picture"—with some sense of a starting point. We cannot overstate the importance of presenting the rationale for your work in the introduction: *Why did you do what you did?*

The Experimental Section

Like the introduction, the experimental section does not contain research results. It does, however, describe how the results were obtained. A good rule of thumb is this: Provide sufficient detail to allow the experiment to be conducted by someone else with at least the same trend of results.

Some of the parameters that count are temperature, pressure, flow rate, pH, concentration, dimensions (area, length, etc.), time duration, time interval, sources of nonstandard materials (company names and locations), and the suppliers of key items of equipment (company names and locations). There may well be other important parameters in your work; at any rate, make sure you define your procedure.

The Results

Uninterpreted data are useless to most readers. When presenting your results, you must remember that even though you are usually writing to an experienced technical audience, what may be clear to you after thinking about the subject day in and day out for months or years may not be obvious to the typical reader. Assuming too much knowledge can be a big mistake, so explain your results even if it seems unnecessary. If you can't figure them out, say so: "The mechanism is unclear and we are continuing to examine this phenomenon."

Often the most important vehicles for the clear presentation of results are figures and tables. These are usually the "guts" of scientific reporting. Each should have a descriptive title, and column heads in tables should accurately describe what's below. Detailed suggestions for presenting data in figures follow.
(Refer to figure 1.)

1. Always plot the independent parameter on the x axis; always plot the dependent parameter on the y axis.
2. Try to arrange your figure so that the y axis is the long axis. That way, the figure will be oriented conveniently on the page and the reader will not need to turn the page sideways to read the graph.

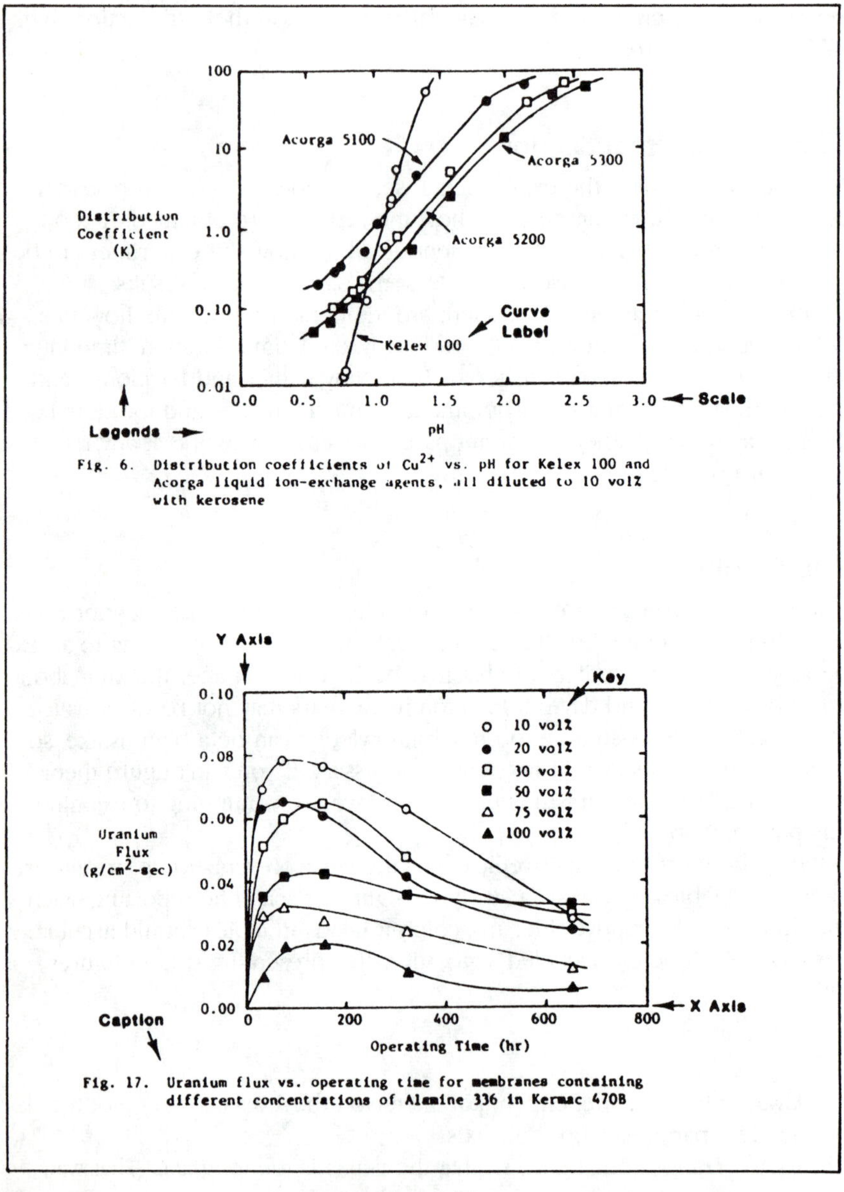

Figure 1. Graphics terminology and recommended format for figures.

3. Try to use at least four tics, but fewer than ten, for each coordinate. There may be exceptions (e.g., pH scales). Multiples of 1, 2, or 5 are good increments for axis numeration. Avoid 0, 3, 6, 9 or 0, 4, 8, 12, as they make interpolation unnecessarily difficult. And it is hard to envision the justification for such oddball increments as 0, 7, 14. If any number in a graph (or table or the text of a paper, for that matter) is less than 1, it should start with a zero and a decimal point (e.g., 0.5).
4. In applying curves to your data, try to follow these rules:
   a. Always show the data points. Five to 10 data points show the essential trends of most functions. If you have gathered more than 10 points, you may have done unnecessary work; if you have fewer than 5 points (unless there is a simple linear relationship at work), your result is usually in doubt.
   b. Do not extend the line much beyond the ends of the data points. If for some valid reason you find it necessary to extend the line substantially, use a dashed line to indicate it's an extrapolation.
   c. The origin is frequently a "free" point. If you are certain that $y = 0$ when $= x = 0$, put the line through the origin. If you are uncertain, don't use the origin; stop the line slightly below the lowest point. Some judgment is required here.
5. Use a minimum variety of symbols for your data. Usually filled and open circles, filled and open squares, and filled and open triangles (i.e., six different symbols) are all that one graph can handle. If you have more than six types of information, break the plot up into two or more plots. Avoid the use of X's to denote data points.
6. Whenever possible, label curves individually, even if you must use arrows to match the lines with the labels. Use a "key" in your figure only as a last resort.
7. Try to avoid presenting the same information on a graph and in the text, and remember that the figure should contain enough information to stand alone—especially if there's a chance it will later be used by itself (e.g., as a slide).
8. In providing legends, try to use the written name for the quantity plotted, and then present its dimensions in parentheses. For example, use "Time (days)" instead of merely "Days" and use "Plasticizer Content (wt%)" instead of "Wt% Plasticizer." Avoid ambiguous shorthands like "MW $\times$ 10^{-3}; use "D(10^{-5} cm2/sec)" which is unambiguous. Abbreviations such as *mg*, *cm*, and *hr* do not take periods. Author guidelines should be consulted for the type of units preferred by each journal.

9. Position the data on the graph (i.e., adjust the scales) so that the curves are not bunched near the top, bottom, or one of the sides. Don't run the scale up to 100 percent if your data go up only to 38 percent. The only time white space serves a valid function in a graph is when you are comparing one graph with another graph that makes use of the full scale.
10. In writing captions, avoid lead-ins like "Plot of hydrocortisone released . . ." or "This is a plot of. . . ." Simply say "Hydrocortisone released vs. . . ."

The Conclusions

The conclusions section is where you should concisely restate your answer to the "What do I know now?" question. It is not a place to offer new facts, nor should it contain another rendition of experimental procedures or rationale.

The References

A reference cited in a formal list should be publicly available and described in sufficient detail for the reader to obtain the source with a reasonable effort. References to personal (not "private") communications, proposals, or unpublished data are best kept to a minimum; if used, such citations should contain names, dates, titles, and affiliations.

—Mark H. Henry and Harold K. Lonsdale (#97, 12/83)

Editor's Note: Henry and Lonsdale originally sent a reprint of the Elsevier journal article to *The Eye* with the suggestion that we encourage our readers to "accept the challenge of breaking into the hundreds of specialized professional journals being published today."

They also noted that response to the article—reprint requests have exceeded 10 percent of the journal's circulation—indicates that (1) "the ability to write well is indeed recognized as an important professional skill" and (2) "communicators who have something valuable to say about their craft should do so in as many arenas as possible."

To obtain a free reprint of the original "Researcher's Writing Guide" published by Elsevier, send a stamped, addressed #10 envelope to Mark H. Henry, Director of Communications, Bend Research, Inc., 64550 Research Rd., Bend, OR 97701.

---

*This article is drawn from an inhouse writing guide developed for Bend Research, Inc., a small Oregon firm that specializes in synthetic membrane research and development. A somewhat longer version was published earlier this year in Elsevier's international *Journal of Membrane Science*, the only "non-membrane" piece published in the 8-year history of the journal.

We found the guide so useful for both writers and editors that we decided to share it with our readers. The copyright remains with the authors.

Book Review: Graphs, Charts, and Figures

THE VISUAL DISPLAY OF QUANTITATIVE INFORMATION, by Edward R. Tufte. Cheshire, CT: Graphics Press, 1983, 197 pp.

This is an exceptional book in which the author truly achieves his aim to influence readers so that "they will never view or create statistical graphics the same way again." Viewers and makers of images will indeed be changed by the insights of this erudite author, who never condescends but lifts the graphics novice to a level of expertise by the sheer skill of his exposition. The book itself, produced by the author's own press, is a work of art. Anyone who works with publications will delight in reading, and can benefit from studying, this book.

The first half of the book surveys good and bad graphics since the 18th century, including an instructive exposé of what passes as graphic art in the world's leading newspapers and magazines. The second half explains how to create good graphics and, from the editor's perspective, how to improve bad ones.

Problems and Their Sources

What's wrong with so many of the graphics in *The New York Times* and *TIME*? With copious illustrations and clear, nontechnical prose, Tufte shows how many graphics distort the data (sometimes by tenfold exaggeration) or miss the real news in the data.

Why do artists draw graphics that lie, and why do respected publications publish them? Tufte blames graphic mediocrity on the illustrators' lack of substantive skills. ("Nearly all those who produce graphics for mass publication are trained exclusively in the fine arts and have had little experience with the analysis of data.") He also points to their dislike of quantitative evidence (they consider statistics unfailingly "boring") and their contempt for the intelligence of their audience (they believe that "graphics are only for the unsophisticated reader").

Some Solutions

If statistical integrity and graphical sophistication are to be achieved, Tufte argues, substantive and quantitative expertise must also participate in the design of data graphics. His argument will delight editors who know that clarity, conciseness, simplicity, and directness are essential to all good communication—including graphics. He sets forth a number of principles:

- The representation of numbers, as physically measured on the surface of the graphic itself, should be directly proportional to the numerical quantities represented. Graphics should demonstrate data variation, not design variation. In other words, if you use a vertical inch to equal $8 in one place, do not use a vertical inch elsewhere in the same graphic to equal $3.92; if you use a horizontal inch to represent 5 years in one place, do not use a horizontal inch elsewhere in the same graphic to represent 0.57 years.
- In time-series displays of money, deflated and standardized units of monetary measurement are nearly always better than nominal units. One of the main problems in graphics, Tufte notes, is that artists often employ only the simplest designs and show unstandardized time-series based on only a handful of data points.
- The number of information-carrying (variable) dimensions depicted should not exceed the number of dimensions in the data, for the simple reason that the eye can confuse changes in design with changes in the data.
- Graphics must not quote data out of context. "To be truthful and revealing," says Tufte, "data graphics must bear on the question at the heart of quantitative thinking: 'Compared to what?' The emaciated, data-thin design should always provoke suspicion, for graphics often lie by omission, leaving out data sufficient for comparison."

Creating Good Design

Tufte devotes the latter half of his book to illustrating how good graphic designs can be created, based on the principle "Above all else show the data." Ink that fails to depict statistical information can clutter up the data, as in the case of a thick mesh of grid lines; hence, he argues, "erase non-data-ink."

Similarly, Tufte suggests erasing gratuitous decoration and reinforcement of the data measures, what he calls "redundant data-ink." For example, he notes, a labeled, shaded bar in a bar chart locates the altitude in six ways:

(1) height of the left line, (2) height of the shading, (3) height of the right line, (4) position of the top horizontal line, (5) position of the number at the bar's top, and (6) the number itself. Tufte argues that any five of the six can be erased and the sixth will still indicate the height.

Tufte summarizes the characteristics of the "friendly" data graphic in this way:

- Words are spelled out; mysterious and elaborate encoding is avoided.
- Words run from left to right, the usual direction for reading Western languages.
- Little messages help explain the data so the viewer does not have to make repeated references to scattered text.
- Elaborately encoded shadings, cross-hatching, and colors are avoided; instead, labels are placed on the graphic itself. No legend is required.
- The graphic attracts the viewer and provokes curiosity.
- The colors, if used, are chosen so that color-deficient and color-blind people (5 to 10 percent of viewers) can make sense of the graphic. For example, most color-deficient viewers can distinguish blue from other colors.
- Type is clear, precise, modest; lettering may be done by hand.
- Type is upper and lower case, with serifs.

—Priscilla Taylor (#104, 6/84)

Test Yourself

On Graphs and Charts

Identify the type of graph or chart.

a. Pie chart
b. Zero-line bar graph
c. Pictorial chart
d. Compound bar graph
e. Multibar graph
f. Simple bar graph or columns chart
g. Compound line graph
h. Zero-line graph
i. Multiline graph
j. Simple line graph
k. Combination bar and line graph

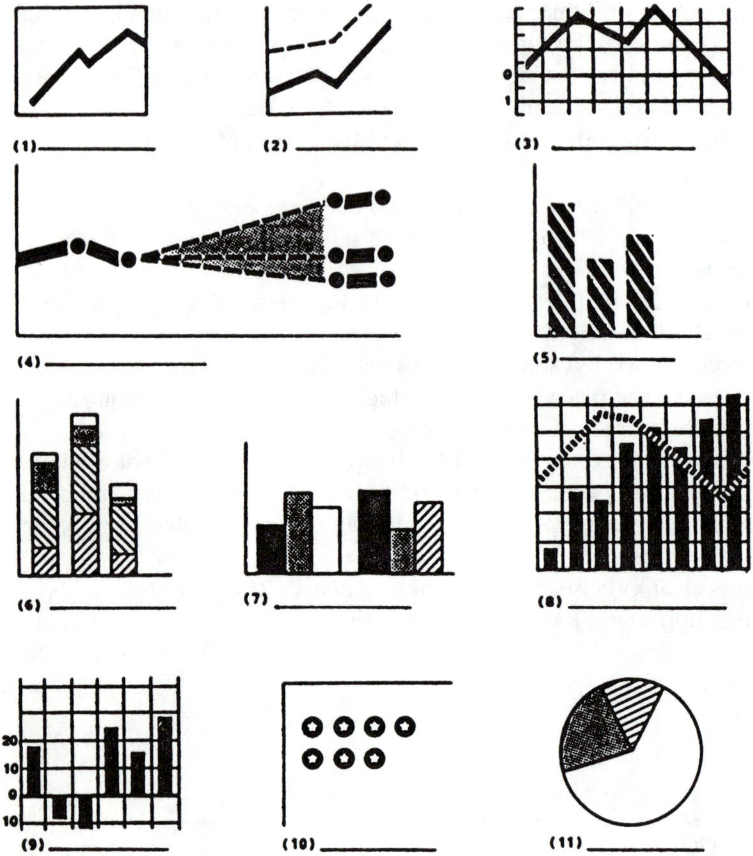

Answers

1. j 3. h 5. f 7. e 9. b 11. a

2. i 4. g 6. d 8. k 10. c

(#93, 9/83)

Document Design: Putting Information Where Readers Need It

Insurance policies, technical manuals, employee benefits handbooks, and most other types of instructions are reference documents that readers want to dip into to find what they need in a hurry. Putting such documents into clear language means more than writing clear sentences and using understandable words—the information also must be organized to answer readers' questions.

The Document Design Center (*Simply Stated,** Aug. 1983) describes the following seven research-based principles it uses to help organizations produce documents that will cut down on calls to a hotline and improve customer relations:

1. *Set the context.* Tell the readers at the beginning of a document what is in it, why they might choose to read parts of it, and what you expect them to get from it. "Don't just tell people how to do something. First tell them why and under what circumstances they might choose to do it, rather than something else."
2. *Set up signposts.* "Tables of contents, indexes, and tabs all help readers find their way. But the headings or entries must be informative. Even within sections you can give directions about the structure of the information that follows."
3. *Limit the organizational information you give at any one time.* Use no more than one level of subheads in the general table of contents; put more detailed listings of subheads at the beginning of each chapter.
4. *Write informative headings.* "The most helpful headings are those that match the readers' questions. Using questions themselves as headings is an effective technique." For example, instead of "Coordination of Benefits" use "What if someone is covered by two group health plans?"
5. *Put information everywhere a reader may need it.* "Don't be afraid to repeat sentences, paragraphs, or whole pages if it will help your readers get what they need efficiently."
6. *Organize the material for more than one audience.* "Charts, summary lists in the text or on a separate card, diagrams, and notes in the margin

are good ways to condense information for more knowledgeable readers."

7. *Make the organization of the material graphically explicit.* "Distinguish different levels of headings by type size, position, or color. Use pictorial or thematic symbols to visually cue readers that they are moving from one section to another."

(#95, 10/83)

*The monthly publication of the Document Design Center is available from American Institutes for Research, 1055 Thomas Jefferson St., NW, Washington, DC 20007.

Checking Out the Grammar Hotlines

When should I use *lay* instead of *laid*? Should I use a dash or parentheses in this sentence? Should I say *none are* or *none is*? How do I know if the subject of my sentence requires a singular or a plural verb? The answers to questions like these are merely a phone call away.

Twenty colleges and universities in 15 states have grammar hotlines that answer questions on English grammar, usage, punctuation, and spelling. The hotlines are staffed by instructors and graduate students.

Four Questions

To check on the reliability of their responses, *The Eye* called six hotlines in different parts of the country and asked them the same four questions on grammar and usage. The hotlines called were (1) the Writing Center Hotline of Auburn University, Auburn, AL, (2) the Grammar Hotline of Moorpark College, Moorpark, CA, (3) Rewrite of York College of the City University of New York, (4) the Writing Center Hotline of Cincinnati Technical College,

(5) the Learning Line of San Antonio College, and (6) the Grammar Hotline of Tidewater Community College, Virginia Beach, VA.

The first question was on subject-verb agreement: "The new model as well as several older models (*is* or *are*) included in the proposal." All hotline answerers correctly maintained that *is* is correct. They were quick to explain that *together with*, *as well as*, *along with*, and *in addition to* are regarded as merely intervening phrases; only *and* can create a compound subject.

The second question was about a slightly more difficult question of subject-verb agreement. This time the construction in question was *one of the* or *one of those*: "John is one of the students who (*talk* or *talks*) too much and (*work* or *works*) too little." All hotline answerers replied that the correct verb choice would depend on the antecedent for *who*. Four hotlines agreed that a plural verb was needed because the antecedent is *students*; some suggested finding the subject by turning the sentence around: "Of the students who talk too much and work too little, John is one." The exceptions were the San Antonio College Learning Line and Moorpark College Grammar Hotline, which recommended using a singular verb because the antecedent of *who* is *one*, and *of the students* is merely a prepositional phrase giving more information about the noun. "*One* absolutely, definitely requires a singular verb," said Michael Strumpf of Moorpark College. The Cincinnati Technical College Writing Center Hotline and the Tidewater Community College Grammar Hotline explained that a singular verb would be used if the sentence read "John is the only one of the students. . . ."

The question is thorny. Wilson Follett, in *Modern American Usage*, states that the words *one of the*, *one of those* "introduce the most widespread of all defiances of rudimentary grammar: the coupling of a plural subject with a singular verb." Follett, Fowler, and Bernstein all recommend using a plural verb in sentences like ours. "Doubt about the correct number of the verb often arises with such sentences," says Roy Copperud, in *American Usage and Style: The Consensus*. According to Copperud, four critics and the American Heritage panel hold that the verb should be plural; four others say that although the plural is strictly correct, the singular is often used and is acceptable. (Ed. Note: *The Eye* holds with the strict constructionists.)

Although the third question dealt with a similar problem, it produced a greater division of the house. Our question dealt with verb agreement when using *the number of* and *a number of*: "The number of polluted rivers (*has* or *have*) increased and a number of ways of fighting pollution (*has* or *have*) been suggested." Three of the six grammar hotlines answered correctly, explaining that the singular verb is used with *the number of* and the plural verb is used with *a number of.* Fowler suggests substituting *numerous* for *a number of,* leaving no doubt that the verb must be plural.

The last question concerned the current usage of *hopefully* to mean *it is to be hoped* or *I hope.* Most hotlines objected to this current usage. York College called it "an ugly formation" but offered the helpful interpretation that the usage has become widespread because this floating adverbial modifier is needed. Like its parallels—*happily, regrettably,* and *presumably*—*hopefully* is probably headed for acceptance as standard usage.

What Dictionaries Do the Hotlines Use?

Dictionaries most often used by the hotline respondents include *American Heritage Dictionary* (because of its usage notes), *Webster's International, 3rd edition, Random House,* and *Oxford English Dictionary.* In addition to the well-known usage manuals by Fowler, Follett, and Bernstein, the hotlines recommended *Advanced English Grammar* by George Kittredge and Frank Farley, *Usage and Abusage* by Eric Partridge, *Standard Handbook for Secretaries* by Lois Hutchinson, and *Modern Business English* by Wittenberg and Boiles. The hotlines cited the grammar handbooks by Prentice-Hall, Harcourt Brace Jovanovich, and Little, Brown, which are used in English classes at the colleges.

Most commonly asked of the hotlines are queries on subject-verb agreement, spelling, usage, and punctuation. All hotlines said they try to give both current usage and prescriptive answers, allowing the caller to make the choice. Callers often ask for help with editing sentences or setting up form letters. Many hotlines consult *The Writers' Hotline Handbook,* a list of grammatical rules published by the University of Arkansas at Little Rock.

Who Calls the Hotlines?

Most hotlines were originally established to help college students with their writing, but the clientele has broadened over the years. The hotline at Moorpark College, which Michael Strumpf started 8 years ago, is the oldest in the country and has been widely publicized. It receives 100 to 150 calls a week—from judges, writers, even the White House, as well as from students.

The York College hotline receives 15 to 20 calls an hour, but more come from the community than from students. Secretaries often call about errors in their bosses' prose. The San Antonio College hotline averages 10 to

15 calls a day, most of them from college students needing help with basic grammar.

The hotline at Auburn University's Writing Center receives 8 to 10 calls a day from business people and state and local government officials, as well as many architectural and engineering students who need help writing technical reports.

The Cincinnati Technical College hotline (one of three hotlines in Cincinnati) receives at least 10 calls a day from students working on assignments in the cooperative employment program. As a reminder that writing assistance is available by phone, stickers with the hotline number are on the phones in many Cincinnati offices.

For a directory listing 20 grammar hotlines, phone numbers, and hours of service, send an addressed, stamped envelope to Donna Friedman, Grammar Hotline, Tidewater Community College, 1700 College Crescent, Virginia Beach, VA 23456. Friedman compiled the directory as a public service.

—Janet S. Horwitz (#104, 6/84)

■ Cadence: The Key to Effective Speech Writing

David Gergen, former presidential speech writer and director of communications in the Reagan White House, calls speech writing "an unnatural act." He's right. It is an occupation fit only for masochists, having all the frustrations and problems of "real" writing and none of the rewards. Writers get bylines; speech writers get anonymity. When the speech goes well, the speaker gets all the credit; when it flops, the speech writer gets all the blame.

Yet there are rewards. Some are overt. A few top corporate speech writers earn six-figure salaries; many earn more than $50,000 a year. Sometimes the satisfactions are less tangible but just as real. If you work for a politician who is elected to high office, your words can reach millions. And, there are special satisfactions that go with mastering the craft itself.

Writing for the Ear

But writing speeches is also a potential minefield for the unprepared writer. Part of the problem is that many newcomers to speech writing, even though they may be fine writers or editors, know little about the nuances associated with preparing public addresses.

The most critical difference, of course, is that writing for a live audience means writing for the ear. Many a well-formed written sentence falls on the ear like a brick; many fine speeches, when transcribed, read as if they had been written by Morpheus himself.

Guidelines on writing for the ear can be found in the myriad books on speech writing on the market today. Only a few are worth reading all the way through, but among the more helpful is Dorothy Sarnoff's *Speech Can Change Your Life* (New York: Dell, 1972). (The best texts, of course, are great speeches.) There you will read about using familiar words, simple ideas, and short sentences, and avoiding tricky words such as homonyms, words that are hard to pronounce, and double entendres. But most of these books either ignore or gloss over the most helpful element in creating a speech that is easy to listen to and that sticks with the audience: cadence.

Cadence

Cadence is critical to speeches because from it arise audience involvement, force, harmony, dignity, and, in truly great speeches, majesty. All languages have distinctive rhythms and cadences when well spoken, and English is no exception. The basic natural rhythm of English is found in the simple declarative sentence. The direct oral style is more appreciated in American English than in French or German, for example.

The most effective cadences in speaking are found in the single direct statement and the simple variations that can be made from it—what I call the double and the triple. Simple statements fall most powerfully on the ear:

> "Carthage must be destroyed."—Cato
>
> "I have a dream."—Martin Luther King
>
> "But let us begin."—John F. Kennedy

Simple statements are most effectively used either to introduce a point in a speech or to sum it up. Many speech writers use simple sentences as a set of bookends for a particular paragraph or as a form of verbal punctuation for several related points. In this latter regard, one of the most effective (though overshadowed) uses of such statements is Martin Luther King's use of "Let freedom ring" in his renowned "I Have a Dream" speech.

There are several kinds of doubles, but they are usually used either to offer a contrast or to provide balance to a sentence. The opening line of Kennedy's inaugural address provides an excellent example:

> "We observe today
> not a victory of a party, but a celebration of freedom—
> symbolizing an end as well as a beginning,
> signifying renewal as well as change."

The basic rhythm here is provided by the sets of pairs, which provide both opposition and apposition. Each of the three sets presents a different contrast, but together they compose a satisfying progression to the speaker's theme for the entire speech—America's entry into a new era.

Several structural devices can be used to set up doubles: either . . . or; neither . . . nor; not (only) this . . . but (also) that; if . . . then.

The double can also be used to contrast ideas and is particularly effective when alliteration can be used to set the contrast off, as in Lincoln's remark: "There can be no successful appeal from the ballot to the bullet; and those who take such an appeal are sure to lose their cause and pay the costs." Here, we have three doubles—a set of balanced clauses, each focusing on an alliterative pair.

John Kennedy was a master at using the rhythm of the triple to drive home a point. In his inaugural promise to the peoples of the Third World, for example, he pledged American help ". . . not because the communists may be doing it, not because we seek their votes, but because it is right."

But when using doubles and triples to establish cadence, speech writers should take care that they establish the right order of the elements. Put the big idea at the end. Patrick Henry did not say "Give me death or give me liberty"; Thomas Jefferson did not write, " . . . we mutually pledge to each other our lives, our sacred honor, and our fortunes."

Sometimes a fourth, fifth, or even more elements can be added to a triple to extend the cadence, change the pace, and offer the speaker a chance to drive home a point. Winston Churchill did this most dramatically in his famous speech to the people of Great Britain following Dunkirk. Notice how, in this passage, the word "fight" marks the cadence and carries a sequence that for many speakers might be too long:

"We shall go on to the end, we shall fight in France, we shall fight on the seas and oceans, we shall fight with growing confidence and strength in the air, we shall defend our island, whatever the cost may be, we shall fight on the beaches, we shall fight in the fields and in the streets, we shall fight in the hills; we shall never surrender. . . ."

Recite!

Writers interested in adding the power of cadence to their repertoires would do well to recite aloud the speeches of Lincoln, Churchill, and Franklin Roosevelt, as well as those of the speakers quoted before. Properly phrased, their powerful sentences have the ability to sweep the reader and all else before them. The remarks of these leaders are truly excellent examples of the art of speech writing. Another superb resource for developing a feel for cadence are the *Psalms* and the *Book of Common Prayer*, which contain some of the most satisfying rhythms in the English language.

Mastering the art of creating cadence will not transform your speaker into another Churchill or King; that takes natural gifts on the platform as well as effective prose. But establishing the right rhythms can help your speaker so to measure out the stream of words that those who hear will not only attend the message but will also know they could not have said it better themselves. And that is the first step toward eloquence.

—Bruce O. Boston (#114, 2/85)

II. THE WRITER'S CRAFT

How to Resuscitate Smothered Verbs

A strong verb can be smothered by an abstract noun in a phrase.* The cure for the problem is to uncover the strong verb and discard the rest of the phrase. Before the cure, of course, must come the diagnosis.

Smothering phrases often begin with a form of *be, give, have, make,* or *take.* The noun in the phrase often ends with *ion* or *ment.* Here are some obvious examples of smothered verbs. (Uncovered, the first and second would be *agree* and *attend.*)

be in agreement
be in attendance
be in possession
be in receipt of
give authorization
give consideration
give a description
give encouragement
give instruction
have a belief
have a need
have a suspicion
have a requirement
make an adjustment
make an assumption
make a choice
make a decision
make a determination
make a comparison
make provision for
take action
take into consideration
arrive at a conclusion
arrive at a solution
come into conflict
effect an improvement
extend an invitation
hold a discussion
put in an appearance
render assistance
try an experiment

Some verbs look nothing like the noun in the phrase that is smothering them:

be cognizant (know)
be in accord (agree)
be of the opinion (believe)
have the capability (be able, can)
present a picture similar to (resemble)
take appropriate measures (act, do)

Prepositional phrases can smother verbs; for example:

before your departure (before you leave)
in accordance with your request (as you asked)
to the effect that (showing, stating, resulting)
with the exception of (excepting, excluding)
with the knowledge that (knowing)

An *of* phrase in a clause ending with a word that means *done* is a prime clue that a verb needs to be freed to breathe:

Reconstruction of the building has been effected. (The building was reconstructed.)
Distribution of the documents was accomplished. (The documents were distributed.)
The success of the project was achieved. (The project succeeded.)

And here is the prize of all smothered verbs: serve the function of being (be)

—Peggy Smith (#81, 11/82)

*For more on smothered verbs, see chapter 3 in Jefferson Bates, *Writing with Precision* (Washington, DC: Acropolis Books, 1980).

Test Yourself

On Changeless Verbs

Some verbs keep the same form in the infinitive, the past tense, and the past participle; for example, to cast, I cast yesterday, I have cast. Some offer alternative past participles: bid/bade, forgot/forgotten, knit/knitted, slit/slitted, spit/spitted. We know of only one that changes its pronunciation (to read, I read, I read yesterday). Can you identify 15 with no alternatives or changes in pronunciation?

Answers

burst, cast, cost, cut, hit, hurt, let, put, rid, set, shed, shut, spread, sweat, thrust

(#106, 7/84)

Précis-Writing Takes Speed

Although précis-writers at international meetings must produce an accurate English summary of up to 50 minutes of multilingual discussion, often within a few hours, many précis-writers have never learned shorthand. Yet this apparent disadvantage actually forces the writers to be more efficient at their job, which is not stenography but highly specialized editing.

Précis-writers work by ear. A spoken cliché like "I cannot emphasize too strongly" automatically goes down on the précis-writer's pad as "stressed." But cutting must be judicious. Delegates to international meetings hunt for their own words in the summary, and if they don't find them, they may return to the sponsoring organization a record bristling with corrections.

The writer of a précis thus must compress and clarify the speeches of delegates while keeping as many of the original words as possible. Paraphrases and synonyms (except alternatives for "said") must therefore be used sparingly. Yet summary records are generally more readable than verbatim records, because the writer has quietly removed whatever impedes the speaker's train of thought.

Ideally, précis-writers dictate straight from their notes to a typist, but even the fastest writer may have to fill gaps. After the "take" of a meeting the précis-writer has three main sources to check what was actually said:

- The delegate's own text, borrowed immediately after the speech. The problem is that some delegates use their text as basis for improvisation.
- The typed English transcript of a speech delivered in another language. This may not reach the précis-writer for an hour or more after the "take," and may contain gaps or confusions of sounds—like one memorable sentence from the transcript of a Vietnamese speaking in French, which was translated "We must remove all threats of war, whether from imperialists, expressionists, or other reactionary forces." (The culprits meant were "expansionists.")
- Tapes in the original language, which take time to use and demand a good ear for the language, but are the most reliable source.

(#51, 11/80)

Orwell on Politics and Language

LOGO•PHILE

"That year" is upon us. The cultural and political mavens have unleashed a barrage of commentary, firing in Orwell's direction ("Orwell was wrong") as well as at their own favorite targets ("Orwell was talking about you"), reminding all within earshot of "what Orwell really meant" and cautioning readers that, although Big Brother may not have arrived, Doublethink and Newspeak have. As a metaphor, "1984" has predictably been debased to the status of cliché; its very abuse has become an example of the muddled thinking that Orwell was trying to unmask. These days, (and, one fears, until 1985 arrives to deliver us) speakers and writers feel entitled to throw "1984" at whatever they happen to dislike, from network TV to telephone answering machines.

But professional writers and editors have to be more discriminating. Our legacy from Orwell is neither debased sociology nor muzzy political analysis. The flame we are bound to keep alive is not the blazing torch of prophecy but the steady glow of quality in the written word. Thus, we need to remind ourselves that, regardless of his accuracy as a prognosticator, George Orwell was perhaps the finest English essayist in this century. And that is why our required reading this year should be not *Nineteen Eighty-Four,* but his essay—now a classic—"Politics and the English Language."

In nearly five decades, this masterpiece has not lost its power to satisfy and sting. It is filled with so many aids for recognizing sins of omission and commission that, if there were a penitential season for writers and editors, this essay could easily become part of the liturgy. Throughout, Orwell is concerned with combating the "half-conscious belief that language is a natural growth. . . ." What language is, he says, is "an instrument which we shape for our own purposes."

That statement, of course, is both the good news and the bad, because language and thought interact. Language "becomes ugly and inaccurate because our thoughts are foolish," he says, "but the slovenliness of our language makes it easier for us to have foolish thoughts." He argues that the two most common writing problems—those with the highest potential for foolishness—are staleness of imagery and lack of concreteness. Orwell counsels avoiding the following at all costs:

- Dying metaphors (*bottom line, free lunch, doing your homework*)
- The routine interment of verbs (*exhibit a tendency to, under the direction of, make mention of*)
- Pretentious words (*effectuate, ineluctable, Weltanschauung*)
- Meaningless words (one of Orwell's examples is superb: "Comfort's catholicity of perception and image, strangely Whitmanesque in range . . . continues to evoke that trembling atmospheric accumulative hinting at a cruel and inexorably serene timelessness. . . .")

As aids to concreteness, he offers six rules. I commend them to every editor and writer in 1984; they fit quite nicely on a 4x6 file card, suitable for tacking above the desk at eye level:

1. Never use a metaphor, simile, or other figure of speech which you are used to seeing in print.
2. Never use a long word where a short one will do.
3. If it is possible to cut a word out, always cut it out.
4. Never use the passive where you can use the active.
5. Never use a foreign phrase, a scientific word, or a jargon word if you can think of an everyday English equivalent.
6. Break any of these rules sooner than say anything outright barbarous.

The common sense tucked away in the last of these sets Orwell apart. He recognized that, although his rules were elementary, their adoption required something akin to a religious conversion. He was also aware that there would be not only much backsliding but also much worshiping of false gods. Writers need to beware the ritualistic avoidance of the passive and the mechanistic reductionism of the readability formulas. Slavish adherence to rules like these results in the death of style. For their part, editors should never forget that style sheets are conventions, not Commandments. They do not so much define orthodoxy as defend against heresy.

As the Orwell revival gets underway, writers and editors have better credentials than most for participating. We have every right to claim him as our own, and to admire and learn from his penetration into the profound relationships between our times and the fragile web of words we use to announce and describe them.

 (#98, 1/84)

Black Eye

"Use of trite expressions shows the writer is in a rut."

—Postal Service Accident Investigation (#22, 2/79)

Modifier Madness

LOGO•PHILE

The ability of one part of speech to fill the shoes of another is one of the most delightful features of English. Using adjectives as nouns ("seeing red") or verbs as adjectives ("open door") makes for much creativity and flexibility. Among the most common crossovers is the use of nouns as adjectives. In English, any noun can be used this way, and there is no end to the useful—and quite appropriate—constructions that can be cobbled together by pressing nouns into service as modifiers: "house party," "love story," "Bronze Age," "postage stamp."

But things have gotten out of hand. Modifier madness is starting to overload the conceptual circuitry. We can still handle tripartite phrases like "test ban treaty," "silicon floor wax," or "aluminum rocket booster"; these are small potatoes. By the time we move on to constructions like "Steamfitters Union Perpetual Insurance Income Fund," queasiness begins to set in. And a chasm separates these from the advertisement for a recent colloquium offered by the Goddard Space Flight Center: "Erasable Gigi-byte Magneto-optic Data Storage Discs."

Noun Strings from Wall Street

But the Gigi-byters are still playing in the bush leagues compared to the Wall Streeters. This whopper recently found its way to the top of the in-basket: "By pooling the resources of many investors into a limited partnership, it is possible for individuals to benefit from the multimillion dollar data management peripheral equipment leasing industry."

I count eight modifiers: one article (the); one adjective-adverb combination (multimillion); two "pure" nouns (dollar, data); two nouns derived from verbs (management, equipment); one verbal noun (leasing); and one borderline adjective-noun (peripheral). All these are stacked atop a single noun, whose knees are clearly at the buckle. The construction is a ponderous inverted pyramid, in which all the conceptual weight bears down on a hapless "industry."

The result is a mountain of conceptual rubble. Does the industry under discussion manage data or lease peripheral equipment? Or does it lease peripheral equipment that manages data? It is the peripheral equipment that is in the multimillion-dollar range in terms of its value, or the industry as a whole in terms of its revenues? Or is it only important to know that, whatever is going on, there are big bucks to be made?

The Cause: Need for Brevity

So much of this kind of language comes at us from advertising ("New Formula Instant Chicken Noodle Soup Mix!") and newspaper headlines ("Chemical Waste Disposal Task Force Convenes") that it can't be avoided. The need for brevity jams words and ideas into the closest possible proximity, the better to blitzkrieg the reader. And, like an airborne virus, modifier madness infects everyone in the village sooner or later.

Beyond the ads and the newspapers, modifier madness is nurtured by the fact that English is not only enormously flexible but endlessly forgiving. A sentence whose nouns are freighted with modifiers can remain impeccably grammatical, even as it mounts its assault on rationality. Words, unlike mathematical symbols, do not always gain elegance from brevity. Stacking nouns and adjectives does achieve brevity, but beyond a certain point, what is gained to brevity is lost to clarity. Our Mother Tongue may be endlessly forgiving, but in the end it's the reader who always pays the price for her sweet disposition.

 (#99, 2/84)

■ In Defense of the Passive

Have you ever wondered why some editors rigorously excise passive constructions wherever they turn up, regardless of sense or sensibility?

Recently, I was asked to review an article for publication. The article was a delight—it had rhythm, style, variety, imagination, and elegance of expression—in its *unedited* state. The editor, in a fit of conscientiousness (perhaps brought on by having read the advice of too many proponents of the short and simplistic), had diligently changed all passive voice constructions to the active, with the result that the author's vigorous style was drained of vitality.

Now, the editor cannot be held entirely to blame. Any "effective writing" manual you pick up—starting with the estimable *Elements of Style*—tells you to prefer the active voice. The key word here is "prefer," which means "like better; choose above another," not "adhere to mindlessly." Yet many editors respond to passives with a pencil-jerk, apparently not pausing to consider that the language probably would not contain a passive voice if it were never to be used.

All right, you challenge, give me one good reason for using the passive. I'll give you several.

First, the active voice, as we all know, is strong because it allows an actor to *do* something. But sometimes your sentence simply does not need an actor—as illustrated in the previous paragraph in the clause "the language probably would not contain a passive voice *if it were never to be used*." If the infinitive phrase were rendered in the active voice, the only possible actor would be the ubiquitous "one" (as in "if one were never to use it"), and "one" is overworked to begin with.

Second, the passive voice can be used to describe a situation in which the thing acted upon is more important than the actor. "The enormous diamond had been given to her on her 40th birthday, but she chose not to wear it until her 75th." Certainly the sentence would make sense if it began "She received the enormous diamond. . . ," but that would shift the focus away from the stone which, in this case, is the more important element in the sentence.

Third, the actor may be obscure, unknown, or unimportant or may wish to be anonymous or transparent. This kind of passive construction occurs most often in scientific or technical material, as in "The mice were fed a solution of gin and vermouth and were observed to behave in bizarre ways." The passive should be allowed to stand, except when it gets in the way of comprehension or produces weird constructions, such as "It was felt that the mice were drunk."

And fourth, sometimes a passive construction can help you achieve a desired cadence. Robert Frost could have written "I took the road fewer people traveled," but that's hardly as rhythmic as "I took the one less traveled by." In deciding whether to change passive voice to active, be guided by your ear, as well as by your training. Read the sentence out loud. If you can't understand it, it may need active voice (and perhaps much more). But if the rhythm is pleasing and the sentence makes sense, leave it alone.

Passive constructions are not evil in themselves; only the misuse and the overuse of the passive have given it such a bad name. Remove it carefully and with much thought; you may be pulling up a wildflower instead of a weed.

—Mara Adams (#108, 9/84)

How to Abstract a Scientific Paper

Robert A. Day, in his book *How to Write and Publish a Scientific Paper* (Philadelphia: ISI Press, 1979), tells about a journal abstract written many years ago by Albert Einstein. The abstract said only this:

$$E = mc^2.$$

According to Day, it's the shortest scientific abstract ever written. It is concise, but it simply won't do, not these days. In an age when abstracts increasingly must serve as temporary or permanent substitutes for "the real article," and when they accumulate by the hundreds of thousands in computerized data bases not even accompanied by their parent articles, no responsible journal editor should let even an Einstein get away with writing a skimpy abstract that can't stand by itself.

Unfortunately, the instructions to authors in many scientific journals give little or no guidance on writing the abstract, except to state that it *must not exceed* a certain length (emphasis theirs). But length is not the main problem; abstracts can always be edited to size. The problem is abstracts that fit in the allocated space but fail to tell the story.

I can testify after working nearly 2 years as technical reviewer on a project supplying journal article abstracts for a computerized scientific data base, and after reading the major parts of more than 4,000 journal articles, that probably no more than 5 percent of authors write adequate abstracts of their own research reports.

In the great majority of cases, abstractors either have to modify the author's abstract or write a completely new one. The good abstractors are almost always better at summarizing scientific reports, although most abstractors have little or no scientific background. How can English majors with only a smattering of science write better scientific abstracts than scientists? Answer: They know what kind of information a good abstract should contain and they have learned where to look for it in the main article.

How an Abstract Is Organized

Any abstract of a research paper should have this basic organization: a topic sentence, a description of methods, a summary of results, and a conclusion. Those elements parallel the organization of the main article itself, which makes sense when you consider that the abstract is so often a surrogate for the article. The task of the editor or abstractor is to find the paralleling elements in the main article and incorporate them in the abstract if they aren't already there. Fortunately, all these elements can, with high predictability, be found in specific places in the article.

1. *The topic sentence* states the purpose of the research. What was studied? What hypothesis was tested? All schoolchildren are taught to start writing with a topic sentence, but experienced abstractors know that if a scholarly author leaves anything out of an abstract it will most likely be a simple opening statement telling what the research was about. An abstractor or a journal editor who finds this void can nearly always fill it by looking in the last paragraph of the introduction, right after the background of the research has been laid out. If the information is not there, the topic must be divined from the results and conclusions.
2. *A brief description of methods* is another essential that authors frequently leave out of abstracts. Since an entire section of most scientific articles, labeled "Materials and Methods," covers this topic, the job of the abstractor is to select only enough information from that section to give the reader some idea of the *general* approach the researchers used. What kind of subjects were used? How were the control and experimental groups treated? What was administered, how often, and in what dosages? Two or

three sentences are usually enough, because anyone who wants to repeat the research will always go to the main article for full details on procedure. The abstract should contain only enough about methodology to provide a context for the results, which are presented next.

3. *Summary of results*. Authors are usually very good at summarizing their results in their abstracts, and many author-written abstracts consist of no more than this summary. But what good is an abstract that merely lists results and can't stand alone as a substitute for the article? If you have to read the article to determine the context and meaning of those results, you might as well skip the abstract.
4. *A conclusion*. Surprisingly, authors' abstracts don't always have a conclusion, even though their articles invariably do. Concluding statements are always found in the last section, labeled "Discussion." To save time, go directly to the last paragraph where conclusions are most likely to be found. Look for sentences that begin, "We conclude. . . " "Our results show. . . " "These findings suggest. . . " "The data are consistent (or inconsistent) with the hypothesis that. . . ." Some journals are considerate enough to have a short final section labeled "Conclusions."

In short (and I do mean short), an abstract should tell a story—with a beginning, a middle, and an end, and always with this "plot": *This is what we studied; this is how we did it; this is what we learned; this is what it means.* Since scientific authors so often forget this scheme, journal editors ought to repair defective abstracts or at least suggest repairs to their authors. Fixing an abstract is seldom difficult. Some scientific training is bound to be helpful, but I have seen many beautiful abstracts written from scratch by people who barely understood the article they were abstracting. They just knew where to look, a skill that increases rapidly with practice.

The fact that scientists are putting out journal articles at an unprecedented rate—faster, indeed, than even the colleagues in their subspecialty can assimilate them—makes the abstractor's skill more important than ever. Tomorrow's Einsteins may be able to reduce the mysteries of the universe to equally brief equations, but they will still need a good abstractor.

—Peter L. Petrakis (#118, 6/85)

Black Eyes

From the Health Corner

Surgery We Could All Use
Another advantage is that it allows patients without third party coverage to make exact financial arrangements well in advance of surgery which can potentially reduce bad debts.

Diet Trends
One month after the second surgery, she developed necrosis of the liver and diet.

. . . .

The panel's specific advice for a healthier diet included this guideline:
Reduce fate intake to 30% of total calories.

Those Problem Patients
"We think there is less of a problem with the vein as an outpatient than as an inpatient," he said.

Cures Worse Than the Illnesses
On the other hand, nausea and headache appeared less commonly in urine users.

. . . .

He had a history of adult onset of diabetes mellitus treated with diet and mild hypertension.

—From a hoard of typos, misplaced modifiers, etc., collected for an inhouse monthly on language usage, submitted by Byron Breedlove, Atlanta, GA

(#86, 3/83)

Kinds of Abstracts

Generally, an abstract should concisely present a document's objectives, scope, and findings while retaining the basic tone and emphasis of the original document. An abstract also should be self-contained so that it will be useful if published by itself. Here are eight types of abstracts:

1. Title only—a bibliographic reference that can be used for indexing;
2. Mini abstract—one to two lines, useful if the document is unsuitable for a more informative summary;
3. Statistical or numerical abstract—concise, tabular form;
4. Descriptive or indicative abstract—brief description of the document's contents without giving results or conclusions;
5. Informative abstract—summary of the document's major arguments, data, and conclusions;
6. Critical abstract—condensation of the document and evaluation of the work and the way the material is presented;
7. Extended or synoptic abstract—a longer abstract that contains up to 3,000 words and may include artwork; and
8. Extract—use of one or more portions of a document to represent the whole.

—Dorothy J. Buchanan-Davidson, University of Wisconsin, Madison, Center for Health Sciences (#83, 1/83)

Tips on Proposal Writing

The worst waste of your time and money is to prepare a proposal when you shouldn't. If the job is 'wired' for another company, if your firm is not qualified to handle the work, or if the competition is just too great, don't waste your time.

Don't give up too easily, though. Sometimes a good proposal will get you a job even if the client hasn't heard of you before. Sometimes also you have to invest in a proposal to get your firm known so you can be considered for future jobs even if you don't win the first one.

A second major mistake is being "unresponsive," or not following directions. Usually the request for proposal (RFP) gives detailed, precise instructions for the form and content of your proposal. You will be ahead of much of your competition if you merely read the RFP carefully and do what it says.

Reread the RFP often during proposal development and then again when your proposal is finished to make sure you are addressing every single client requirement. It seems basic, but stick to the job at hand. Don't ignore any requirements and try to avoid taking issue with any client "musts."

If possible, find out the client's budget for the job and make your approach fit that budget. Cost out your proposal before you do too much writing. (If the budget or other job requirements are totally unrealistic, make sure you can persuade the client to change or don't waste your time on a proposal.)

Pay attention to the criteria the client will be using to evaluate the proposals. If the client is kind enough to spell out what qualifications are most important, then respond by showing exactly how your firm meets and even exceeds them. A discussion of your company's philosophy is not a suitable substitute for requested details of previous similar projects.

Content

First, use your proposal to tell just what you will and will not do. Detail your plan. "Quantify as much as possible," recommends Washington proposal expert Herman Holtz. "You'll add to credibility, get a baseline for costing, and provide the basic objectives and controls to plan and manage your project later."

Your proposal is also a sales and educational document. It must show the client that you know exactly what you will be doing, that you are the best qualified, and that your price is reasonable and realistic.

Personalize the proposal. It would be foolhardy to write every proposal from scratch, so you must develop and use boilerplate material that outlines your experience and other aspects of your work. Don't fall in the trap of reusing that boilerplate unchanged for each proposal. Treat your boilerplate as your starting draft and modify it to match each job you are bidding on. Pick out the most directly related projects and highlight them. Rewrite résumés to stress directly relevant experience.

Modern word processing equipment can make "global" changes—it can, for example, change the word "Army" to "Navy" every time the former appears. With or without such equipment, a human being should carefully reread every draft to make sure no inappropriate references remain.

Keep a file of old proposals so you can adapt old material for new proposals. Index the proposals not only by client but by type of project and skills required so the needed information can be found easily.

Writing the Proposal

Appoint a proposal manager to be in charge of the whole effort, from strategy to delivery. Also designate an editorial/production manager for the proposal. If your firm has an editorial staff, it should put one person in charge.

The proposal manager should also appoint one person from the proposal team to interact with the editorial/production manager. The most likely candidate for this role is the lead writer—someone who knows enough about the proposal in general to answer questions. The proposal manager will probably be too busy with costing, staffing, and other work to be the point of contact.

The contact should be available to answer questions about editorial and production matters at all times the proposal is in process, including and especially nights and weekends, when critical editorial or production steps may be taking place.

A well-written, nonresponsive, overpriced proposal will lose to a poorly written responsive one. A well-written on-target proposal, of course, will do best of all. Here are some tips for writing.

Have as few people as possible writing. Choose writers who are knowledgeable about the parts they write. Make sure the writers can give the proposal work priority. If they are so overcommitted with project or other work, they will put off their writing until the last minute and disrupt the rest of your proposal schedule. If necessary, get a professional writer to meet with your technical staff, get their ideas, and prepare the drafts for review.

If you divide the writing, don't let it be done by committee. Hold meetings to discuss approaches, but then assign only one person to prepare each draft or section. Let other group members review and revise that draft.

Get a professional editor to help smooth out the proposal. If possible, involve this person from the start to help proposal organization and structure.

Especially if you've had more than one writer, make sure to have only one editor. Try not to start editing until writing is done. Make sure the same person reviews the entire proposal—business and technical. Look for and ensure consistency among the parts—especially on details of scheduling and hours to be spent.

Organization and Style

Follow all instructions in the RFP. If the RFP specifies an order for the proposal sections, follow it.

Deviate from this rule only to add a summary up front if one is not requested. Your goal should be to let the proposal's reviewer know within 2 minutes exactly why your firm is best for the project. Also include a table of contents.

If no proposal order is specified, follow this one:

- Introduction
- Statement and Understanding of the Problem
- Technical Approach—how you would do the job, step by step
- Management—quality control, project organization
- Personnel—who will do the job, project manager, key staff
- Budget—in the required format and level of detail
- Appendix—for backup materials, but make sure these are summarized and referred to in the text

Give your proposal a central, unifying theme. Without such a theme, it will appear to ramble erratically and make few points clearly.

Don't be long winded. Use short words, sentences, and paragraphs. Keep sentences under two or three typewritten lines; paragraphs under a half page. Use headings and underlining to highlight important points.

Don't be formal or bombastic. Write the way you talk. If you're having trouble writing the proposal, dictate it first and work from a transcript.

If you are submitting a large proposal with detailed technical specifications that each require detailed discussion, start each discussion with a statement that you are in compliance with the requirements so there can be no question on the part of the reader.

If any nonspecialists will be included in the proposal review team, be sure to explain all terms and processes they might not understand.

—Laura Horowitz (#32, 9/79)

■ Proposal Production

The best scheduling advice is to start early. Don't wait until the last minute.

As soon as the proposal team is assembled and the writers are appointed, prepare and distribute a realistic, written schedule for writing, reviewing, editing, typing, and checking each section and draft of the proposal.

If any requirements such as size, content, deadlines, and assembly change, be sure to tell the editorial/production manager so production scheduling and staffing can be changed accordingly.

Allow some leeway in your deadlines for machinery breakdowns. Have backup capabilities and arrangements.

Post the schedule prominently and check off completed tasks. Seeing others in the company meeting their deadlines can spur team members on, for no one wants to appear as a bottleneck.

On drafts especially, leave wide margins with plenty of room for comments. Minimize capital letters to make the text easier on the eye.

Opinions vary on single or double spacing, but the overall effect should be a neat, carefully prepared, easy-to-read proposal.

Try to use some charts and other illustrations to help the reader visualize your approach and schedule. Be sure to use descriptive captions on all artwork. Try to keep all artwork vertical so the reader won't have to turn pages around. If you must have horizontals, be sure all of them face in the same direction.

Limit the number of drafts. Aim for a maximum of three. Have only the proposal manager review the final draft.

Date each draft so you don't lose track of which one is current. Have reviewers initial each draft. Use yellow paper for preliminary drafts and then switch to white paper for the final draft.

Use word processing equipment especially for company capability statements, lists of past projects, and résumés. With a minimum of rekeyboarding, you can rearrange the projects listed in these to be responsive to the client you are proposing to.

If you use word processing, don't become so enamored of the machines' revision capabilities that you waste hours on revisions when the original marked up draft should be discarded and reinput.

Finally, set the proposal aside for at least a 24-hour cooling-off period at the end and then reread it. Allow time to make the revisions after this final review, for that is when embarrassing and sometimes fatal errors are caught.

As Holtz says, "it is not the proposal writing that produces winners; it is proposal thinking."

—Laura Horowitz (#32, 9/79)

Reprinted with permission from *Professional Services Management Journal* (PSMJ), a monthly newsletter on managing, financing, marketing, staffing, and otherwise running a planning, design, architectural, or research firm.

PSMJ also sponsors seminars on proposal preparation, project management, and financial management. For more information on the seminars or to get a copy of PSMJ, write Box 11316, Newington, CT 06111.

Writing Responsive Proposals

The key to writing a successful proposal is responsiveness to the requirements of whoever is seeking a contractor. But more than half of the proposals submitted each year are rejected as nonresponsive, according to the late Jim Beveridge, an expert on the anatomy of winning proposals.

Responsiveness

And what is "responsiveness?" A responsive proposal—whether a 5-page grant application or a 2,000-page system integration solution—tells how the offeror will carry out every task to be done and service to be supplied, as described in the request for proposal (RFP). The RFP and any amendments provide a nonnegotiable baseline of information the offeror must include, specifically and completely, to be considered for program award.

All this seems like common sense; why, then, are so many proposals nonresponsive? The proposal can run off the track when the offeror does any of the following:

- misinterprets the client's needs and offers to provide the wrong service;
- decides the direction the RFP gives is confusing or nonsensical and assumes conclusions about the program that are not necessarily true;
- thinks of a "better way" to do the work and proposes *that* way;
- plans a new schedule for the work and sets milestones different from those stated in the RFP;
- disagrees with the proposed qualifications or composition of the staff and proposes a project team similar to but not the same as that asked for; or
- neglects to address all of the requirements.

Enthusiasm, not incompetence, is often to blame. Consider a typical scenario: After a corporate decision to bid on the work, proposal managers and contributors read the RFP superficially, think they understand the client's needs, and immediately begin to plan a creative response that fits their own image of the program or, more likely, their own capabilities. These solutions can be innovative and clever but completely off target.

Techniques

Here are some techniques proposal writers and managers can use to avoid nonresponsiveness:

1. Read, reread, and study the RFP. Be sure you understand fully what the client needs. Visit or call the contracting officer for clarification. You may also prepare formal questions and request an extension of the deadline to allow time for response. Use examples to illustrate your questions.
2. Identify conflicting RFP instructions that cloud the nature or direction of the work required and ask the client to resolve the conflict. Clients will feel embarrassed if you point out many scrambled instructions and may even tell you to "figure it out for yourself." But a little humor and persistence—and a humble attitude—may convince the client of your sincere interest in understanding the requirements. If an RFP contains too many traps, however, you may want to reconsider your decision to bid on the work.
3. Stick to the client's proposed work plan, even though you may devise one that seems better. By showing how the RFP work plan can be carried out, you demonstrate a cooperative attitude. You can submit and defend an alternative plan in a separate proposal or in an appendix. Be sure to note the availability of your alternative in your response.
4. Develop your work schedule within the client's time frame, even if it is not one you would voluntarily adopt. Demonstrate the most efficient way to meet the client's milestones for the project. Use personnel loading charts to show, task by task, how you'd staff the project *to complete all requirements*. You can also show your planning ability and concern for the client's budget by providing a more logical and more economical schedule.
5. Comply *exactly* with the staff composition the RFP calls for. If the RFP proposes a staff of two systems designers, a data base expert, three systems programmers, and five applications programmers familiar with IBM mainframes, *that's* the staff you propose. Your staff resumes should reflect the levels of competence, education, specialized technical or managerial knowledge, and years of experience called for.
6. Devise a fail-safe plan for proposal management to be sure you address all requirements. Several time-proven methods exist.

- Develop a detailed outline, keyed to the RFP, from which you write all responses. Double-check them against the RFP to be sure no elements are missing.

- Use a "storyboard" or proposal response form that assigns a topic sentence to each RFP requirement. The form serves as a focal point around which you write supporting text and plan illustrations.
- Create a system to trace RFP requirements by assigning a number or keyword to each one. Track that number or keyword onto all drafts of the proposal. If you write to each requirement, you should be able to build a matrix at the end of the effort that includes proposal text references to all numbers and keywords. This careful cross-check of your responsiveness is especially useful with large, complex proposals. Many offerors submit the matrices with their proposal to help the client evaluate it.
- Recruit a "red team" of two or more knowledgeable professionals to read and grade the final draft of your proposal against the RFP. Their mandate is to ensure responsiveness to requirements. Build in time to act on the red team's suggestions.

Style

As with any writing task, writing proposals in response to RFP requirements calls for straightforward, concise language that incorporates appropriate technical terms. If the requirement is to "describe the software development methodology you will employ for each subsystem," don't say,

> Extensive consideration was given to the mandated requirements to describe the software development methodology to be employed for the implementation of each subsystem. . . .

Instead, say, "We considered several plans for developing the software for each subsystem. . . ."

Remember to respond to requirements using paraphrases, not the exact language, of the RFP. For example, if the RFP says, "Offeror must comply with the requirement to provide a redundant system in case of system failure," you might respond with: "We will design and install redundant equipment to provide continuous operation during times of primary system downtime" (and then tell *how*). When paraphrasing, be sure to retain key technical terms; in the example, "redundant" remained because it has an important, specific technical meaning in this instance.

Use artwork to illustrate your responsive text, providing the client with a picture of your plans for meeting requirements. Well-executed organization charts, flow diagrams, concept illustrations, and skills matrices all strengthen a response. Writing a responsive proposal is not, in itself, a guarantee that you will win a contract, but it will give you an edge on at least some of the competition.

—Barbara Anderson (#115, 3/85)

Test Yourself

On Editorial Trivia

1. What is the name for this symbol: # ?
2. What is a *balaam*?
3. What was the name of the first electronic novel ever published?
4. What is the derivation of the term *freelance*?
5. Give the ZIP code abbreviations for Maine, Minnesota, Mississippi, Massachusetts, Alabama, Arkansas, Arizona, and Alaska.
6. List five of the ten most commonly used English words.
7. Choose the correct word: (Who) (Whom) do you believe is telling the truth?
8. What does ISSN stand for?
9. What does the abbreviation "cc" stand for at the bottom of correspondence?
10. What does the acronym RADAR stand for?

Answers

1. octothorp
2. term for a journalistic filler
3. *Blind Pharaoh*
4. In the Middle Ages, mercenary soldiers who were unattached to a liege lord were called *free lance* soldiers.
5. ME, MN, MS, MA, AL, AR, AZ, AK
6. The ten words are *of, and, a, to, in, is, I, that, it, the.*
7. Who
8. International Standard Serial Number
9. It is the plural of the Latin abbreviation for *copia*, as "pp." is for *pagina* and "ll." is for *linea.*
10. RAdio Detection And Ranging

(#103, 5/84)

III. PLAIN ENGLISH

Clear Writing in Government Communication

If government regulations are going to be written in plain English, team efforts are needed. Writers and public relations specialists must be on the team from the start, not brought in at the end to translate what legal and technical experts have already written.

This was the advice of Fred Emery, editor of the *Federal Register*, at a National Association of Government Communicators (NAGC) workshop in Washington, DC, in 1978.

Author Jefferson Bates agreed that writers need to be elevated from what a member of the audience described as "second-class status in government agencies" and brought into the regulation-writing process early. It has long been considered easier to train a liberal arts-oriented writer in science than to turn a scientist or engineer into a writer, he noted.

Avoid the "Dumb and Unenforceable"

The goal of regulations is voluntary compliance, *Federal Register* attorney Rose-Anne Larson noted. If regulations are written clearly, people will comply, she said. But the person challenged to translate complex regulations into simple language often discovers that bad writing is covering up bad logic. When requirements are revealed to be "dumb and unenforceable," the product must be rewritten from scratch, not just simplified, she continued.

Bates blamed much of the bad writing on regulations drafters who are not sure of their audience and use lawyer-to-lawyer or scientist-to-scientist language instead of a government-to-individual tone. Moreover, he said, most regulations fail to address the basic who, what, where, when, and why queries.

How can the product be improved?

- Avoid the use of multiple negatives.
- Write in the singular.
- Require people who draft forms to fill out the forms once themselves.
- Read all regulations aloud before promulgating them.

Try-outs May Be Needed

The ultimate solution, according to Emery, may be for the government to field-test its regulations, much as businesses test-market their products. Toy manufacturers, for example, hire customers to test-assemble their toys from written instructions in the kits to see where problems arise. Similarly, the government needs to test its regulations on sample groups of machine shop operators or pension plan holders who will have to use the regulations formulated for them.

(#19, 12/78)

■ Plain English Movement Progresses

The effort to simplify U.S. government writing has grown during the Carter administration. From an attack on obscure language in government regulations, the plain English movement has expanded to a general improvement of memos, reports, and whatever else government writers produce, according to a panel at the National Association of Government Communicators' annual conference in Washington, DC, in early December 1980.

In a workshop on promoting plain English, Ruth Ralph, associate professor of communication at American University, noted that the Office of Management and Budget now requires annual reports of agencies' progress toward plain English. Agencies showing particular progress in the November 1980 report include the following:

- Department of Health and Human Services, where Operation Common Sense has clarified documents in programs for serving the handicapped, Social Security applicants, and students seeking loans.
- Environmental Protection Agency, which, said Ralph, has produced some outstanding writing guides.

- General Services Administration, which has trained hundreds of employees in plain English techniques and has improved the guide to its regulations and the regulations themselves.

Ralph also discussed the plain English movement at the state level. New York, Maine, Connecticut, Hawaii, and New Jersey, for example, have passed laws to control the language of consumer contracts, particularly mortgage and insurance agreements. Fines for failure to use plain English in consumer contracts are small, she noted, but the laws aim to establish the principle that merchants and lenders should use language that people can understand.

Plain English Practitioners Wield Clout at HUD

The plain English program managers at the Department of Housing and Urban Development (HUD) "are unpopular, but very powerful," said panelist Robert Wulff, senior program analyst and plain English project officer for the HUD Office of Policy and Program Development.

Instead of emphasizing revision of the regulations themselves, as President Carter's 1978 Executive Order dictated, HUD has focused on clarifying the forms and other documents that program participants must use. In fact, if the plain English reviewers do not approve those documents, the programs will cease until the documents are revised to meet reviewers' objections.

Wulff blamed HUD lawyers for most of the problems his office has met in its pursuit of plain English. Program people and communications experts, he said, happily accept the editors' work and are delighted when applicants can complete the necessary forms easily.

Lawyers, in contrast, constantly argue that any simplification of legal language not only will open the Secretary of HUD to legal liability but also will negate 600 years of jurisprudence and jeopardize "all of Western civilization."

Wulff noted that his office used to be somewhat intimidated by lawyers' arguments about the immutability of certain legal language. The editors' attitude changed when several lawyers once disagreed so violently over their interpretation of the word *premises* that it became clear that the language was just as imprecise as the nonlawyers had always suspected.

Now, Wulff commented, his office takes the offense against arcane language and negotiates successfully with lawyers to change it. Wulff cautioned, however, that "real legal liability problems" exist in translating consumer documents such as mortgage notes into understandable English beyond a certain degree. Some Latin terms are so complex that they cannot be precisely summarized in English and it's better not to try.

U.S. Army Program Marches Apace

"The Army mirrors society, and people can't read," said panelist Dottie Nicewarner, who directs the Army's plain English program through the Office of the Adjutant General. So, Nicewarner said, the Army launched its plain English offensive in 1977, several months before President Carter entered the fray.

The goals of the 34 editors under Nicewarner are to write regulations in plain English and to reduce the number and bulk of Army publications. Like HUD editors, the Army group has clout. The editors have to justify what they do and negotiate with the writers, but any writer who refuses to accept editorial changes must "get his General to write to our General for an exception" to the plain English policy, said Nicewarner. At that point, she added, writers usually decide to cooperate.

Using a readability formula devised by Rudolph Flesch, the Army's editorial office has greatly reduced the reading level of 600 Army regulations. Nicewarner's office has also trained more than 1,000 regulation writers in clear writing techniques.

Nicewarner noted that her office is meeting less resistance as time passes and as the advantages of the revised regulations become evident to users.

"The readiness of the Army depends on how well the soldiers understand what they learn through training manuals, repair manuals, and the like," she said. The Army spends much money on its publications—and that money is wasted if the publications cannot be used. The editing, therefore, "pays for itself."

—Priscilla Taylor (#52, 12/80)

Black Eyes

"The Unknown Aspects of Incoming Orders"

MEMORANDUM September 29, 1982

To: All Employees
From: Vice President/Finance
Re: Incoming Investor Cash

The flood of incoming orders, particularly with this investment program seems to arrive at too many locations other than Order Processing. Because of the unknown aspects of just when the last order will arrive, please expedite the checks and orders to Order Processing as you happen to receive them. Please hand carry all orders to Order Processing to insure them being included in that day's volume.

—Submitted by Sarah H. Bulgatz, Emeryville, CA (#81, 11/82)

Wonder if Cats and Dogs Own Fish and Gerbils?

On October 29, Friday, at 7:30 PM, I am inviting all pet owners, and that means cats as well as dogs, to meet in Studio 46 . . . to put our heads together and discuss these problems.

—Pet Peeves notice to tenants in Alexandria, VA, apartment house (#81, 11/82)

The Bigger the Heading, the More Likely the Error

Vocabulary, Grammer, Spelling,

From a U.S. Department of Agriculture Graduate School catalog (#81, 11/82)

Ballot

Following is an alphabetical list of nominees for the Board of Directors and the Nominating Committee. (Incumbents are indicated by an asterisk.) All candidates' biographies are 40 words or less and have been unedited.

I think "unediting" is what sometimes happens to a carefully edited technical paper after the review board has finished with it.

—Sue Budlong (#81, 11/82)

Plain English Supply-Side Style

Although the Carter administration gave a large boost to the plain English movement, the movement was not born with that administration, nor will it die with the passing of the Carter regime. Nevertheless, Reagan administration budget cuts have taken some of the wind from the plain-English sails, and changes in policy emphasis have somewhat altered the movement's course, at least as far as government English is concerned.

The Reincarnation of the Carter Order

In April 1981, President Reagan replaced Carter's Executive Order 12044, *Improving Government Regulations,* with Executive Order 12291, which bears the same title but does not mention plain English. Some people believe the omission may have been inadvertent rather than deliberate; others believe it reflects the overall change in philosophy of government.

According to Robert Wulff, a former project officer for the plain English program in the Department of Housing and Urban Development, the plain English movement at HUD was the victim of a "double whammy": the movement's association with Carter and its association with consumerism.

"The economists who wrote the new Executive Order were more concerned with other things," says Warren Buhler of Management Design, Inc., a consulting firm that has worked with the Reagan administration. "Many of the projects that had high visibility under the Carter administration continue today," Buhler maintains, "buried in the regulatory process."

Janice Redish, director of the Document Design Center, American Institutes for Research, believes the new Executive Order aims to reduce the burden on people who are required to fill out documents for the federal government and that plain English is still a good way to accomplish this purpose. "Although deregulation means less regulatory activity in general, clear English still makes good business sense," says Redish.

Redish's office has been working with the Department of Education to improve the forms that colleges and universities use to report to the federal government on student loans. The Document Design Center team has removed some extraneous material from the forms and has reorganized the remaining material so people can find what they need more easily.

Although public information offices in government agencies are drastically reducing their staffs, Redish notes, agencies still publish some documents for public consumption. Redish's office recently worked to improve a Federal Trade Commission manual to help businesses. "English for the sake of the consumer has gone out of fashion," she says, "but plain English is good for business and hence is not out of step with the Reagan administration."

Some Programs Bow to Budget

The *Federal Register,* which has trained hundreds of employees in plain English techniques, discontinued its document-drafting workshops with the beginning of the 1982 fiscal year because of budget cuts. Rich Claypoole, deputy director of the Executive Agencies Division, says the Federal Register's program to simplify and clarify the language of regulations began in 1975-76; the Carter administration's Executive Order just enhanced a program already in place.

The *Federal Register* continues to offer technical assistance to agencies that need help in writing regulations, Claypoole says. To any disappointed would-be trainees interested in self-help, he recommends the *Document Drafting Handbook* (published by GPO). This manual covers much of what was taught in the workshop classes.

USDA Agencies Maintain Standards

The U.S. Department of Agriculture prides itself on having had a plain English focus since 1905, when it first began publishing bulletins for farmers. Although all USDA agencies have their own publication standards, all USDA publications must also meet criteria for clarity and effectiveness established by the Office of the Assistant Secretary for Governmental and Public Affairs.

Nelson Fitton, head of the Office's publishing center, credits Carter's plain English initiative with stimulating some improvement in the writing of regulations. Last year, USDA hired an information specialist to train technical people, managers, and others to write more effectively. Instruction, for example, may be tailored to meet the needs of particular groups of scientists or technicians. Fitton notes too that USDA has been working with its Graduate School on a training program to improve regulation writing.

Bonnie Whyte, deputy director, Office of Public Information for the USDA Food and Nutrition Service, says her staff has always tried to write in plain English. Public affairs specialists considered the Carter initiative to relate chiefly to editing regulations and technical publications with which public information people are not directly concerned.

Mixed Progress Elsewhere

Outside the federal government, plain English in government documents is still plodding along. In 1981, Minnesota became the sixth state (joining Connecticut, Hawaii, Maine, New Jersey, and New York) to pass a law to control the language of consumer contracts. In Maryland, however, 1981 was the third year in a row in which special interest lobbies defeated the efforts of plain English committees appointed by the governor.

In the District of Columbia, a 1979-80 proposal to require that legislation be drafted in plain English was not adopted, chiefly because of the fiscal impact it might have had. The timing of the proposal proved unfortunate in that the code of the District had just been amended, and it was feared that adoption of this proposal might have required a complete rewriting.

—Priscilla Taylor (#70, 3/82)

Plain English: Dollars and Sense

Commerce Secretary Malcolm Baldrige, who 2 years ago ordered his staff to stop sending him correspondence written in bureaucratese, is widening the war against obfuscation. The Commerce Department recently sponsored a 1-day forum, "The Productivity of Plain English," emphasizing government cooperation with the private sector to establish plain English communication with consumers.

Forum chairman Alan Siegel, president of Siegel & Gale in New York, told representatives from leading U.S. companies and associations, "Up to now, the plain English movement has focused on the social benefits of plain language. . . . For the movement to survive and grow, attention must be given to the economic benefits of plain language."

Siegel added that "Secretary Baldrige's effort will amount to no more than a few syllables dropped in a bucket until our government and corporate leaders finally recognize that regulations, forms, contracts, letters, and other communications in plain English save money and time."

Approaches to Plain English

The forum consisted of three panels. The first included representatives from five private-sector organizations who discussed their organizations' approach to plain English programs. Grant Denison, vice president of Pfizer, Inc., said the plain English focus of his pharmaceutical-manufacturing company has been on improving consumer information in instructions and advertising; Pfizer now pretests its literature to be sure consumers can understand it.

Alexander Liosnoff, editorial coordinator of consumer forms for the Bank of America, reported on his firm's efforts to improve the language of its forms. John Horton, manager of forms for the St. Paul Fire and Marine Insurance Company, discussed his company's improvement of the language in its policies.

Richard Jilbert of General Motors Service Development Center discussed his company's use of the Star readability program, which is based on Rudolf Flesch's plain English guidelines.

Hazel Schoenberg, director of consumer information for J.C. Penney, Inc., discussed Penney's improvement of information to consumers about auto repairs as an example of her company's emphasis on plain English.

Plain English Laws

Speakers on the second panel included Peter Sullivan of the New York State Assembly, who discussed the plain English law enacted in his state several years ago. Participants in this forum pointed out that although business people had feared an increase in litigation if plain English laws were adopted, in fact, to the extent that absence of litigation can be measured, the opposite seems to have occurred.

Measuring Marketplace Results

Panelists representing the American Council of Life Insurance, Shell Oil Company, and Yankelovich, Skelly and White, Inc., discussed anecdotal evidence on how plain English can improve productivity, but agreed that it is hard to measure the cost-effectiveness of new bank forms or the amount of litigation forestalled by clear language.

Joseph C. Jones, Jr., corporate advertising manager for Shell, said that the "Come to Shell for Answers" information campaign had been very popular with consumers. During this campaign, Shell published a series of pamphlets about car care for consumers that discussed in simple language arcane subjects such as gasline freeze and disc brake repair. Market analysis shows that more people now recognize and respond favorably to Shell. Jones noted that the information campaign had been stimulated by the oil crisis of the mid-1970s, which made "Buy Gas" advertising inappropriate.

Panelists generally agreed that more research is needed on the cost effectiveness of plain English, and that more communication is needed among people and organizations working to encourage the use of plain English. Secretary Baldrige recommended establishing a committee consisting of representatives of government and private-sector organizations to coordinate further plain English activities.

(#84, 2/83)

Book Review: Plain English

HOW PLAIN ENGLISH WORKS FOR BUSINESS: TWELVE CASE STUDIES. Washington, DC: U.S. Department of Commerce, Office of Consumer Affairs, 1984, 102 pp.

Designed for business managers, this useful book tells how a dozen corporations and trade associations fought their way to a better bottom line by simplifying consumer documents and product-information brochures.

The book is a product of the Department of Commerce, the one federal agency that seems to be serious about cleaning up its language act. Secretary Malcolm Baldrige has acquired a reputation for covering subordinates' memos with red marks and editorial comments. This book is an outgrowth of his influence.

The book explains in detail how such corporate giants as Aetna Life & Casualty, Citibank, J.C. Penney, Sentry, and Shell paved the road to greater profits with plain English. The profit lies in streamlining procedures, eliminating unnecessary forms, and reducing customer complaints.

Case Study #7, for example, discusses how Roche Laboratories developed a multimedia campaign to tell the public how to use prescription medicines safely. The "What If" brochures developed by Roche answered important questions about medication. It was so successful (24 million copies) that a follow-up campaign was launched with a "How To" booklet, using the same Q&A format.

The public's perception to the contrary, no other sector of business pays as much attention—now—to plain English as the insurance industry. The plain English movement of a few companies like Sentry attracted the attention of major industry associations, and easy-to-read policies soon became an industrywide priority. Today, more than 95 percent of insurance companies have revised their policies.

Sentry's experience (Case Study #8) is particularly instructive. It took a team of two attorneys, a former English teacher turned business communicator, and two marketing specialists more than 1,500 hours to rewrite Sentry's basic automobile policy. The policy was reduced from an imposing 12,000 words in 8-point type (31 pages) to 6,500 words in 11-point type (23 pages). There was another leap forward when eight different terms for vehicles were reduced to *car* and *utility trailer*. Consumers' fears about "the fine print" were reduced considerably by eliminating it. And the policy was personalized; the insured became *you* and the company became *we* or *us*.

The case studies are valuable to any business or organization that wants to communicate more clearly, effectively, and profitably. One helpful appendix explains the Flesch Reading Ease Test, and another provides a checklist for managing a corporate plain English project.

—Bruce O. Boston (#110, 11/84)

(Ordering Information: Superintendent of Documents, U.S. Government Printing Office, Washington, DC 20402, Stock #003-000-00631-0)

Baldrige Bearish on Bull

Plain English is still alive and well in Washington thanks to Secretary of Commerce Malcolm Baldrige. Not only has he issued a directive instructing those who write his letters to use simple, concise language, but he has also fixed some Commerce Department word processors to stop and flash "Don't Use This Word!" when they encounter a forbidden expression. These measures are reported to have reduced late answers to letters from 140 a day to 10.

Here are his guidelines to writers:

- Answer questions specifically.
- Respond in no more than one page, where possible. When answering a series of questions, prepare a brief cover letter and attach specific answers.
- If the response is negative, be polite, not abrupt.
- Avoid wordiness. Keep sentences lean and short.
- Use the active rather than the passive voice.
- Use no unnecessary adjectives or adverbs. Write with nouns and verbs to strengthen the letter.
- Do not use nouns or adjectives as verbs, such as:

to optimize	to finalize
to impact (or to impact on)	to target
to interface	to maximize

- Use the precise word or phrase.

datum (singular)—data (plural)
criterion (singular)—criteria (plural)
subsequent means *after*, not *before*
different *from*, not different *than*
insure means to guarantee against financial loss, *ensure* means to make sure or certain [GPO to the contrary notwithstanding].
effect as a noun means *result*; as a verb, to *bring about*, to *accomplish*
affect means to *influence*, to *act upon*, to *alter*, to *assume*, to *adopt*
think is mental; *feel* is physical or emotional (think thoughts, not feelings)

- Please stop using affected or imprecise words. Some examples:

viable	effectuated
input	output
orient	prioritize (not a word)
hopefully (use *I hope*)	hereinafter
ongoing (prefer *continuing*)	parameter (use *boundary* or *limit*)
responsive	
specificity	image
utilize (prefer *use*)	delighted (use *pleased* or *happy*)
glad (use *pleased* or *happy*)	
thrust	inappropriate (overused)

- Please stop using the following phrases:
  I share your concern (or interest or views)
  I appreciate your concern (or interest or views)
  I would hope (use *I hope*)
  I regret I cannot be more responsive (or encouraging)
  I am deeply concerned
  Thank you for your letter expressing concern (use *Thank you for your letter concerning*. . .)
  prior to (use *before*)
  subject matter
  very much
  bottom line
  best wishes
  at the present time (use *at this time*)
  as you know, as I am sure you know, as you are aware
  more importantly (use *more important*)
  needless to say
  it is my intention
  mutually beneficial
  contingent upon
  management regime
- Avoid redundancies, such as:

serious crisis	enclosed herewith	future plans
personally reviewed	important essentials	end result
new initiatives	final outcome	great majority

  untimely death (Has there ever been a timely death?)
- Do not use a split infinitive (placing an adverb between *to* and the verb).
- Do not use addressee's first name in the body of the letter.

- Do not refer to the date of the incoming letter.
- Stop apologizing, such as: I regret the delay in responding to you.

The Secretary describes the style he prefers as "halfway between Ernest Hemingway and Zane Grey with no bureaucratese." Baldrige is reported to have said that when he came to Washington he noticed "many people spoke in multisyllabic words and phrases that I'm not sure even they understood completely."

He is quoted as saying, "The only reason I could see for them talking that kind of talk was a subconscious urge to cover one's self. There is a kind of protection in statements and a recommendation so vague that it can be interpreted two or three ways on a single issue. That's not communication; that's covering one's flanks."

Is that closer to Grey or Hemingway?

(#63, 9/81)

Test Yourself

On Words About Time

Fill in the appropriate letter. Note that letters can be used more than once.

1. biannual ________	a. daily
2. biennial ________	b. weekly
3. continual ________	c. every 2 weeks
4. continuous ________	d. every 2 years
5. decennial ________	e. twice a year
6. diurnal ________	f. every 5 years
7. fortnightly ________	g. every 10 years
8. hebdomadal ________	h. every 20 years
9. millenary ________	i. recurrent
10. quinquennial ________	j. uninterrupted
11. quotidian ________	k. continuing through centuries
12. secular ________	l. 1,000 years
13. sennightly ________	
14. vicennial ________	

(#42, 4/80)

Answers

1. *biannual* (e) twice a year; 2. *biennial* (d) every 2 years; 3. *continual* (i) recurrent; 4. *continuous* (j) uninterrupted; 5. *decennial* (g) every 10 years; 6. *diurnal* (a) daily; 7. *fortnightly* (c) every 2 weeks; 8. *hebdomadal* (b) weekly; 9. *millenary* (l) 1,000; 10. *quinquennial* (f) every 5 years; 11. *quotidian* (a) daily; 12. *secular* (k) continuing through centuries; 13. *sennightly* (b) weekly; 14. *vicennial* (h) every 20 years.

(#43, 5/80)

PUBLICATIONS MANAGEMENT

I. RUNNING THE SHOP

Writing is basically a solitary task; publishing (or better, the publication process), because it usually happens in a context of barely controlled chaos, is a collective task that requires orchestration.

In this section we explore some of the techniques, strategies, and tactics for maintaining that control and for giving the appearance of knowing what is going on when all around you are obviously losing the few marbles they have left.

Because working with language is more art than science, standards of performance have always been difficult to come by.

- Is it possible to devise an editing test that will tell you whether a job applicant really can edit?
- How would you go about hiring a proofreader?
- Why is there no limit to the number of times authors and clients will change their minds?
- How fast and accurate should keyboarding be?
- How do you estimate the time, and therefore the cost, of editing, and why is it that everyone always underestimates the amount of time a given job will take?
- How do you keep the arms of the eternal editorial triangle—time, cost, and quality—in some kind of balance?

The answers to these questions are the essence of successful publications management. They don't come easy, and when they come, they don't always stay. You'll find a few of them on the following pages.

Lessons from 50 Years' Editorial Experience

"I have not made any novel discoveries or found any magical remedies. What I *have* done is to survive 50-plus years of trying to be a communicator—and still like what I'm doing."

With these words, Lola Zook introduced a talk on "Lessons Learned," delivered at the International Technical Communications Conference in May 1980. Here is the essence of her talk:

Lessons I Wish I Hadn't Had to Learn

1. There is absolutely no limit to the number of times authors or clients will change their minds.
2. The more firmly an author or client says that all the copy will be ready for you by a certain time, the later the material will be.
3. The rule on the innate perversity of inanimate objects applies. When I am in no hurry, the copying machine works perfectly. But if I need 20 copies for a meeting that starts in 3 minutes, a demon takes over.

   Likewise, all machines for putting words on paper—from linotype to photocomp—are, on occasion, possessed by demons. Surely, in a proposal, no *human* mind could take the phrase "government duplication" and change it into "government duplicity."
4. You can't have everything. What is essential is to *recognize* this fact—to be aware that you must choose, but that *this gives you the opportunity to take control.*

With a tight budget, you balance the advantages and the costs of color work, quality of paper stock, and so forth. You can't have everything, but you can have a satisfactory product.

With a tight deadline, you decide where the limited time can be used to best effect. You can't do everything, but you can make your time count.

Lessons I Wish I Had Learned Sooner

1. It is impossible to overestimate the infinite capacity of things to go wrong.

2. It is impossible to overestimate the capacity of people to do something you don't expect.
3. When you are trying to tell graphics people how you want something done, one layout is worth 10,000 words.
4. There is one absolutely universal shortcoming that afflicts everyone in the publications business: *Everyone* underestimates the amount of time a job will take.

Lessons I Never Did Learn

1. I never did learn to spell supersede.
2. I never did solve the problem of he/she usage.
3. I never did learn to abhor the passive voice. I prefer the active voice; I know it is more vigorous and all those good, strong things. But still, there are times when what-was-done is more important than who-did-it. So I confess: Now and then, I put a sentence in the passive voice—deliberately!
4. I never did convince myself that shortest is best. I do indeed believe that good technical prose should not slop around with extra words and meandering sentences. But I have wasted many an editorial hour struggling to make sense of a passage where the author was determined to obey the rules and Be Concise, Brief, and To the Point. Unfortunately, in so doing, the author forgot the reader—and omitted the transitions, the explanatory phrases, or the line of reasoning that provided the base for an assumption or conclusion.

So, when someone sings the glories of conciseness, I still tend to say, "Wellll, yes, but it's not that simple."

Lessons I Am Still Trying to Learn

1. For one who works with words, the ultimate goal is to produce a sentence that sounds as if it could have been written no other way.
2. One of the best ways to judge whether prose is effective is to use your ear. Listen to the rhythm of the sentence, the sound of the words, the cadence of the paragraph. If the words are awkward neighbors, if the breaks are too close, the flow is interrupted. That may be just what you want—but do it on purpose and not by accident! *Hear* rhythm and flow and contrast; use them as tools to make the language harmonize with the meaning.

3. A good way to improve editorial skills is to teach someone else in a one-to-one, tutorial relationship. With a bright, assertive apprentice who questions and challenges every aspect of the work, you'll find yourself reviewing rules you've grown careless about, looking up items you've taken for granted, sharpening style—all because you had to take a fresh look at things that had become so familiar you didn't even see them anymore.
4. Borrow the first step of the Scientific Method: Define the problem. If you are having trouble, back off and consider: What *really* is the problem? If you can't focus the writing, is the problem in the writing, the reasoning, or the organization? If the author has specified one audience but written for a different one, is the problem in the perception of the audience or in the writing? If there is too much work and not enough time to produce a big job, should you sound the alarm for emergency help, or try to get someone to take a hatchet to the size of the job?

   And, be sure that problem definition moves in two directions: You must know management's problems in a project, and you must inform management about problems *you* face that could endanger success. A problem is not likely to be solved unless the right people know it exists.
5. As an editor, you must be aware of what you do *not* know about a technical subject but not let yourself be intimidated.

   Poor organization is poor organization whatever the subject matter. Bad grammar or careless documentation has to be corrected in any discipline. Preparing a manuscript for publication is the same process whether it deals with maintaining tanks or projecting energy demands.

   What you must do is keep sharply aware of technical danger points. *Of course* the subject matter specialist is afraid of what an untested editor might do to technical statements. When you show that you are sensitive to these hazards, you are likely to get more freedom.
6. Remember: *You, the editor, are a bridge between two people, the person who has written and the person who will (or may) read.* Everything else in the process is simply a means to that end.

   There is a corollary to this lesson. Every editor must like working with words, but to be fully effective an editor must also like working with people.
7. Keep a sense of perspective. The editor who sets a goal of perfection is in for a lifetime of disappointment. Set a goal that is reasonable, and then take pride in reaching it.

   Accept the fact that authors and production people have their own problems, and that your problem may be pretty far down in their priorities.

Take time to *enjoy* what you are doing. If this is your chosen work, presumably you like doing it, or at least most of it. Yet some of us are so tense, so upset over every trifle, that the job sounds like punishment. We need to establish that sense of perspective.

And, always, we need to keep an eye out for the funny side.

(#44, 6/80)

Publications Management Lessons and Warnings

Always

- Plan for the worst; hope for the best.
- Hand-carry finished work.
- Keep records.
- Give and solicit feedback.
- Determine the audience, purpose, and distribution of your documents first.
- Consult your designer and printer early in the project.
- Allow enough time for reviews and clearances.
- Get your instructions from the persons who will have to approve your work.
- Put agreements in writing.
- Plan for interruptions and downtime.
- Use checklists to itemize tasks to be done on a job.
- Develop and use style sheets.
- Have one person responsible for each project.
- Have back-ups for each person, including yourself.
- Leave a written record of what you did and why.
- Keep all drafts of a document until it is finished (but cross through old drafts so you know which is the current one).

- Have checkpoints. Insist on work samples and reviews.
- Know where all things and key people are, and how to find them.
- Spend extra time carefully planning your project; you'll save time later.

Never

- Believe people who tell you there will be no revisions or AA's.
- Believe people who tell you a manuscript has been "perfectly" edited.
- Believe people who claim their manuscript needs only a "light edit."
- Expect a neatly typed manuscript to be well edited.
- Overplan your day.
- Believe an author who swears all the material will be in by the deadline.
- Believe you are going to get a job until you have it all in your hands.
- Accept oral estimates or quotations without written confirmation.
- Hire people without checking references, reviewing work samples (including résumés), or testing.
- Expect a good writer to be a good editor, or vice versa.
- Expect a former English teacher to be able to write a simple declarative sentence.
- Expect a former typing teacher to be a good manuscript typist.
- Assume anything.
- Expect your messages to be received.
- Expect two people in the same office to know what the other is doing.
- Expect a typesetter or typist to make all marked corrections.
- Jump to conclusions. Always check out the other side.
- Trust the mails. Keep a protection copy of your material.
- Make the same mistake twice (there are new ones waiting to be made).
- Believe repair people when they say your machine is fixed. Make them watch you use it for a few minutes before you let them leave.

Lessons

- When you order two batches of paper for one job from one sample book, the colors won't match.
- When the equipment salesperson swears you can count on maintenance within 2 hours, you can hope that what he or she means is 2 days rather than 2 weeks.
- If you schedule two big jobs in sequence so you can readily handle both, the first job will be delayed and the second will come in early.

- Former English majors or teachers cannot necessarily write, edit, proofread, or type.
- Management consulting firms cannot necessarily manage publication departments.
- Word processing is not a panacea.
- A broken machine will work perfectly when the repair rep comes.
- 80 percent of the problems are caused by 20 percent of the work or workers (and vice versa).
- If there is only one error, it will be on page one or the cover.
- Love is Blind Principle: Don't expect a good substantive editor to do a good job of copyediting his or her own work; or a good typist to do a good job proofreading his or her own work.
- If you use standing material for the front matter in a series, there will come a time when the printer strips in the negative backwards—and that will be the one time nobody checks a page proof.

And Finally, Applicable Murphy's Laws

- Everything takes longer than you think it will.
- If anything can possibly go wrong it will.
- Whatever you've planned to do costs more than the original estimates.
- Whatever project you set out to do, some other project must be done first.

And Lest You Give Up

- Precise planning, minute attention to detail, and exact timing never succeed like dumb luck!

—Laura Horowitz (#4, 4/78)

Special thanks to veterans Lola Zook and Peggy Smith for their contributions, and to the Drawing Board catalog for its statement of Murphy's laws.

Strategic Planning in Publishing

What benefits does strategic planning hold for the field of publishing? Consider the following example: The revolution in communications technology affects everyone working in publishing today. You know you must exploit the new technology, but how? What kind of systems should you use? How powerful should they be? How should you structure your work to fit them? What will be the long-term impact of these choices for you?

If you are a manager in publishing, the key to these and similar questions is strategic, or long-range, planning. It offers a way of testing whether your short-term solutions are sound, and it helps you—as a manager—make the transition from crisis management to concentration on your organization's long-term success and welfare.

What Strategic Planning Is

Formal strategic planning is several things: a process, a structure, a managerial philosophy, a mental discipline. George Steiner, a pioneer of modern planning theory, calls it "inventing your own future." Peter Drucker calls it "what you do to deserve a future."

In essence, strategic planning provides a framework for systematically considering current decisions in the light of their implications for future decisions. Planning helps you to break free of the all too common passive-reactive style of management and to take active control of your organization's destiny.

A major not-for-profit publisher recently had dramatic proof of the value of planning. For many years, this organization had avoided a certain line of publishing because of "competitive factors." A planning exercise showed that the competitive situation had been badly misinterpreted; the publisher is now providing a new, worthwhile service that contributes substantially to its financial base.

What Strategic Planning Is Not

Much of what passes for planning is really just extrapolation colored by optimism or wishful thinking. Proper planning is not—

- anticipatory decision making;
- forecasting, or extended budgeting, or R&D (although all these may be tools);
- "blueprinting" of the future (nobody can do that); or
- preparing of massive, complex, incomprehensible planning documents.

How You Start

Your planning system should be tailored to your kind of publishing, the characteristics of your organization, and the people who will be involved. Before you work out the specifics, though, you should take these preliminary steps:

1. Learn something about planning concepts and techniques.
2. Decide who should be involved in the planning process. Although planning is the responsibility of top management, the process works best when it involves the line managers who will be executing the plans.
3. "Plan to plan." Develop ground rules, schedules, and assignments for participants. In doing so, you should consider questions like these: How should the organizational climate be prepared? How formal should the process be? What interval should it cover? What are likely to be the obstacles to planning? How should financial data and analysis be handled? If yours is a subunit of a larger organization that does not plan, what should be the scope of your efforts? These questions must be answered case by case; there are no pat prescriptions.

The Basic Planning Steps

Although planning can benefit all kinds of organizations, procedures and emphases vary. Still, certain basic steps are common to all successful approaches:

1. Always begin with the definition of long-range goals or missions. (I like to think of this as the institutional equivalent of "What do I want to be when I grow up?") This crucial step is virtually guaranteed to change the way you see your organization.
2. Look at where you are now. (This step is called the "position audit.") Examine your organization's strengths and weaknesses (internal factors), as well as opportunities and threats (external factors).
3. Once you know where you want to go and where you are starting from, formulate strategies for the journey. Weigh and test alternatives, then pick the most promising or least problematic.

4. Prepare your plans: first, the long-range (usually 3 or 5 years), then the short-term (usually 1 year).
5. Implement the short-term, or operational, plan.
6. Monitor performance and experience under the plan.
7. Start all over again. *This step is absolutely essential*; successful planning is a never-ending, self-correcting process. Inevitably, adjustments must be made to take account of changing conditions and information, and as each new year arrives, the long-range plan must be extended another year into the future. Most planning systems work on an annual cycle, coinciding with the fiscal year.

In both the preliminary steps and the planning process itself, it is often helpful to have a facilitator—either an outsider who understands your business (the outsider's detachment is actually an advantage) or an inhouse professional who is not in line management. The important thing is to begin. The payoffs are real. Don't delay; dig in.

—John M. Strawhorn* (#82, 12/82)

*The author, a consultant in the Washington, DC, area, recommends works by John Argenti, Russell L. Ackoff, Peter Drucker, and George A. Steiner.

Successful Newsletters: Advice from the Experts

What makes a newsletter successful? A newsletter should be "utilitarian, reader-minded, [and] forward-looking," and should serve as "an aid to the decision making capability of the subscriber," says Austin Kiplinger, publisher of the *Kiplinger Washington Letter*. Emphasis on what readers need has helped make Kiplinger's *Letter* one of the most successful newsletters ever published, as judged by standards of both longevity and editorial excellence.

Kiplinger's advice is quoted by Frederick D. Goss, director of the Newsletter Association of America, in *Success in Newsletter Publishing, A Practical Guide* (Washington, DC: Newsletter Association of America, 1982, 195 pp.). This book is one of several new or recently reprinted how-to manuals offering advice on success in newsletter publishing.

The books can be divided into three groups: those especially useful for noncommercial newsletter editors and publishers, those primarily for internal organizational use, and those for commercial newsletter editors and publishers.

Books on Noncommercial Newsletters

Editing Your Newsletter (Portland, OR: Coast to Coast Books, 2nd ed., 1982, 122 pp.) by Portland writer and publisher Mark Beach, is the most comprehensive of the books in the noncommercial category. Although intended for newsletter editors who have little training in writing or production, the book contains so many hints on effectiveness that it is an excellent reference for more experienced people.

Beach's book features an attractive 8½″ × 11″ format, quotations from working newsletter editors supporting his points, an informal writing style, and discussions of writing without bias and of using text-editing equipment. The real strength of the book is its advice on graphics and production. Beach explains the types of illustrations useful in newsletters and the equipment needed, and gives examples from the newsletters he discusses.

Beach's "Tips for Graphics" section includes this advice:

- Be careful not to overdo it. Keep designs simple and images clear. Flowery graphics, like flowery words, may confuse your readers.
- Use graphics to draw attention down the page and to the right. Clip art especially should be placed to emphasize the least-read area of the page [the far right-hand corner].
- Be sure blacks are dense and uniform, edges sharp and clear. With copy lacking dense blacks and sharp edges, try outlining with pen and shading with lines or dots.

Writing advice is the principal strength of *The Newsletter Editor's Desk Book* (Kansas City, MO: Parkway Press, 1982, 133 pp.). The authors are Marvin Arth, who edits *Newsletter Forum*, a commercial newsletter emphasizing aspects of writing and editing, and Helen Ashmore.

The *Desk Book* also is intended for editors with little training and covers much of the same material as the Beach book—defining the purpose and audience for newsletters; getting organized and getting help; collecting newsletter news; reporting, writing, and editing; writing headlines; and designing, printing, and distributing the newsletter. The section on reporting and writing for newsletters includes good advice on maintaining objectivity, gathering news, doing interviews, writing features, and rewriting.

On interviews, Arth and Ashmore give these useful tips:

- Successful interviewers psyche up for an interview. First, they fix clearly in mind why this person is a good source—what the person knows that the readers will want to know. This helps the interviewer decide what questions should be asked. . . .
- Set a specific time for the interview. Allow time to ask enough questions to over-cover the subject because it is always better to have too much information than not enough.
- Taking notes and running a tape may be the best policy. This way, the writing is started, and the high points are on paper. The tape will serve as a back-up only, not as the principal source.

This book also contains a concise summary of legal considerations for newsletter editors—libel, privacy, and copyright.

A useful appendix contains a model stylebook, headline schedule, some formula stories (how to report personnel news, meetings, speeches, reports, notices, controversy), a form contract for use with suppliers, and lists of copyediting and proofreading symbols.

Inhouse Instructional Booklets

There are many short instructional books and pamphlets that organizations originally created for their own use and then distributed more widely. One such booklet is *A Practical Guide to Newsletter Editing and Design* (Ames, IA: The Iowa State University Press, 1979, 5th printing, 50 pp.). The author, LaRae H. Wales, senior publications editor at the Vermont Agricultural Station, subtitled her book "Instructions for printing by mimeograph or offset for the inexperienced editor." This book, which is intended for novices with small budgets, concentrates on the how-to aspects of production.

Books on Commercial Newsletters

Although the books just mentioned are useful to commercial newsletter editors and publishers, they do not discuss two subjects of primary importance to these people—subscription promotion and business management.

Fortunately, two excellent new books offer guidelines for launching a successful commercial newsletter. Both contain chapters on direct-mail strategies and management.

Publishing Newsletters (New York, NY: Charles Scribner's Sons, 1982, 205 pp.) was written by Howard Penn Hudson, publisher of *The Newsletter on Newsletters*, lecturer in the field, and founder of the Newsletter Association of America. Hudson relates how to find and judge your market; how to determine editorial style, composition, and printing; and how to advertise, use direct mail, and keep subscription records.

Hudson's hard business sense makes his chapter on judging the market one of the best in the book: "The word 'market' has various shades of meaning. What you are really seeking is what I call your universe—the number of people who appear to be reasonable prospects for your newsletter. Here you must start dealing with specifics. It is not enough to say your newsletter is aimed at people who are interested in money. You have to find these people by name and address."

Hudson's directness gives life to the book. "Too much involvement in production," he says, diverts editors from "their primary job, which is to write and edit." On direct mail, Hudson comments, "The rules for successful direct mail are deceptively simple. Locate your target audience—mail to it, and measure results—if it works, mail again. It is similar to poker in that you can learn the rules in 5 minutes, but it takes a lifetime to play well because there are infinite variations and combinations to be studied and mastered."

Frederick Goss, in *Success in Newsletter Publishing, A Practical Guide,* which was mentioned earlier, says a lot in a small space about design and production, but he devotes most of his attention to newsletter promotion and management.

On renewals, Goss says, "Editorial quality is the single most important factor in determining successful renewals, not the design of the renewal series." However, to help renewals along, he adds, "One school of thought holds that the best time to get an additional order is when a prospect is in a buying frame of mind. As soon as you receive an order, or within a month or so, may be a good time to send out an early renewal offer."

In addition to covering subscription promotion and renewal, Goss discusses electronic editing, newsletter accounting and financial operations, the legal aspects of newsletter publication, and the buying and selling of newsletter properties.

Goss quotes from managers of prominent newsletter publishing firms and from well-known consultants in the field. Unfortunately, the book has no index.

Success or Failure for Your Newsletter?

The past decade has witnessed a phenomenal growth in the number of newsletters published. Many fail in the sense that they do not achieve the goals set for them—they are not read, used, or referred to. The main difference between commercial and noncommercial newsletters is that commercial newsletter publishers become aware of their failure faster because of low subscription rates. Those newsletter editors and publishers who want to minimize their chance of failure should read some of these recent books on the subject.

—Nan Fritz (#87, 4/83)

■ Guide for the Perplexed

A national survey by Opinion Research Corporation found that 93 percent of financial analysts believe that the annual report is the "most useful written communication" companies publish. The same could be said of many associations and nonprofit organizations. But editorial staffs seldom have useful resources (aside from last year's report) to guide them through the process of putting an annual report together. According to Marty Ochs, author of *Planning Your Annual Report*, the last book published on annual reports came out in 1961. His own 48-page brochure is recommended as a guide for the perplexed and as fortification for the intimidated. It is available from Ochs Publishing Co., P.O. Box 2083, Littleton, CO 80122.

Rule 1 of annual report writing is divide and conquer. Think of the annual report as two distinct documents. The first document, on corporate operations, should include the president's report, special features, and a review of operations and activities. The second document is devoted to financial statements and explanatory footnotes. The lawyers and accountants will insist on writing them anyway, so give them room and rewrite later.

Rules 2 through 5 have to do with what editors know how to do best: assure brevity, conciseness, concreteness, and liveliness. These goals are especially important for annual reports because the review cycles inevitably produce verbal excess. An inhouse editor will have to be able to make a strong case against the assault of vice presidents and chief executives.

But where most people need help is in design and production. The annual report is, after all, a presentation piece. It is the company or organization dressed in its Sunday best. The basic rule here is that the art, design and layout, photography, paper, and typography make the difference between a report that induces yawns and one that begs to be read.

Experienced editors maintain files of other companies' annual reports, which they regularly raid for ideas. Investor relations departments of the *Fortune* 500 companies are happy to send copies of last year's report on request, as are the public affairs departments of large associations, foundations, and nonprofit organizations.

The Ochs brochure shines in its design and production; it practices what it preaches, and beautifully. Among its other preachments are discussions of art and typography, copy preparation, and paper selection. Putting pointers into print means being abreast of the graphics trends. These trends include using full color throughout, with bigger and better pictures; more special photographic effects; more bleeds; fewer head shots and more "team" shots; more location photography; 2- and 3-column formats, ragged rights, and unjustified bottoms; sans serif faces (usually Helvetica); 10-point type and larger; bold and abundant use of white space; and higher quality paper stock.

Much of this design advice translates into higher production costs, a factor that has made printing the sixth-largest business in the United States. Avoiding extra costs will include such steps as finding the right printer, which often means shopping nationally; making sure everything is perfect before printing; learning to use your suppliers as educators and sources of information; understanding trade customs and practices thoroughly; and making rigorous estimates.

The Ochs brochure offers excellent advice on mailing lists, including techniques for report and proxy mailing and a very valuable listing of suggested extra audiences. Editors should also prepare a final review checklist, a planning and operational timetable, and (very important) a checklist of the requirements of the Securities and Exchange Commission on annual reports.

—Bruce O. Boston (#101, 4/84)

How to Devise an Editing Test

How can you judge the editing ability of applicants for a publications job? Assuming that the resumes and cover letters show the applicants to possess a working knowledge of the English language, you may wish to administer an editing test geared to your organization's special needs. The test, or battery of tests, must be scrupulously objective; the test must be administered to all applicants under the same conditions and graded according to a point-weighted answer key. How do you devise such a test?

Your first step is to define the level of editing you are seeking. You may need an all-purpose test including simple spelling, proofreading, and copyediting problems, or you may want a more substantive test including more difficult wording, organization, and rewriting problems. Perhaps you will need both kinds.

All-Purpose Test

The all-purpose test should probably include the following:

1. A list of spelling demons, preferably one in which the test takers must choose among variant spellings.
2. A short paragraph in which there are a few misspelled words and some correctly spelled but tricky words (such as "fluorescent") that applicants must mark as correct, incorrect, or "D" (for "I'd look this one up in a dictionary").

3. A group of sentences demonstrating common editorial problems: nonparallel constructions, subject-verb disagreement, style inconsistencies, dangling modifiers, misplaced modifiers ("I found the pearl necklace swimming out by the raft"), windy phrases, and the like.

Substantive Test

This test should include the all-purpose test plus a longer document—perhaps several pages or a chapter from a manuscript your organization has already published—containing errors of fact, ambiguities, errors of logic, organizational problems, tabular material, and notes or references. The material should reflect most of the problems you want a substantive editor to be able to handle. (Drafts of government publications—which are in the public domain—often make good editing tests.)

Test Conditions

The conditions under which any test is given must be identical for all test takers. That is, if you administer the test to one applicant in the middle of a noisy, busy office, all applicants must take the test in the same noisy, busy office. Ideally, you should set aside a quiet area specifically for testing and instruct employees who work nearby to be especially quiet during testing periods. Have available to the people taking the substantive test such reference books as *The Chicago Manual of Style,* the *GPO Style Manual,* the dictionary you prefer, and your house style manual if you use one. To decide how much time to allow, have two or more of your editors take the tests and average the length of time it took for each.

Scoring System

For the all-purpose test, devising an answer key is simply a matter of marking what is correct and what is not. Assign a point value to each error and set a maximum on allowable errors: on a 50-point test, for example, 5 errors (10 percent) would be a reasonable maximum.

For the substantive test, devising an answer key is more difficult. Edit the document yourself as thoroughly as you would like to have applicants edit it. Assign a point value to each change according to its importance. For example, you might subtract one point for each error left uncorrected ("the sun threw *it's* rays") and a half-point for each desirable change not made (such as removal of sexism). You might not count at all changes that really are niceties (changing *towards* to *toward*), or you might give extra points or half-points (pluses) for them.

EEI's scoring system includes both pluses and minuses: Applicants lose points for not making essential changes, for introducing errors, and for not following directions, but gain points for especially good rewording or querying.

Conclusion

Administering and grading editing tests take a considerable amount of time. For an editorial business, testing is an essential investment in the service it supplies. For any organization with a publications or public relations program, testing can help managers pick the editors best able to produce clear, literate, and even elegant prose.

—Mara Adams (#94, 10/83)

■ How to Hire a Proofreader

There seem to be as many ways to hire new proofreaders as there are employers of proofreaders. A review of the scant literature on hiring proofreaders and a survey of some Washington-area firms found a wide range of hiring practices and standards.

Some employers will consider inexperienced applicants, test them for aptitude, and then train those they choose. Others require applicants to have particular academic backgrounds—English or journalism perhaps—or proofreading experience or both. These firms also test applicants and hire only those who demonstrate professional expertise. Most firms' applicant requirements fall somewhere between these two practices.

Define Your Needs

Before you start looking for a new proofreader, decide exactly what you will expect of the person you hire. Will the person's duties be proofreading only? Will they include administrative or production duties? Do you expect to promote the proofreader eventually to other responsibilities? Do you want one-person or team proofreading? Write a job description; it may help determine the type of person you should choose.

The Ideal Proofreader

The stereotypical proofreader is mousy and bookish, but in fact such a person usually doesn't make the best proofreader. One authority on proofreading describes the ideal proofreader as a college graduate who majored in English and who has experience as a compositor. Lacking a candidate with this background, he looks for appropriate aptitudes—a feel for the language and an eye for detail. Most good proofreaders like to read and care about the quality of the final product; they are perfectionists but also realists.

Other characteristics a proofreader should have include intellectual curiosity, a sense of humor, patience, meticulousness, and the abilities to work under pressure and to understand and follow directions. If you require team proofreading, look for someone who is compatible with others and can read aloud accurately and rapidly. A lone proofreader probably should be less people-oriented than a team proofreader, because the isolation of the job might be a hardship.

A proofreader should have good eyesight—with or without glasses. Neither gender nor age correlates with proofreading ability.

The Selection Process

Most employers begin with newspaper advertising; then they screen the résumés they receive in response and test the most promising candidates. But within that structure lie many variations.

One employer who tests aptitude rather than established proofreading skills uses an oral test. Candidates read aloud a paragraph containing many complex words. James L. Harrison, Jr., author of *How to Find, Hire and Train Proofreaders* (National Composition Association, 1978) suggests testing proofreading aptitude with a three-part written test that includes number and name comparisons, simulated filing, and spelling, in addition to an oral test.

A consulting firm uses as its proofreading test two pages of single-spaced typewritten copy in technical language that is to be compared with a messy, space-and-a-half draft copy. Would-be proofreaders must use standard marks to correct deviations from the draft, word divisions, and format inconsistencies. They must also know when and how to query.

This firm receives 200 to 250 responses to its ads and invites about 15 applicants to take its test. Of those tested, three usually pass. The final selection is based on personality; this employer prefers a strong (but not overbearing), meticulous person who asks questions and is eager to do the job right.

The publisher of a national magazine looks for an English or journalism degree and professional experience and tests those applicants with five pages of typeset copy to be compared with typewritten copy. There is no time limit, but most applicants complete the test within 2 hours. About 3 in 10 pass the test. Usually, the more professional experience the applicant has, the better the test score.

A research and development firm considers only applicants with a college degree and consulting firm experience. This employer's proofreading test has so many errors that no one has ever caught them all. The test is scored by number and kind of missed errors (some errors are considered more serious than others). About 2 applicants in 10 pass the test and are hired.

A consulting firm that doesn't often promote proofreaders to editing warns, "Look for someone who wants to proofread and will be happy to continue to proofread." This firm uses a one-and-a-half-page test that does not involve comparison. The test contains about 60 errors, and the best score so far has been 8 misses. On the average, only 1 person in 10 passes the test.

Getting Down to Work

When you have screened and tested your applicants, made your selections, and are ready to hire, always do so on a trial basis and plan a structured program to orient new proofreaders to your shop. Tour the office and explain the publications operation and how proofreading fits into the total picture.

Give new employees a procedures manual, however informal; preparing one will force you to organize the orientation. Keep the manual up to date by revising it as your operations change. Supply samples of typefaces and lists of proofers' marks, printing terms, and style rules.

Reread all the copy your new employees proof during the trial period to find out if their work is satisfactory. Set standards and make them clear to new workers. Look for patterns in missed errors and point out these patterns so new proofreaders will know when to exercise special care.

With thorough orientation and ample feedback during the trial period, you can hire on a permanent basis, knowing that new employees can meet your proofreading needs and standards.

—Mary Bodnar (#62, 8/81)

How Do Editors Read Résumés?

Surveys show that on initial screening, potential employers will spend an average of 10 seconds on a résumé, 20 at most. Editors with positions to fill are just as busy. The aim of the editor's first brief review is to eliminate patently inappropriate or otherwise unacceptable résumés. Here the editorial eye comes into play immediately. Typographical, spelling, and grammatical errors will immediately cause an editorial job seeker's résumé to self-destruct. (I've seen too many descriptions of editors' duties cite "liason" [*sic*] with vendors and authors.) Inappropriate use of passive voice, smothered verbs, noun strings, and lack of parallelism will probably relegate your résumé to the very bottom of the pile. Lack of parallelism is particularly noticeable in descriptions of responsibilities ("Duties included technical writing, editing manuscripts, analysis of data, preparation of technical proposals, graphics, coordinating and supervision of production"). Redundancy and ornate prose also create an unfavorable impression. Descriptions must be concise. In short, the language in an editor's résumé must be nothing short of perfect.

This requirement is not so hard-hearted as it may seem. Aspiring editors' cover letters and résumés are their best work samples. If their own marketing tools are careless and imprecise, how can they bring perfection to documents in which they have no vested interest?

Catching the Reader's Eye

To get the reader's attention, emphasize the most important information. A definite attention-getter is a list of qualifications that match my requirements precisely. Thus, the conventional wisdom applies: Find out exactly what the employer's needs are and stress how your qualifications can help meet those needs. Candidates should not talk about what they want but what the employer needs. It is ridiculous to emphasize painstaking editorial work on a scholarly journal in the humanities when applying for a job as a technical writer or production coordinator in a proposal shop.

Along this same line, résumés should show candidates to their best advantage. I want to notice job titles first, then specific skills (proofreading, design, paste-up), professional development, increasing responsibilities, and special achievements, such as awards, promotions, or merit increases. I'm also impressed by experience at doing the impossible. Names and dates are helpful but should not overshadow good titles or directly applicable skills.

Once the writer has my attention, the way to get me to pick up the phone is to entice or challenge—create a desire to find out more about what the editor can do for me.

Against the Current

Thus, the trend among career counselors—to start the résumé with a job objective—doesn't work for me, especially when the goal statement is so broad it is meaningless ("An opportunity to be associated with a substantial firm in a position utilizing my creative communicative abilities with progression to leadership"). I prefer seeing an introductory item, such as "Skills Summary" or "Expertise," that tells me immediately whether the applicant can solve my problems with little orientation. But I expect every skill claimed to be supported by experience stated.

If possible, draw the reader's eye to job titles, not to dates or organizations, unless the title does not reflect responsibilities. The résumé should contain a brief, well-written description of the organization, the publication, and duties. The description should not be overdone or boastful. Publications managers know what "substantive editing" is; don't translate the term. And save the superlatives for the interview.

Editors Aren't Writers

When seeking an editor, I am unimpressed by a candidate's writing skills. Most writers are poor copyeditors; I want a critic, not a creator. I am more impressed with skills that indicate that the candidate can pick nits, impose consistency, and improve—not rewrite—an assignment. Candidates who list only their doctoral dissertations, master's theses, or college term papers, but no real editing experience to support their editing skills, don't get past the door.

I am interested in skills at tasks that people consider routine, the ones they can do with closed eyes; the ability to go on automatic pilot at deadline time can be a real asset. In addition, tasks that you consider mundane may show the reader your versatility and knowledge of the entire publication cycle. Were you responsible for granting reprint permissions or for securing copyrights? Soliciting advertising? Supervising and hiring advertising representatives? Working on page dummies? If so, say so.

It is also helpful for me to know the types of publications an applicant has worked on—magazines, newsletters, proposals, brochures, book manuscripts—and how they were produced so that I can see if their skills are readily transferable. The résumé should also give me an idea of the editorial environment in each job the applicant has had: Did the editorial staff consist of 30 persons or was it a 1-person show? Was there an inhouse graphics shop or a designer?

Format

I prefer chronological résumés. I've seen enough functional ones to make me suspect a coverup. A chronological résumé immediately shows me progression of experience and responsibility and a consistent career path. All this tells me better than the writer what the next step should be.

Last Things First

The main element that will get me to inspect a résumé is a good cover letter. Like the résumé, it should be the applicant's best work; even more so, because so many résumés appear to have been prepared by professionals. A good cover letter brings out the writer's personality and piques my interest. It can highlight skills and experience directly applicable to the job. I also want to see the letter addressed to me by name, by title, or at the very least, by company name.

Good openings tell me about special recognition, "a penchant for accuracy," "attention to detail," "love of the written word," "commitment to excellence," or "ability to work under pressure and meet deadlines." The letter should then allude (briefly) to the contents of the résumé, stating how qualifications can meet my needs or solve my organization's problems; it should appeal to my self-interest. Ending the letter with a challenging thought might arouse my curiosity and make me want to read further, or set up an interview.

But no matter how effective your written introduction, a sterling résumé and cover letter can never replace strong credentials.

—Bita Lanys (#119, 7/85)

II. PRODUCTIVITY STANDARDS

Editorial Productivity Standards

How many pages should an editor/writer be able to complete in a day?

From 8 to 80, depending on how "dense" and how bad the text is, according to an organization called Writers Inc. (WI).

Hugh Nugent, a partner in the group, shared with *The Editorial Eye* the standards he has developed in working with clients (including, appropriately enough, the National Commission on Productivity). These standards are presented in the following chart. Definitions explaining the kinds of text and work follow the chart.

(As with other standards *The Eye* has printed, we do not necessarily endorse or agree with these. We present them to begin a discussion. We welcome contributions of any standards you have devised.)

Writers Inc. Editing Standards

	Normal Text		Dense Text	
	Pages/ hour	Pages/ day	Pages/ hour	Pages/ day
Proofreading	15	120	10	60
Simple edit	10	80	6	48
Sentence edit	6	48	4	32
Paragraph edit	4	32	3	24
Rewrite	2	16	2	16
Major rewrite	1½	12	1½	12
Total rewrite	1	8	1	8
Original from client's materials	¼	2	⅛	1
Original	⅛	1	⅛	1

Writers Inc. Definitions

Proofreading—Checking copy against original text for conformity to text, spelling, punctuation.

Simple Edit—Checking copy for spelling, grammatical errors, conformity to prescribed style.

Sentence Edit—Improving sentence structure by improving choice of words, flow of sentences, use of parallelism, etc. The basic sequence of sentences remains unchanged.

Paragraph Edit—Improving paragraph structure by changing sequence of sentences within paragraph, changing paragraph breaks. Includes sentence edit.

Rewrite—Retaining overall structure and flow of discussion while moving materials within major sections. Includes sentence and paragraph edits.

Major Rewrite—Retaining some of the original structure but moving materials from section to section. Includes sentence and paragraph edits.

Total Rewrite—Using material of the original but with complete freedom to restructure. Includes all the above edits and rewrites.

Original from Client's Materials—Organizing and writing new manuscript using material supplied by client.

Original—Researching, organizing, and writing new manuscript on topic requested by client.

Normal Text—Text written for the general reader, that is, the intelligent but not technically trained reader. Ratio of tables to pages of text is greater than 1:3. Footnotes do not exceed an average of two lines per page. A normal typewritten page is double spaced and contains about 300 words.

Dense Text—Text written for the technically trained reader. Ratio of tables to pages of text is 1:3 or less. Footnotes exceed an average of two lines per page. A dense typewritten page contains more than 300 words. Single-spaced pages are treated as two pages.

(#7, 6/78)

Black Eyes

Yep, Our's Will Be Better Than Your's

"Each of our machines has it's own private work area . . . and our staff is always avialable to answer questions and solve problems. . . . Most importantly, because you're doing the work, you can guarantee that your final draft will be letter perfect."

—From a word processing rental firm's promotional letter (#78, 9/82)

How to Succeed at...?

SEXUAL HARASSMENT and other books that can make you a better manager.

—From a book advertisement (#78, 9/82)

Invisible Braves Are Trend In Adult Orthodontics

Has Sitting Bull been notified?

—Submitted by Rick Rommel, Newark, NJ (#115, 3/85)

IPO's Board of Directors will make the final selection. The winner will receive $1000 and a plague next spring at ceremonies on Capitol Hill.

How about if you just mail us the check?

—Submitted by Judy Sokoll, Vienna, VA (#115, 3/85)

How Fast and Accurate Should Keyboarding and Proofreading Be?

The average error rate in keyboarding is one or two errors in 1,000 keystrokes, and the average in proofreading is one or two uncaught errors in 7,000 characters (two full-size galleys), according to the National Composition Association (NCA) newsletter.

Informal polls of NCA seminar participants and detailed information from several companies provided the data for an article titled "Production Standards: Grappling With the Amorphous, Undefinable Beast" (*NCA Quick News,* July 1980).

Keyboarding Speed

Reported keyboarding standards include rates on a well-known photocomposition machine and for cottage labor with typists producing copy for electronic optical character recognition (OCR).

For sustained work on straight text and simple copy in excellent condition, keyboarding averaged 12,500 to 14,500 keystrokes an hour. The low hourly rate was 7,000; the high, 24,000.

One company figures a basic rate at 11,500 keystrokes an hour to allow for lulls in the workload.

Proofreading Speed

Proofreading takes two-thirds to three-quarters of the time it takes to keyboard. One company reported a basic rate of 14,000 keystrokes an hour for proofreading directly on a video display terminal (VDT), including minor corrections by the proofreader.

Proofreading accuracy is directly related to keyboarding accuracy. Proofreading is slowed if the original input contains many errors, says the NCA article.

Penalties

Jobs with many typographic commands usually take proportionately less proofreading time than keyboarding time. Other conditions that slow the work and produce "penalty copy" apply equally to keyboarding and proofreading.

Richard Matthews of Corporate Press reported to NCA a comprehensive list of penalties in three main categories—manuscript condition, content, and format:

Manuscript condition	Penalty
8½″ × 11″ pages, minimal editing	none
various size manuscripts, medium editing, light copy	8%
printed copy, all caps, all italics, heavy editing, blurred or pasted-up copy	17%
illegible editing, handwritten copy, cards, computer printouts, manuscript out of sequence	125%
Content	
foreign language	100%
technical	20%
excessive pi characters (characters that do not appear on a standard keyboard)	10%
Format	
rule forms	200%
tabular forms	100%
outline format	25%
caps and small caps	10%
excessive coding: for each 15 codes per page	1%

EEI Standards

Editorial Experts, Inc. (EEI) expects team proofreading to go at the rate of 5,000 words an hour; one-person proofreading at 4,000 words an hour. An average of one "miss" an hour is the minimum proofreading standard. EEI usually has a checker review proofreaders' work to catch these misses and expects to catch 95 percent of the errors after one round of proofreading and checking. To improve the percentage rate, EEI recommends at least two formal rounds of proofreading and checking.

In addition to the problems that cost the penalties named by Matthews, EEI finds that proofreading is slowed by the need for many queries, text in sans serif type, an unusual typeface, wide measure, or a type size smaller than 8-point.

EEI expects its keyboarders to type at least 80 words a minute with no more than one uncorrected error per 8½″ × 11″ double-spaced page. At 80 wpm, they usually turn out at least six double-spaced pica pages an hour from drafts with no penalty factors.

Other Standards

Standards from other sources are as follows:

One typo per page "is a reasonable norm in all but the most precise works," says *Association Trends* (Sept. 19, 1980).

More than two uncaught errors in 10,000 ems of type is unacceptable proofreading, according to James Harrison of Waverly Press, author of *How to Find, Hire and Train Proofreaders* (NCA, 1978).

—Peggy Smith (#55, 3/81)

■ How Much Newsletter Copy Can You Turn Out in a Year?

One editor can write the entire copy for either one weekly or two biweeklies in a narrow focus area, says Eric Easton, executive editor, Business Publishers, Inc.

This level of productivity assumes the use of a lot of derivative copy from other sources, plus production of 25 percent to 40 percent of copy.

Ash Gerecht, publisher, Community Development Services, expects a reporter to produce about 200 pages of copy a year, say an 8-page biweekly.

—*Hotline* from the Newsletter Association of America (March 1980) (#42, 4/80)

Estimating Editing Time

Estimating the amount of time that will be needed for editing—whether the estimate will be used for a job price, a proposal budget, or a department budget—has long tended to be more intuitive than structured. But many estimators apparently have developed reasonably workable systems, according to their responses to a questionnaire distributed after a panel discussion arranged by Alberta Cox, Mary Fran Buehler, and Lola Zook at the 29th International Technical Communications Conference in May 1982; additional questionnaires were sent to about 30 readers of *The Eye* following an invitation to participate.

People who systematically analyze manuscripts to estimate editing speed consider the complexity and length of the manuscript, the condition of the tables and figures, their previous experience with the author, the intended audience, and, of course, the level of edit required. Some typical responses:

- "We have a levels-of-edit framework. We provide an estimate of the time it will take to return [the manuscript] to the author for review of editing, and an estimate of total time it will take to [produce] camera-ready copy (work time, not elapsed time). Our estimate is based on what's happened on earlier work."
- "I give authors several options—e.g., it will take 3 days for substantive work, or 1 day for a light edit. Otherwise they may expect that their manuscripts will receive more attention than is possible with time constraints."
- "We review a manuscript for level of difficulty, subject matter, audience intended, and overall sentence and paragraph structure."
- "We not only have levels of edit, we have a computerized unit cost program that tells me the rates for the different levels, per input unit (a page of text or piece of artwork). I can make an estimate very quickly, and so can the editors."
- "We use a computerized cost reporting system from which unit costs are selected to guide the estimate."
- "We consider previous experience with type of report; author; amount of external work involved (e.g., map production, figures, and photos); and length of report."

- "We spot-check the text for clarity and evaluate tabular and illustrative material for complexity, and we use rule-of-thumb estimates (depends on what editor is assigned)."
- "I make my own levels-of-edit decisions, according to how much time I have. I edit according to what's possible."
- "We determine general level of editorial quality required, consider apparent condition of manuscript, and estimate a per page editing time based on these two factors. Then [we] use total number of pages to estimate editing time."

Bases of Methodical Procedures

Of the people who reported methodical procedures, six link their estimating systems directly to the levels-of-edit concept, and five apply the concept less formally in their calculations. Here is one description:

> We have levels-of-edit guidelines. We also have a project planning form, which we review with the author, product manager, and other appropriate parties. The form covers levels-of-edit as well as production plan, product release schedules, necessary reviewers, art required, etc.
>
> Time estimate is a factor of the condition of the manuscript (typed, handwritten, already online in a word processing system we can use), the competence of the original author (judged by completeness of manuscript, accuracy of text and examples as determined by spot checking), previous experience with the author, size of project (very small jobs have high fixed overhead, but very large jobs are complicated by size of task—optimal size is 50 to 75 pages), method of production, and work required for our group (i.e., level of edit required).

Seven respondents reported using a standard pages-per-hour figure for estimating. One uses a rate of two-and-a-half draft pages per hour, two use four pages per hour, and four use about two pages per hour. One uses a precise "15 manuscript pages, typed and double spaced, per day per editor, minus 1 day in every 10 for vacation leave and sick leave." Obviously, organizations using a standard number of pages per hour or day have fairly homogeneous manuscripts, and little need to adapt to wide variations.

Some Survey Statistics and a Hint for Managers

Of the 62 technical editors and managers who responded to the questionnaire, 51 reported that they had had experience in estimating the time required to edit a given manuscript. Well over half of the respondents (30 out of 51) reported having a methodical estimating procedure; 20 in this group use a formal process based on statistical experience, while 10 use a systematic analysis of the elements of the manuscript. The remaining 21 were divided between those who use a less formal approach and those who admit that, essentially, they're guessing.

One observation regarding the fact that one-sixth of the respondents had had no experience in estimating: In routine operations, managers can give their editors valuable experience by having them estimate the time they will need on a manuscript, and then comparing this estimate with the work record. Even if such estimates will not be used in pricing, this exercise alerts editors to time factors and to choices and helps them pace their work.

—Lola Zook (#83, 1/83)

Black Eyes

An "It's" Collection

. . . announced that, effective immediately, his new syndication firm has changed it's name to *SUNSHINE SYNDICATION SERVICES.*

I am interested in your program to help new writers get started. Please send me your free Writing Aptitude Test and 28-page illustrated brochure describing The Institute, it's Course, Faculty, and the current market for children's literature.

Hirschfield Brook:
It's Historic Past

Baltimore Reclaimed It's Waterfront

—Submitted by Erwin S. Koval, New York; Helen Brown, Atlanta, GA; and others

(#83, 1/83)

III. PRODUCTION

■ Typesetting: More Economical and Readable than Typing and Photoreduction

Why should a firm typeset its publications instead of typing and photoreducing them?

The chief reasons are more economical compactness and better readability. For example, a double-spaced pica manuscript page, when typeset 9/10 Times Roman, shrinks 73 percent; a single-spaced, elite manuscript page, 35 percent.

And studies have proved that the proportional letterspacing provided by typeset copy reduces eye travel and so helps readability.

George A. Boucher advised typesetting for economy and readability when he spoke at the seventh Annual Word Processing Equipment Exposition and Workshop in Nov. 1978. He pointed out that any user of word processing can take advantage of phototypesetting quickly and economically.

In fact, once clean copy is captured on a magnetic medium, the copy can be transferred directly to computer systems, to TWX or Telex systems, to electronic mail systems, to other word processors, or to phototypesetting, without rekeyboarding or reproofreading, he said.

Proofreading, a Hidden Cost

Proofreading, Boucher pointed out, is a major expense, often "hidden" in word processing or typesetting costs. Typesetters estimate that, on any given job, 30 percent of their costs are for keyboarding, 22 percent for proofreading, and 14 percent for corrections, he said. Sending clean copy electronically to a typesetter can result in a savings of 40 percent in these three areas combined.

WP–Typesetting Interface

There are now several ways a word processing machine can interface with a phototypesetting machine:

- A word processing machine may interface directly, actually driving a phototypesetting machine;

- Copy typed in an OCR (optical character recognition) typeface, which is read by a machine, can be used by a typesetting machine;
- A word processing machine can be connected with a typesetting machine by a telephone modem;
- A computer-activated makeup system (CAM) enables a word processing operator to make up a page directly on the screen.

Boucher thinks that telecommunication is the most practical interface for most users and that it provides the word processing operator with complete control over the work's content. Format is determined by a series of codes that serve as type specifications for the phototypesetter. The codes are usually set up by a typographer; then they can be input by the word processing operator or by the typesetter.

No matter who inputs, coding is done after the copy has been proofed and corrected. Once the codes are set up, input, and proofread, the copy is ready to be phototypeset—with no additional keyboarding or proofreading.

—Lee Mickle (#18, 12/78)

Knowledge of Production Helps Editors

A solid knowledge of production is a tremendous practical advantage to an editor.

Initially I didn't have any choice; first I went to a school of journalism that believed in giving all students broad basic training in publications, and then I served a long stint in small-town newspapers where an editor also wrote news and laid out ads and read proof and ordered supplies and kept books and dummied the front page and helped "put the paper to bed."

When the aftermath of World War II tossed me into technical editing, I found that I had considerably more background in publications production than most editors had at that time, and it was a real advantage to me.

Although the editor's first responsibility is to deal with the words in the manuscript, nevertheless an editor with a realistic knowledge of production can help an author in many ways—planning presentations and illustrations, setting up schedules, anticipating problems, aiding the whole process of getting the project into print.

The gulf between editor and production began to narrow with the advent of cold-type composition and offset presses, and it narrowed even more as we moved on to magnetic tape and photocomposition. Now in many cases the editor is really caught up in, and an integral part of, the production process. In fact there can be a danger that in the urgency and fascination of the physical creation of the product, the editor's first responsibility may be overwhelmed by events. Judging from the number of errors in spelling and syntax that I see daily in supposedly good publications, the function of editing seems to have vanished in some cases. When I see a nicely printed announcement for a Christmas program that says the chorus will sing "mid-evil" carols, I think that the situation may be getting serious.

In any event, as the years go by every editor needs to make a continuing effort to stay informed about changing trends and new techniques in production. Your own niche may be comfortable and well worn and presumably safe from erosion. But the world changes, and organizations change, and needs change—and your niche might be worn away, or you may just get tired of it. When you poke your head up to look around, better be sure you know what's going on in the 1980s.

—Lola Zook (#46, 8/80)

■ Stretching Your Production Dollar

An organization's publications are often the first to feel the budget pinch. Faced with cost cutting, publications managers are searching for ways to reduce expenses without sacrificing quality. The goal is to get the most out of your budget—to produce effective publications for the smallest possible amount of money.

First, you will have to convince "the powers that be" in your organization that the meat-ax approach to budget cutting may also cut communication between the organization and its audience. Moreover, careless budget slashing in the publications program can increase program costs in other departments.

Start with Basic Questions

Effective, economical publications are planned that way. Begin with a meeting of everyone involved—writers, editors, designers, printing specialists, program officials. Exchange ideas and assumptions. Ask three important questions about each of your publications:

What goals are we trying to achieve with it?
Who is our audience?
Is this one really necessary, or could we achieve our purpose some other way?

The answers to these questions will give you some clues about potential savings. If you have a small, highly targeted audience, you can reduce your press run. If the document will be thrown away, you can use throw-away stock. If your audience is elderly, you might reduce the number of pages, but you would not want to reduce type size. If you have a technical audience, you may want to reduce type size but maintain the number and quality of tables and figures. Find ways to keep in touch with your audience to evaluate what is effective.

Practice Good Management

Good office management—work-flow patterns, time management, motivation, scheduling, and budgeting—can save money. Consider your staffing, for example. Do you have adequate staff for the job? Are they trained properly? Are you making the most of outside resources? Could you use student interns?

Keep up with technological developments, and update your equipment, if necessary. . . . Your savings in time and labor may more than pay for the cost of buying or leasing new equipment.

Know what your vendors can and cannot do. Make sure your bidding specifications are clear, and get all estimates in writing, especially complicated ones. Beware of printers who promise low prices, top quality, and quick turnaround. They may be able to deliver on two of the three claims, but delivering consistently on all three is highly unlikely. If you have a rush job, be prepared either to sacrifice quality or to pay extra for it.

Keep your perspective. It may be less painful to cut a full issue of your periodical than to snip away at each one until the overall quality suffers.

Also, see if you can pass along some of your costs to other programs or departments in your organization. For example, if the insurance department wants to print a special brochure, that department should contribute to the cost.

Ways to Trim

Each stage of the publications process offers opportunities for saving money without diminishing the quality or effectiveness of your publication.

Copy Preparation

- Research your subject thoroughly before you begin to write. Doublecheck citations and references, and make sure all the facts are correct so you won't have to return to libraries or interview sources for a second time.
- Question the need for additional or special sections—appendixes and summaries, for example.
- Edit yourself and others ruthlessly. Tight copy saves space and reads better than rambling copy. Also, correcting wandering commas and inconsistencies after typesetting can be very expensive.
- Obtain all clearances before you type or typeset. Educate authors about typesetting costs. Ask writers to minimize their alterations of typeset copy.
- Copyfit carefully; you will find it hard to use up half a page of surplus typeset copy.
- Proofread carefully before copy goes to the printer. If you are the writer or editor, get at least one other person to read proof.
- Make a checklist, and check everything on it before copy goes to the printer. Every time you find a new category of error in your printed copy, add it to your list for next time.
- Send the printer a clean, double-spaced draft. Leave ample space in the margins for your instructions and write those instructions legibly and clearly. Number all pages. Submit copy on a single size of paper.
- Write a clear specification sheet. Include a sample, if possible.

Typesetting

- Submit all copy at the same time. Avoid paying minimum charges for less than minimum amounts of copy. If you have a lot of display type, put it on a separate sheet.
- Set department heads for a periodical for the whole year, and use the repros for pasteup.
- Set copy unjustified. If you set justified right columns, you may have to reset or run out a whole paragraph to fix a mistake in one line.
- Consider reducing your typeset copy before printing. Your typesetting costs will be a bit higher, but you will print fewer pages and save on paper, binding, shipping, and postage.
- Investigate word processing systems with typesetting capabilities. Even without your own system, outside resources may be able to translate your disk or tape into typeset copy. If you do not have a word processing system at all, you may be able to use an optical scanning system that can "read" typewritten copy and set it in type.
- Set type solid, but use typefaces that emphasize readability.
- Ask the typesetter for fewer galleys or copies. Have several readers share copies and mark with different colored pencils.

Design and Layout

- Consider a standard design for all printed documents. Using the same logo, type, stock, and colors simplifies preparation and reduces paper waste. Standardization also gives your publications immediate identity.
- Whenever possible, use standard sizes cut from standard press sheets with a minimum of waste trim.
- If you always use the same printer, design your publications to fit that printer's equipment.
- Try doing your own designing; keep a reference file of layouts and whole publications you like.
- Try to do your own mechanicals. Get the proper tools, and practice.
- Use preprinted (nonrepro blue) layout sheets.
- Give the printer camera-ready artboard with all elements—type, logo, photos, reverses—pasted into exact position so the printer can shoot only one or two pieces of copy instead of several.

Illustrations

- If you give the printer separate photos, be sure they are keyed, cropped, and scaled properly. Give the printer the percentage reduction, if you know it; if not, give the finished measurements.
- Avoid silhouette photos.
- Have your staff take photos rather than hiring outside photographers.
- Reuse the same photos in several publications.
- Use fewer halftones and more line art.
- Try to gang photos for reduction.
- Avoid special effects such as line resolutions.
- Avoid retouching.

Paper

- Try to use lighter weight stock to save postage costs. Ask to see a printed sample, however, to make sure the print will not show through the paper.
- Use the same stock for several publications to take advantage of quantity discounts. If you have a cool, dry place to store the stock, buy a year's supply in advance.
- Investigate buying stock directly from the manufacturer.
- Use bond paper with a low rag content; but don't skimp on rag content if a document is to last several years.
- Plan distribution carefully, and order your paper accordingly.

Printing

- Don't skimp on bluelines, brownlines, or color keys; the mistakes that might slip through are expensive to correct.
- Print two sides if possible.
- If your masthead is a different color from the body of your text, have mastheads preprinted in the second color.
- Avoid reverse type.
- Eliminate duotones. Instead, use a screened tone of the color ink for emphasis, or ask your printer about adding color to black ink to give a duotone effect without the cost of making a negative.
- If you have several color photos and you are using a four-color process, have two copies made of each photo and paste them up on your artboard

so the printer can make a single separation rather than individual separations of all photos.

- Ask your printer about gang runs of small jobs.
- Compare prices of printers with web presses against those of printers with sheet-fed equipment.
- Save negatives; you may want to run more copies in the future. The printer may claim the negatives, but some will sell them to you. You may want to have your negatives made by a service that will allow you to retain the rights to them.

Binding

- Glue throwaways instead of stitching them.
- Use self-covers.
- Avoid using hard covers if possible.
- Use adhesive binding instead of sewing. The quality of adhesives has improved vastly.
- Avoid embossing and die cuts.
- Do hand operations inhouse. Often, you can insert, fold, and collate for much less than a bindery would charge.

Distribution

- Use self-mailers.
- Cull your mailing list periodically, and screen all additions.
- Use lettersize envelopes instead of large ones for releases.
- Plan distribution to avoid excess storage.
- Keep fewer back issues and eliminate unused old copies—but don't lose track of the information entirely.
- Mail bulk rate.
- Use the right ZIP Code and the Postal Service standard two-letter state abbreviations.
- Print permits on envelopes and self-mailers to avoid hand-stamping individual pieces.

—Nan Fritz (#68, 1/82)

Production Planning to Meet Your Deadlines

Picture the scene: You have a weekly newsletter coming out tomorrow, a monthly magazine with a still-unapproved feature story going to press next week, a membership directory being updated by computer and scheduled for the printer on Monday, and three books in various stages of unreadiness. A colleague pokes his head in your door and says, "Got a minute? I want to talk about that new PR brochure we're writing."

According to Barbara Oliver, manager of editorial services for the Washington Hospital Center, your answer should be an unequivocal "not now." A "yes" answer or a casual approach can lead to missed deadlines, endless corrections, and wasted time and money, said Oliver in a June 1982 workshop of the Washington chapter of the Education Press Association.

Start with a Planning Meeting

When you say "not now," tell your colleague that you will be glad to sit down later and discuss the project and set a specific date and time. Prepare an agenda for the meeting and invite others who may have something to contribute. At the meeting, try to make your colleagues focus on a series of basic questions:

- Who is your audience?
- What is your message?
- What is the best medium for the message?
- When is the piece due?
- What is the budget?

From a well-conducted planning meeting you will emerge with a clear idea of what will be produced and how.

Now you can break the information you have gathered into manageable parts and devise a production schedule for the job. Robert Baker, writing recently in *IMPACT**, a communications newsletter he edits and publishes, advocates keeping track of these individual tasks "in an orderly, foolproof visual way."

Keep a Detailed Chart

The best method is to make yourself a chart—it should be a standardized one that you can photocopy and use for all your projects—listing each element in the production process. For each project, you add the dates by which the steps in the process must be complete, working backward from your due date. Include time for printing, typesetting or producing camera-ready copy, proofreading, designing, editing, and getting clearances. Ask each vendor to provide a schedule along with the bid; sometimes a vendor's ability to do your job—as well as the amount you will be charged—depends on what else is in the shop; so you may get a price break if you can allow a lot of time.

Stay on Schedule

But making a schedule and enforcing it are two different tasks. First, do not keep your schedule a secret, says Oliver. Make sure that everyone who has anything to do with the project has a copy of your timetable.

Always build extra time into your schedule, so that when the typesetter's air conditioning system fails and the machines won't function, it's not a disaster. Plan for the unexpected: you get sick, the person who needs to approve the final draft goes away, a touchy political situation arises, the manuscript arrives late. Know the people you're dealing with, so you can build their idiosyncrasies into the schedule, particularly if you have to depend on several people for clearances.

Expedite Clearances

To expedite clearances, Baker suggests several useful tactics:

- Make as many copies of the work as there are people who must approve it, to avoid the "criticism begets criticism" syndrome.
- Hand-deliver the copies.
- Review changes face to face, if possible.

Oliver adds what she calls "an 'I will assume' memo" whenever she sends a piece for review. Her note announces, "Unless I hear from you by deadline date, I will assume that you approve and I will proceed accordingly." People respond to a deadline more rapidly when you make clear that the responsibility for errors is theirs; you should be very clear in explaining the consequences of late changes, she says.

What if someone does miss a deadline? Baker follows up with a visit or phone call to ask why; Oliver lets the miscreant know that she is not pleased and that missing a deadline, however valid the reason, costs both time and money.

—Mara Adams (#76, 8/82)

*For a copy of this excellent article on production planning, write *IMPACT,* 203 N. Wabash Ave., Chicago, IL 60601.

Ten Tips for Cutting Newsletter Production Costs

It would be nice if all editors commanded budgets that allowed typesetting, unlimited original artwork, six colors of ink, glossy paper, and other luxuries. Fortunately for the creative process, poverty budgets are more common. Here are some tips for upgrading quality while controlling costs:

1. To avoid typesetting charges, use a typewritten format.
2. To avoid retyping, plan each article ahead of time and type it in columns appropriate to your publication. Your newsletter can be printed from clean typed copy if you use good-quality paper. Ragged right margins are easier to work with than justified margins.
3. Preprint the first page with banner and other standing material in color. You can then print each issue in black ink and you'll have only one ink color to pay for per issue.
4. Use only standard paper sizes and an even number of pages. Unusual paper sizes are more expensive than standard 8½″ × 11″ or 17″ × 22″. Varying the number of pages makes budgeting difficult. An odd number of pages requires the extra step of inserting the extra sheet of paper.
5. If you use 8½″ × 11″ paper, skip the folding process and just staple the newsletter together in the top corner. If you use 17″ × 22″ paper folded at the side for an 8½″ × 11″ publication, skip the pasting or saddle-

stitching step in 8- or 12-page newsletters. (The folding process usually holds the inside sheets in place, especially if the newsletter is a self-mailer.)

6. To save on envelopes, make your newsletter a self-mailer. If the information isn't timely, mail the newsletter third class bulk, with the mailing indicia printed in the mailing label area.
7. Use clip art generously. Either subscribe to a clip art service for a year or buy a few packs of appropriate material from an art supply store. Unlike photographs, which involve an extra production process and thus an extra charge per photo, clip art is camera ready and there is no charge for reproducing it on the page.
8. If press-apply or rub-on lettering is too expensive or time-consuming, have a set of department heads typeset. Some clip art books provide department heads for predictable categories such as "Letters to the Editor," "News," and "President's Message."

   In Washington, the average charge for an hour of typesetting is $30 to $35, but prices vary nationally. For a more professional look, have article heads typeset and paste them up yourself.

   Another alternative for headlines is Kroy type. The machine is relatively expensive, but you might be able to share the machine and its print wheels with another editor to reduce costs.
9. Use quick-print shops to reproduce material and print your newsletter. Full-scale printshops can be more costly for a small publication.
10. Invest a few dollars in several rolls of rule tape at a graphic arts supply shop. It's amazing how much a few carefully applied boxes and lines can jazz up a page. The tape comes in a wide variety of fun-to-use designs and costs only a dollar or two a roll.

The real key to saving money is organization. The more carefully you plan each issue, the smoother the production process. The cost of making changes increases dramatically when newsletters are typeset and professionally produced; organization can reduce these costs.

Small community newspapers often look for newsletters to typeset and paste up at lower costs than established houses. The more a paper can use its equipment the better, and if you can help them make a few more dollars on off-days, everyone benefits. Try swapping free ads for type services.

You *can* produce a newsletter on a tight budget. It may take more work, but the results can be more satisfying.

—Ruth Thaler (#103, 5/84)

■ Rules for Good Typography Revisited

Copy that is typeset flush left and ragged right, with uniform four-to-the-em wordspacing and full hyphenation, has everything to recommend it. The format is especially good for setting type from computer (or word processor disks or interfaces) because electronic "compositors" do not always adjust lines well in justified copy.

Peter Smith of Peter Smith Associates is an editor and graphic designer who has shown many people how to work with words—how to write and edit them and how to present them in type effectively.

At the May 1984 meeting of the Washington chapter of the Society for Technical Communication, Smith reminded the audience of some of the rules for readable, attractive typography:

- Don't exceed the maximum easy-to-read line length of 65 characters (2½ alphabets). Longer lines cause a reader to "double"—read the same line twice.
- In body copy, don't use less than the minimum easy-to-read line length of 35 characters. Shorter lines cause sentences to be broken into so many lines that thoughts are difficult to grasp.
- Use italics only for a few words on a page and only when essential. Long stretches of italic type are hard to read.
- Reserve boldface mostly for heads and subheads; in body copy, use it for only a few words. Lines of boldface in body copy "flimmer"—the letters fill in and vibrate.
- Avoid using all caps; they slow reading speed and take 30 percent more space than lowercase. For display, use caps and lowercase or italics and boldface. For emphasis in body copy, use italics or boldface—but use them sparingly or they become ineffective.

The same rules apply to typewritten copy, with this added injunction: Never justify it. The unequal space between words that results is hard on the reader and makes an ugly page full of holes, rivers, and lakes of white space.

Few designers would argue with any of these rules, but Smith also has some ideas of his own about increasing economy and readability that are worth considering. For example, he prefers a head with just initial caps and the rest of the words in lowercase. He also prefers flush left heads to centered heads. And he may be one of the few designers who have considered the practical uses and the aesthetics of bullets in all their variety.

Shooting at Bullets

"Sometimes typographic bullets can be used to good advantage," says Smith. "Bullets are usually better than abc's or 123's if the letters or numbers have no special significance (such as for reference)."

But Smith believes bullets are often used badly.

"Never, never, never, ***never*** use bullets for a group of items that consists entirely of one-liners," he says.

He also dislikes the popular format in which bulleted items hang and bullets extend to the left of the items. Smith prefers inconspicuous bullets where the bullets are part of the block of text—flush left, with the carryover lines also flush left.

As for line spaces between bulleted items, Smith recommends them only for long items (five or six lines or more).

For two- or three-liners, he recommends indenting the bullets, which is more economical than adding line space between items. "A group like this could go on and on," he says, "but even so, it's best to drop in a subhead here and there."

—Peggy Smith (#106, 7/84)

■ Besting the Big Ape: Tips on Tackling a Gargantuan Editorial Project

Although not every publications manager has faced down a gargantuan project that threatens to assume an uncontrollable and menacing life of its own, most have had nightmares about it.

The gargantuan project might involve a massive report that requires resources exceeding those available. Often it has an impossible deadline. Or it might develop from an unrealistic demand to publish a sophisticated product in large numbers and on short order.

Typically, the Big Project offers one or more of the following:

- shortage of time or money or both;
- multiple constituencies—for example, members of an industrywide committee or several senior officers within an organization; or
- very high stakes for the organization, the manager's supervisor, and the publications manager. The Big Project has the potential to be a career-maker or a career-breaker.

As executive editor for more than a dozen presidential and congressional commissions, among other special publishing projects, I have developed techniques for approaching the Big Project. Call these my rules for survival—the ticket home from a kamikaze mission. This is the thrill side of editing; in addition to working long hours for modest compensation, you get to take *risks*.

Lessons from Risk-Takers

Publications managers can learn from others who take risks in their everyday work: astronauts, submariners, wing-walkers, savings and loan managers in Ohio. Risk-takers who survive follow a few standard rules:

- *Define the risk-taking act precisely*. Faced with the Big Project, the publications manager should identify danger points that threaten schedule, quality, and budget.

- *Practice the risk-taking act.* There is no time for practice when the Big Project arrives; prepare by taking small risks with other projects.
- *Build in redundancies.* Surviving a Big Project depends on establishing backups, photocopying protection sets, and following similar fail-safe procedures.
- *Inspect and test all systems.* Like a wing-walker testing struts, the publications manager should personally inspect and verify all systems (for example, data gathering, read-behind procedures) and generate a stream of reports to supervisors.

Countdown to Press Time

Your first and most important task is to line up resources and establish priorities. The Big Project must have strong support from the top. Meet personally with the boss; describe the steps from startup to final publication; be upbeat about the chances of producing a respectable product given the time and money involved; and be frank about the embarrassments that could flow from failure.

The psychological value of the worst-case scenario is known to every publications manager. In coping with the Big Project, I keep the worst-case scenario on the front burner but do not use it as a threat. Instead, I point out that the project is increasing in velocity while hugging the line that divides success from disaster. Everybody has to understand the growing risks as the project matures. Everybody, especially the boss, has to contribute whatever it takes to keep the project moving at top speed on the success side of that dividing line.

Your most important function is to maintain the network of people who supply resources, make decisions, and establish priorities. In most cases, only you will know the details of production, which means only you can realistically assess options. Thus, your responsibility is to inform, advise, warn, and cajole other people into doing the sensible thing at the right time.

A sense of teamwork is essential. To achieve it, set up a small, informal task force of people assigned to the project. Produce a one-page list of everybody on the team, with titles, office and home addresses, and telephone numbers. The list should include your supervisor and even the organization head, with home phone for emergency decisions. Make sure everybody on the list gets two copies (one for home).

As the coordinator of the Big Project, you should take pains to build a separate set of files, a list of key contacts (usually a lot longer than the team list), and a depository of project documents, including all generations of the manuscript, galleys, page proofs, and project notes and memoranda.

Time may not permit developing a written plan; in any event, you should quickly schedule regular production meetings. When the crunch starts, I hold a meeting of key team members every Monday morning, more often if necessary. I follow up the production meetings with daily chats with team members—this is much more efficient management than additional meetings. Designate a backup in case you become ill.

Throughout the project, it is important to obtain top-level clearance at every step, preferably in writing. Such clearances help to ensure a panel of green lights at press time. In handling multiple constituencies, try to deal with a representative of each faction rather than all members of that faction; in any event, be open and responsive and keep out of policy battles.

Securing clearances by telephone for copyright permissions and one-time uses is fine, but follow them up with written clearances. The extra pressure of a Big Project is no excuse for sloppy procedures that could lead to serious legal trouble.

Show sketches and comprehensives to the head of the organization; otherwise, you will run the risk that the design concept will be rejected at the last minute. Show final artwork only to your immediate supervisor; don't show blues, chromalines, or press sheets to anybody except your designer and team members.

Inspect all prepress proofs and press sheets yourself, even if it means long hours, around-the-clock vigils, or other inconveniences. On extended press runs, be present in the printer's plant or place a trusted aide there while you catch some sleep. The pressure you maintain on the printer, through your presence and constant inspections, may well make your Big Project a winner instead of an also-ran.

As final countdown for the Big Project begins, all of your intense effort will pay off. The critical threats—copy that has not been cleared, permissions that have not been obtained, design that has not been approved (or just doesn't work with the words), and mistakes or poor craftsmanship in prepress—should have been neutralized. Now is the time to meet again with the organization head, to reassure that person about the quality of the product, and to obtain a commitment that no changes will be made. Then you can give the "OK to print" instruction with confidence.

—Joseph Foote (#117, 5/85)

Joe Foote's latest wrestling match was with a gargantua called the *Report of the President's Task Force on Victims of Crime*.

INDEXING

An index, writes June Morse in one of her articles in this section, "provides readers with the scope and content of the entire book in a highly condensed overview, as though the author's outline and treatment were shuffled and reassembled in alphabetical order."

That's a good perspective for those who don't know much about indexing because it lifts the lid that covers an important editorial fact: Indexing is tough work that requires both 360-degree vision and an incredibly orderly mind.

Readers who take indexes for granted should be thankful they did not live before the 17th century, which is about the time that book publishers began to alphabetize subject lists consistently. Before then it was a matter of luck if a book had an index at all, beyond that provided in the table of contents.

Like other back-breaking editorial tasks, indexing is now being done more and more by computers. But as the few articles in this section will show, constructing a good index requires getting inside the reader's head, which requires more than the ability to sort things into bins; it requires real imagination.

How to Recognize a Good Index

Your manuscript is at the page-proof stage, and with great relief you have sent it to be indexed. The index will be the last piece of text sent to the typesetter, and everyone is eager to get the whole thing to the printer and get the book published. But how can you tell if the index is a good one before approving it?

Whether you are an editor, an author, or a reviewer, you should judge by five basic criteria: accuracy, depth of indexing, conciseness, cross-referencing, and logical selectivity.

Accuracy

Accuracy is the most important characteristic of a good index. Without it, nothing else matters. A complete check of accuracy is impractical; it would amount to constructing the index all over again. Test for accuracy, first, by spot checking a few pages. Choose two or three entries in each column and look up all the page references given. Is the subject listed in the index covered on the pages cited? If the index fails this first test of accuracy, all other tests become unnecessary. You and the indexer are in trouble.

Next, verify the alphabetical order. This step sounds like child's play, but alphabetization is a surprisingly complex process. The two basic approaches to alphabetization are word-by-word and letter-by-letter. In the word-by-word style, the space at the end of a word sorts before any ensuing letter or character. The letter-by-letter style ignores all spaces in the index heading. Either style is acceptable, but usage must be consistent within a single index. The difference this style decision can make is shown in the following example from a report on the oil and gas industries:

Word-by-Word	**Letter-by-Letter**
tank cars	tank cars
tank cleaning	tank cleaning
tank trucks	*Tankerman Manual*
Tanker Owners Agreement	Tanker Owners Agreement
Tanker Safety Conference	tankers

Tankerman Manual
tankers

Tanker Safety Conference
tank trucks

Last, because accuracy in proper names is essential, check a few entries to be sure the indexer has followed the author's usage.

Depth

Look at the depth of the index. Is it suitable for the material at hand and the intended audience? This question should have been thoroughly discussed and resolved before the indexer started work; once an index reaches the review stage, it is too late to change its depth. An average index has three to five entries for each page of text; a light one has one to two entries per page. An extremely detailed index for a scholarly work or a technical manual might have as many as 10 entries per text page; an encyclopedia could have 15 or more. The index users' needs govern the depth of the index.

You can assess depth by taking a few sample pages of text, identifying the important topics covered, and looking up the topics in the index to make sure they are included. This test will also reveal how well the indexer has used headings and subheadings to organize the material.

Conciseness

Whether an index is crisp and useful or long and rambling will depend on the choice of terms for headings and subheadings. Consider the following example:

Physicians' offices
  full-time personnel
  scheduling appointments in
  use of microcomputers in

A thoughtful indexer would achieve more conciseness by using tightly worded subheadings, with the keyword placed first:

Physicians' offices
  appointment scheduling
  computer use
  personnel needs

Cross-References

Cross-references are an index's transportation system. A *See* reference leads from a term not used as an index entry to the synonym that is. A *See also* reference leads the reader to related information under another heading. The author or editor should take the time to verify all cross-references to be sure that they lead to additional information and to verify that the *See* and *See also* headings are exactly the same as the actual entries. Nothing is more maddening to the user than a cross-reference loop that leads the reader on a winding path. No index should tell a reader who looks up "Firearms" to "*See* Arms," if "Arms" says "*See* Weapons."

Only necessary cross-references should be included. For a subject entry with no subheadings, it takes less space to insert the page references under two different headings (for example, *users* and *consumers*) than it does to lead the reader unnecessarily from one to the other with a *See* reference.

A *See also* reference must lead to additional information, not to the same page references under a second heading. Accurate, logical, and useful cross-references are the hallmarks of a good index.

Logical Selectivity

The ability to select and organize appropriate headings separates an experienced indexer from a novice. Beginners tend to choose everything that looks like a keyword and use it as an index term. The result is cluttered text. The opposite error is to attach a long string of page references to a single entry, a practice annoying to readers. (No one wants to look up 12 different pages to find a specific piece of information.) Any subject with more than six page references should be divided into subheadings.

The relationship of subheadings to main headings must be logical. One common fault is to use a heading as both a noun and an adjective, as in this example:

Acid
    acetic
    -free paper
    hydrogen ions
    neutralization
    rain
    solutions
    sulfuric

A better solution is to organize the headings this way:

Acid-free paper
Acid rain
Acids
    hydrogen ions
    neutralization
    solutions
    See also Acetic acid; Sulfuric acid

Finally, a good index provides readers with the scope and content of the entire book in a highly condensed overview, as though the author's outline and treatment were shuffled and reassembled in alphabetical order. Like tables of contents, the best indexes give readers all the information they need on what the book contains. If the author and editor are confident on that score, the book—and its index—are ready for printing.

—June Morse (#110, 11/84)

Budget-Conscious Indexing

Many publishers consider an index a luxury, at least for non-reference books and periodicals. Indexing is time consuming and thus prolongs the production process. Indexer time and the pages the index adds to the publication both raise costs. Forced to pinch pennies, publishers may be tempted to pinch the index right out of existence. An index is a useful addition to almost any publication, however, and a must for some. Why not try to reduce indexing costs rather than eliminate the index altogether? Here are some suggestions.

Tailor the Index to Your Audience

The depth (level of detail) of an index directly affects its cost. A very detailed index requires more indexer time than a "light" index, and the extra length will also raise your editing, proofreading, and printing costs. If you understand how your readers will use your index and how much they will depend on it, you can avoid indexing in more depth than is useful.

The Eye index . . . is an example of a very detailed index. Because many readers use *The Eye* as a reference source, we index every word or phrase for which usage or spelling has been discussed, as well as the usual author, title, and general subject entries. Some *Eye* pages generate as many as 20 index references.

A scientific encyclopedia would be indexed in even greater depth. In contrast, a children's book might need only one entry per page. A comprehensive index for the average nontechnical book might require only three or four entries per page, which should not make your budget officer blanch unless the book is very long. The cost of the index will vary with the length of the book, as well as the number of entries per page.

Plan Ahead

Make all necessary decisions before the indexer starts to work. Plan the comprehensiveness, format, length, and style of the index, and review your requirements with the indexer in advance. Rebuilding an unsatisfactory index may be almost as expensive as starting over.

Preparing a long index and then editing it down is neither cost effective nor practical. A good index is a structured whole, built up with cross-references as the indexer works. You might be able to shorten an index by eliminating subentries or by rewording carryover lines to fit a single line, but eliminating entries entirely invites error. You are likely to end up with a cross-entry like *Canines*, see *Dogs*, when the entry for *Dogs* has been merged with *Animals* to save space.

Wait for Final Page Proofs

Too often, editors faced with tight deadlines ask an indexer to work from final drafts or galleys and then add the page numbers when page proofs become available. Many do not recognize that adding or changing page numbers at the last minute adds at least 35 percent to indexer hours.

Consider Using a Computer

Computers can now do much of the routine work of indexing. They are invaluable for large indexes derived from data bases and for indexes that must be regularly updated or cumulated. A human must select index terms and make the editorial decisions, but the computer takes over nearly everything else. It automatically alphabetizes index entries and arranges them in a preselected format. The computer can also enter the editor's and author's revisions and print out a draft ready for typesetting, or even typeset, without additional keyboarding. The potential savings are large, IF the index is long enough to justify the computer costs.

Jay M. Pasachoff and Nancy P. Kutner have described their experience with computer-assisted indexing in *The Indexer*, October 1981. They used a home video terminal to type in index terms, identifying codes, and page numbers. This information was communicated by telephone lines to a large computer at the Rensselaer Polytechnic Institute in Troy, NY. The computer produced a draft index, which took only a few hours to edit.

The amount of computer time used to compile the index was trivial, according to Pasachoff and Kutner. For a finished index of about 4000 lines, the computer time charge was less than $200—a modest amount compared with the cost of manually alphabetizing, typing, and proofreading an index of that length. The largest part of the $200 charge was for connect time (hookup with the home terminal) and for printing time. Programming costs, however, were not included in this figure.

Choose Your Indexer Carefully

Computers may save time indexing, but they cannot by themselves create a clear, logical, and precise index that is suited to the needs of the user. That takes an expert and experienced indexer. Look for an indexer who understands the subject matter at hand, especially if the subject is technical. Don't be reluctant to pay for experience. An inaccurate, inappropriate, and illogical index is an expensive luxury indeed.

—June Morse (#69, 2/82)

Making It as a Freelance Indexer

Indexing is a fertile field for freelancers. Most publishers don't have staff indexers, because indexing usually is a short-term, sporadic need. Instead, publishers turn to freelancers.

The panelists at the American Society of Indexers' (ASI) 1979 Washington, DC, seminar on freelance indexing provided many tips on getting started and on handling some of the problems freelancers face. Here is a summary of their advice.

Finding Enough Work

If you are armed with references from satisfied publishers and an impressive portfolio of published indexes, then canvassing publishers regularly by letter or phone will produce assignments—someone, somewhere, will need an index just at the time you call.

If you are a neophyte indexer, how do you start acquiring this impressive record? Often, it appears, by accident. An author, for example, may be more than happy to have a volunteer index his or her book, and the result is one published index under your belt.

Resist the temptation, however, to do a free demonstration index for a publisher; if you want a publisher to value your time and skills, you must value them yourself.

You will find a list of publishers and sometimes editors in *Literary Marketplace*. Try to contact the publisher's index editor, if any, or the editor in your area of expertise. The ASI member roster is also a good source of referrals.

Pricing Your Index

Whether you price an index by the hour, by the text page, by the index line, or by flat fee, the object of pricing is fair payment for your time. The time indexing takes depends largely on the number and size of book pages and on the density (entries per page) of text.

- *An hourly rate* is useful for estimating a flat fee, but it may cause problems as a basis for payment. Publishers may distrust hourly figures.
- *Page rates* should vary with the density of text. Also, agree in advance on the page count method; publishers may omit figures and tables, even though they must be indexed.
- *A rate per index line* is simple from the indexer's point of view, IF the publisher has not arbitrarily limited the length of the index. This rate should vary with the difficulty of the text.
- *A flat fee* may be the most comfortable arrangement. Do two or three pages to project how much time the book will take; then apply your hourly rate to get a total fee.

One recommended pricing strategy is to give a new client a relatively low rate and raise it with subsequent jobs until you meet resistance. A full-time freelancer will probably make between $18,000 and $24,000 a year, depending on how hard he or she works at indexing.

Billing

Always establish in advance how and when an index is to be done and how and when payment is to be made. An exchange of letters is probably sufficient; in fact, a detailed formal contract may unduly restrict the indexer's work.

The bill itself should be submitted separately on your letterhead. Include an invoice number. Do not combine your bill with comments about the job; the bill may get lost in the wrong file and payment will be delayed.

Pitfalls and Problems

Novices should steer carefully around certain obstacles common in freelance indexing.

- Working from galleys. In order to speed up publication, an editor may ask an indexer to make cards from galleys and fill in page numbers later. Some experienced indexers would refuse the job; others simply require the extra work to be reflected in their pay.
- *Completion time.* Publishers avoid rehiring indexers who don't meet their deadlines. The time to decide and discuss whether a deadline is realistic is before you agree to do the job.

- *Technical subjects*. If possible, avoid indexing technical books outside your own area of expertise. If you do take one on, get from the editor as much guidance as possible on the level and type of entries to include.
- *Indexer standards*. The art of indexing is traditionally underrated. Editors may put index length before quality; authors may request inappropriate entries. Indexers feel these constraints depreciate their skills and judgment. If possible, explain your viewpoint to an editor or author; if not possible, charge extra.

—Charlene Semer (#21, 2/79)

PROOFREADING

Like a brain surgeon, a proofreader can never be too careful. Of all editorial tasks, theirs is the most thankless because their successes are never seen, only their failures. And, what Dr. Johnson once said about lexicographers applies equally well to proofreaders: They cannot aspire to praise; the best they can hope for is to escape reproach.

Given these working conditions, it's a wonder that anyone is willing to read proof at all. Yet proofreading does have its satisfactions, the most obvious of which turns out to be the same one that drives the editorial profession as a whole—an irrepressible drive to get it right.

Perhaps in its perverse way, the attraction of proofreading lies in the very fact of its disagreeableness to the vast majority of writers and editors. Like the fabled Seabees of World War II, who took pride in wading through jobs that would daunt mere combat Marines, proofreaders are ready to tackle anything. As a rule, most writers and editors find proofreading boring, tedious, monotonous—the perfect camouflage to go with the popular misconception of the proofreader-as-drudge. And that is their secret weapon: The animus of the majority is their reservoir of power. They never forget that nothing goes to press until it's proofed.

If, gentle reader, you would like to acquire some of the knowledge that can enable you to talk intelligently with those of our happy band who keep the rest of us from making fools of ourselves in public, read the seven selections in this section.

30 Tricks of the Trade for Proofreaders

If you proofread alone or with a copyholder, here are some suggestions that professional proofreaders have found useful when they compare dead and live copy:*

Follow Proven Procedures

1. Use standard proofreading marks, two for every error (one in the text, one in the margin).
2. Give the typesetter a list of the marks you've used.
3. As you did in the second grade, read one word at a time—the opposite of speed reading. Read unfamiliar words letter by letter.
4. Maintain a good, steady pace, not slow but not so fast that you miss errors.
5. When you work alone, read aloud to yourself, especially when the material is difficult.
6. Do different tasks separately; for example, first look for end-of-line errors; then check for widows* and orphans*; next check the sequence of folios* and, finally, the sequence of footnotes. Combine tasks only when you are sure of your skill. (Partners can do separate tasks so that both keep busy.)
7. Adjust your level of effort to the job. A memo to the office down the hall needs only a cursory check; a legal document or a budget may need team proofreading and several readings.
8. Take a 5-minute break every hour and spend some of the time looking in the distance. Never read for more than 3 hours straight without at least a 15-minute break.

Take Extra Precautions

9. Read everything except boilerplate.* Even with boilerplate, scan for garbled material. Read salutations and signature lines in letters. Don't just mark "wf" on passages set in the wrong font in galleys, but read the passages to spot typos that would otherwise be repeated when the copy is reset.

10. Watch especially for errors where pages, paragraphs, and sections begin; where lines and pages break; where type size or face changes (footnotes, heads); and where other errors occur (typos often come in bunches). Pin up headlines and stand back to read them.
11. Look at live copy upside down and sideways for spacing errors and misalignment.
12. When proofreading columnar material—an index, a table, or a table of contents—read first across to find format problems or dropped punctuation, and then down for content.
13. When you work alone on tables or revises*, slug* them (or put dead and live copy on a light table* to find respaced lines in revises).
14. Doublecheck each handwritten insertion in the dead copy to be sure none was missed.
15. When the dead copy is a collection of scraps of paper, count the number of paragraphs in both dead and live versions to be sure none was missed.
16. If you become fascinated with the content, read the manuscript once for pleasure, then proofread.
17. Never, never put anything that could spill (coffee, tea, food) on the surface with the copy you are proofreading. Replacing damaged copy can be very costly.

Use Many Tools, Not Just a Pencil

18. Keep your place and focus your attention with a guide; use a straightedge, pencil, or mask*, or a T-square for continuous copy.
19. When you're interrupted, use a pencil mark, Post-it®* note, or a colored sheet between pages to note the place you stopped.
20. Use a magnifying glass to help decipher bad handwriting.
21. Check alignment and centering with a pica grid* or a graphic artist's centering ruler* (or check centering by measuring the width of the two margins with the tip of a pencil and your thumbnail against the pencil's body).
22. Use a light table to check the register* of folios, running heads, and running feet and to check that boilerplate matches its model.
23. Use a calculator to check the totals in tables.
24. To flag pages you want to return to (for example, if you plan to write all queries in one step), use a paperclip or Post-it® note or make notes of the page and line numbers.

Make Notes

25. If no style is specified, keep notes, especially on capitalization, compounds, and number style.
26. If you have no specification sheet, make your own for headline levels, size of type, spacing, etc.
27. Keep a list of words often misspelled or found as misprints. Look at them twice when you find them in text. Here's a start: cavalry, calvary; conservation, conversation; from, form; it is, is it; is, in, it, if; martial, marital; or, on, of; simulation, stimulation. The hardest typos to find are real words that are wrong in context. Unless you are somewhat aware of the sense of what you're reading, you'll miss these hard-to-find errors.

Keep Improving

28. Learn from your mistakes. Keep a record of what you've missed. Analyze the record to learn and correct your weaknesses.
29. Improve your eye for letterforms. Collect and classify examples of typefaces (start a file or scrapbook).
30. Read. Study. Learn all you can about language and typography. Keep up with the world. Odd facts, unusual spellings, general information—nearly everything you know comes in handy sooner or later.

—Barbara Hart and Peggy Smith (#86, 3/83)

*For definitions of starred terms, see the "Proofreader's Glossary."

■ Proofreader's Glossary

boilerplate—text standardized for repeated use

centering ruler—a ruler marked with measurements from the center to both edges

dead and live copy—older version and newer version
folio—page number
light table—glass lighted from beneath, used to see a bottom sheet through a top sheet
live copy—see *dead and live copy*
mask (n)—an opaque rectangle with a cut-out area the size of one line of copy
orphan—a page-bottom widow such as the first line of a new paragraph
pica grid—a transparent sheet printed with horizontal lines one pica apart
Post-it® —3M's little yellow notepads with a special adhesive strip that does not permanently stick to or mar the copy
register—exact alignment from page to page
revise (n)—corrected galley or page proof
slug (v)—to compare first words of lines by folding dead copy along its margin and placing folded edge against the live copy
widow—a short line at the top or bottom of a page such as the first or last line of a paragraph.

Common Proofreading Errors

Precisely what errors should beginning professional proofreaders expect to encounter as they work their way through the first allotment of copy? There are some predictable patterns that have been tabulated by the old pros.

The "Top Ten" Errors

A tabulation of errors found by professional proofreaders provides the following "most frequent" errors in written copy:

Letters omitted	14.5%	Word omitted	5.9%
Substitutions	14.1	Small letter for capital	2.9
Space omitted	10.7	Full line omitted	1.7
Punctuation mark omitted	10.5	Spelling error	1.6
Transpositions	6.6	Capital for small letter	1.1

Many common errors can be attributed to some basic human tendencies concerning concentration timespan and the transmittal of messages between eyes and hands. For instance, mistakes are more likely to occur in the latter half of a long line (over 4 inches) and in the middle of longer words.

Specific transpositional errors frequently made include *r* and *t*, *v* and *b*, *n* and *m*, and *s* and *d*. Substitutions are common in both single letters and endings: *e* for *i*, *d* for *s*, *e* and *o*, *d* and *k*, *s* for *ed*, *tion* for *ing*, and *your* instead of *yours*. Predictably, titles and column headings are often ignored by the best of typists quickly scanning the body of their material for minor mistakes. Consistency of format can be overlooked by someone searching for grammatical errors. Punctuation errors are especially easy to miss when dealing with amounts of money, time, percent, and the general use of figures in written material.

Perhaps the most embarrassing and potentially serious gaffes are mistakes in actual content. Consider the case of the $200 scholarship offered by the business school, generously enlarged to $2,000 by a simple typing error. Worse yet, have you ever accepted a luncheon date for Wednesday, Oct. 2, only to check your appointments calendar later and discover that Oct. 2 is actually a Tuesday?

—From material presented at an Altman and Weil seminar (#34, 10/79)

Proofreading: Solo or Team?

Which is better, the time-honored method of proofreading—copyholder and copyreader—or today's more usual method of one-person proofreading?

To answer the question, you have to answer some others first: Which is more important to you, time or money, accuracy or speed? Which method better suits your proofreader's skills and preferences? What kind of material do you proofread most often?

People have strong opinions on which method is more accurate, but I know of no objective study on the question. Cost aside, I favor team proofreading, in part because I do it better and enjoy it more. In this kind of work, those considerations are important. But I have also seen excellent solo work by people who dislike working with a partner.

Defining Terms

Proofreading involves comparing live copy with dead copy, e.g., a retyped manuscript with an edited manuscript, typeset proof with typemarked manuscript, or previously read proof with revised copy.

Dry reading is minimal copyediting, searching for and marking blatant errors in live copy without reference to dead copy.

Silent reading is an editorial review of live copy for sense and policy, not for nitpicking.

Solo proofreading ("horsing," single proofreading) is comparison proofreading done by one person.

Team proofreading (double proofreading, partner proofreading) is comparison proofreading done by two people. The traditional method involves a copyholder who reads the dead copy aloud to the proofreader, who marks errors on the live or proof copy. Variations include having the proofreader read aloud from the live copy or having the marker (live copy) and the holder (dead copy) reading aloud alternately.

Pros and Cons

Assuming easy-to-read dead and live copy, here are some of the arguments for and against solo and team proofreading.

Pro: Properly done, team proofreading is much faster. *Con:* Not that much faster. A fast team can cut a fast solo proofreader's time by only about one-third. If each is paid the same, the team costs one-third more than a single proofreader.

Pro: A second reader improves quality by adding the sense of hearing to the sense of sight. Experiments show that reading aloud activates more areas of the brain than reading silently. *Con*: A second person's voice intrudes on concentration. Besides, solo proofreaders often read difficult copy aloud to themselves.

Pro: Constantly shifting the eyes from dead copy to live copy breaks the flow, tires the eyes, and leads to missed errors, especially omissions and repetitions. *Con:* Experience accustoms the eyes to shifting and teaches solo proofreaders to watch especially for outs and repeaters. A copyholder often breaks the flow by reading too fast or making irrelevant comments.

Pro: A second person's input increases the validity of queries. *Con*: A second person's input slows queries.

Pro: Interaction with a second reader is stimulating and keeps the first reader alert. *Con*: Interaction with a second person is irritating. Working alone establishes the most effective pace.

Pro: Solo proofreading depends much more on short-term memory than team proofreading does. Most people can hold only seven to nine items—words or numerals—in short-term memory. In team proofreading, the proofreading is done as the words are spoken; short-term memory is used only to remember the sense of a sentence until it ends. *Con:* Experienced solo proofreaders can hold up to two sentences in short-term memory, resulting in more intense work, harder concentration, and greater alertness.

Recommendations

The material to be read may help determine the method used. I recommend one-person proofreading for short takes, such as in proofreading advertising copy, and for unfamiliar material that must be read character by character, such as mathematical equations and chemical formulas. I recommend two-person proofreading for inexperienced people and trainees and for extensive tables, long lists of figures, hard-to-read copy (e.g., handwritten copy), and hard-to-handle copy (e.g., index cards, address labels).

Either method requires effective procedures. For example, a good solo proofreader should spend twice as much time as a team on the live copy. A good team allows no one to be idle; while one person looks up words or style points in a reference book, the other rechecks word divisions, initials galleys, or does other tasks.

A third method may work well for some organizations. Tape proofreading involves reading the dead copy into a tape recorder and listening to the tape while reading the live copy. Single proofreaders who prefer to team proofread can also read aloud to themselves. People who use this method may find they can do tape proofreading as fast as their solo proofreading colleagues, and as accurately as with a partner.

Computer spelling programs are very helpful, particularly for the first cut at the job. But they cannot substitute for human proofreading, since no spelling program will catch typos that are themselves words (e.g., reed for red, bead for read, than for that).

With any method, however, quality control is assured only by taking one further step—checking, by a different person. Unfortunately, no method yet discovered, not even repeated proofreading, assures 100 percent accuracy.

—Peggy Smith (#101, 4/84)

Can Proofreading Be Perfect?

Accuracy Standards

"Proofreading standards?" "You mean how many typos a proofer can miss?" "Oh, and format errors too? Well . . . not too many. . . ."

How many missed errors are too many? *The Eye* asked 21 Washington-area typesetters, associations, corporations, and government offices this question in an informal telephone survey.

The answer was usually the same: "We don't have a set policy, but if you come up with some standards, let us know."

Of the 21 organizations surveyed, only one has a quality control measure for proofreaders. Byrd PrePress in Springfield, VA, uses a sliding hourly pay scale based on how fast a proofreader reads computer characters. Five words (50 characters) are deducted for each missed error to arrive at a worker's proofreading speed.

Employers of both inhouse and freelance proofreaders reported a lack of formal standards. Most respondents do monitor the quality of proofreaders' work and provide feedback.

Although Aspen Systems Corp. has no written policy, the company expects some missed errors in complicated, technical material, but none in straight text with clean copy.

The American Psychological Assn. also lacks written guidelines, but considers more than one missed error per page unacceptable.

The *National Geographic* uses team proofreaders, gives everything four readings, and ultimately expects 100 percent accuracy.

Nine of the organizations use full-time, inhouse proofreaders. Seven use whoever is available; their editors, writers, and secretaries proofread. Five regularly hire freelancers to proofread. All pay by the hour.

—Alison Heckler Reier (#25, 4/79)

When Do You Stop Trying?

If two rounds of proofreading catch 98 percent of the errors in a book, is it worthwhile to have a third round and try to catch the remaining 2 percent?

Is there a point where you should stop in trying to achieve perfection?

Is there an "excess perfection syndrome" in publishing, and is it harmful?

Claiming that "it is not possible to ever achieve 100 percent perfection," the May 1978 issue of *Professional Services Management Journal* (*PSMJ*) charges that most technical professionals have an "overwhelming urge to do more than is really necessary on a particular task."

Says *PSMJ*: "In the early stages of a task, increased effort causes pronounced increases in excellence. But as the task approaches 90 percent perfection, the point of diminishing returns is rapidly reached.

"Note we are not talking about perfect vs. imperfect work. We are talking about degrees of excellence," *PSMJ* explains.

"The question the project manager should constantly ask is what level of excellence is really needed on this particular assignment at this particular time," the *PSMJ* article states.

PSMJ is directed primarily at architectural and engineering firms. Do you think its argument is valid in publishing?

(#7, 6/78)

Proverbs for Proofreading

Love is nearsighted. When you are the writer, editor, typist, or typesetter proofreading your own work, you will almost surely suffer from myopia. You are too close to see all the errors. Get help.

Familiarity breeds content. When you see the same copy again and again through the different stages of production and revision, you may well miss new errors. Fresh eyes are needed.

If it's as plain as the nose on your face, everybody can see it but you. Where is the reader most likely to notice errors? In a headline; in a title; in the first line, first paragraph, or first page of copy; and in the top lines of a new page. These are precisely the places where editors and proofreaders are most likely to miss errors. Take extra care at every beginning.

Mistakery loves company. Errors often cluster. When you find one, look hard for others nearby.

When you change horses in midstream, you can get wet. It's easy to overlook an error set in type that is different from the text face you are reading. Watch out when type changes to all caps, italics, boldface, small sizes, and large sizes. Watch out when underlines appear in typewritten copy.

Glass houses invite stones. Beware copy that discusses errors. When the subject is typographical quality, the copy must be typographically perfect.

When the topic is errors in grammar or spelling, the copy must be error-free. Keep alert for words like *typographical* or *proofreading*. Doublecheck and triplecheck.

The footbone conneckit to the kneebone? Numerical and alphabetical sequences often go awry. Check for omissions and duplications in page numbers, footnote numbers, or notations in outlines and lists. Check any numeration, anything in alphabetical order, and everything sequential (such as the path of arrows in a flowchart).

It takes two to boogie. An opening parenthesis needs a closing parenthesis. Brackets, quotation marks, and sometimes dashes, belong in pairs. Catch the bachelors.

Every yoohoo deserves a yoohoo back. A footnote reference mark or a first reference to a table or an illustration is termed a *callout*. Be sure a footnote begins on the same page as its callout. Be sure a table or illustration follows its callout as soon as possible.

Numbers can speak louder than words. Misprints in numerals (figures) can be catastrophic. Take extraordinary care with dollar figures and numbers in dates, statistics, tables, or technical text. Read all numerals character by character; for example, read "1979" as "one nine seven nine." Be sure any figures in your handwriting are unmistakable.

Two plus two is twenty-two. The simplest math can go wrong. Do not trust figures giving percentages and fractions or the "total" lines in tables. Watch for misplaced decimal points. Use your calculator.

Above all, never assume that all is well. As the saying goes, ass-u-me makes an ass out of u and me.

—Peggy Smith (#27, 5/79)

A reviewer adds: *Sweat the small stuff*. A simple transposition turns *marital strife* into *martial strife*, *board room* into *broad room*. One missing character turns *he'll* into *hell*, *public* into *pubic*.

LEXICOGRAPHY

Among all the traits that may distinguish an editor (a reader for pay) from an ordinary citizen (a reader for fun or information), having an attitude about a dictionary is preeminent. Indeed, an editor is likely to be one of the relatively few people who know that there are as many differences among dictionaries as there are among symphonies and sports cars. Not only that, an editor is likely to be not merely opinionated about dictionaries but downright dogmatic.

That's all to the good, but the first thing to remember about dictionaries is that they are really playgrounds. "A Little Experiment," which closes this section, will show you how to play games with your dictionary, a pastime that beats solitaire. A dictionary is fun.

The second thing to remember about dictionaries is that the "descriptive vs. prescriptive" debate generates as much heat as light, and a good deal more smoke. Most important, as Mary Bodnar points out in her article on this issue, is that you understand your goals in using a dictionary and that you find one that will help you achieve them. A dictionary is useful.

Finally, a dictionary, like a friend, ought to be chosen with care, as Peggy Smith points out in her "How to Live with a Dictionary." Whether the friendship blossoms will depend in part on your expectations and how much time you are willing to spend cultivating your friend's strengths and learning how to avoid its weaknesses. A dictionary will treat you as well as you treat it.

How to Live with a Dictionary

We have 18 English-language dictionaries in our house. The count includes facsimiles of Samuel Johnson's and Noah Webster's, G.&C. Merriam's venerable *Webster's II* and Houghton Mifflin's newest that disrespectfully exploits the sobriquet of Merriam's revered tome and calls itself *Webster's II*, all the current big ones, and several editions of publishers' collegiate dictionaries.

Until I read Sidney I. Landau's book *Dictionaries: The Art & Craft of Lexicography*,* however, all I knew about dictionaries came from the miscellaneous file in my head and from the dictionaries' front matter. I didn't know much about dictionaries; I just knew what I liked—and I found none ideal.

Landau, a distinguished lexicographer, is a pleasure to read. He told me much more than I thought I wanted to know about dictionaries and dictionary making, but I'm glad I read every word. I recommend the book to anyone who often uses a dictionary, who writes definitions (as in glossaries), or who enjoys scholarly controversy—or who just likes books about words.

Now that I've read this informative and delightful book, I realize that living with a dictionary is something like a good marriage: when the basis of admiration and respect is strong, there are ways to work around the irritations, as when you patiently put the cap back on the toothpaste yourself.

Choose Your Partner Well

For your mainstay, choose a hardcover copy of one of the big four collegiate dictionaries and be faithful to it until it's superseded by a later edition. (Do as I say, not as I do; dictionaries differ in many ways, and you have to shift several gears when you use one that is different from the one you're used to.)

Decide which you want to live with:

- G.&C. Merriam's intellectual *Webster's Ninth New Collegiate Dictionary* (1983);
- Simon & Schuster's practical, down-to-earth *Webster's New World Dictionary of the American Language*, Second College Edition (1979);

- The *Random House College Dictionary*, Revised Edition (1982), with its scholarly tone; or
- Houghton Mifflin's somewhat flashy *American Heritage Dictionary*, Second College Edition (1982).

Canadians who prefer British usage may want to consider breaking away from *The Concise Oxford* by looking into a couple of worthy newcomers, *The New Collins Concise Dictionary* and the *Longman New Universal Dictionary*. Or they may want the *Gage Canadian Dictionary*, which pays attention to Canadian usage.

To make the most intelligent choice, read Landau's book, which tells you the many ways these and other dictionaries differ from one another. Whatever you do, ignore the hype in ads and on dust jackets. Commercial dictionaries compete for your dollar the same way breakfast cereals do. All the big four collegiate dictionaries are full of nutrition; they just taste different.

Keep the Relationship Happy

Don't take your relationship with your dictionary for granted; you have to work at it. First, you should read the front matter—the articles and the "Guide to the Dictionary." (*Webster's Ninth* calls the guide "Explanatory Notes.") Reading the articles is enlightening; reading them in several dictionaries is the next best thing to reading Landau's book. Reading the guide to the dictionary you live with is obligatory.

Spelling Variants. Among the important things the guide to your dictionary tells you is that many spellings are style choices; there are equally correct alternatives. Learn how your dictionary distinguishes equal and unequal spelling variants, because it's unfair for editors to impose their preferences on an author whose preference is as valid as theirs. Say you choose *Webster's Ninth*. It lists equal variants after the word *or*, like this:

judgment *or* judgement	traveler *or* traveller
theater *or* theatre	upward *or* upwards

If an author uses an equal variant consistently (or most of the time), the editor should go with the author's choice unless spelling style is specified by the publisher.

Webster's Ninth identifies a "secondary variant," which "occurs less frequently than the first," after the word *also*. The statement that "secondary variants belong to standard usage and may be used according to personal inclination" must not be taken salt-free. Some of the *alsos* are merely out-of-date, but some are not yet acceptable except to lexicographers. When enough dolts perpetrate misspellings like *dependance* and *dissention*, those misspellings get into the dictionaries. The *alsos* in *Webster's Ninth* include these two plus the following:

among *also* amongst	woeful *also* woful

Another class of variants is labeled *var of*. These are the ones to shun. If you live with *Webster's Ninth*, I recommend using only the spelling at the main entry or only the one in small capitals at the *var of* listing:

grey *var of* GRAY	momento *var of* MEMENTO
wholistic *var of* HOLISTIC	miniscule *var of* MINUSCULE
racoon *var of* RACCOON	

rime, rimer, rimester *var of* RHYME, RHYMER, RHYMESTER

(Merriam's computerized data base must surely include other common illiterate misspellings that don't get into print—*it's* for *its*, *peice*, *supercede*, *liason*, *preceed* and, of course, *mispelling*. Somebody at Merriam must decide which misspellings make it and which don't; I wish that person were more finicky. So I put the cap on the toothpaste myself; I shy away from a *var of*.)

Sequence of Senses. It's important to know your dictionary's approach to the order of a word's senses. The guide to the dictionary tells you the nature of the order given. In some dictionaries, such as *Webster's Ninth* and *New World*, the first-listed sense of a word is the oldest, and the rest follow in historical sequence. In other dictionaries, such as *Random House*, the first sense is the most common, and the rest are in order of frequency. In still other dictionaries, the definitions are arranged analytically; the *American Heritage*, for example, says its arrangement is "according to central meaning clusters from which related subsenses and additional separate senses may evolve."

Other Features. You need to know whether your dictionary shows end-of-line word division in homographs (prog·ress *n*, but pro·gress *v*), as do *Webster's Ninth* and the *American Heritage*, or whether you're expected to figure it out for yourself, as *New World* and *Random House* expect.

You need to understand how etymology, usage labels, usage notes, and synonyms are treated. Read, absorb, and grow accustomed to the features the guide explains.

But What If Your Lexicographer Doesn't Understand You?

I think Landau somewhat misrepresents the role of copyeditors: "Copyeditors, like teachers," he says, "are devotedly conservative in matters of usage; they are paid to be. It is safer to observe every ancient quibble about usage than to risk an outcry among one's customers."

Not fair! We don't observe *every* ancient quibble; we have a lot of common sense. And few of our customers know enough to raise an outcry if we miss. It's the reader we're thinking of when we undangle modifiers or chop off the *ir* from *irregardless*.

The trouble with dictionaries, and with lexicographers, is that they try to represent both written and spoken English, to the detriment of the written language. Landau says that dictionaries present a distorted picture:

> The fact that dictionaries are dependent on edited copy rather than impromptu speech or unedited writing presents a distorted picture of actual usage, which is far less uniform and far less standard than dictionaries ordinarily represent it to be. Dictionaries should try to segregate their representation of usage information based on edited material from that of unedited sources or naive speech.

I've got a better idea. Forget the unedited sources and naive speech. Give me a dictionary based entirely on well-edited material. (Even a happily married person can daydream of a more perfect union.)

In the meantime, do your darnedest to maintain the "distorted picture of actual usage" or, to put it contrariwise, keep on putting actual usage's crazy-mirror distortions into focus. You work within the constraints of the written language; you don't have an impromptu or naive speaker's range of volume, stress, pitch, intonation, and gesture to express meaning.

And readers are far less patient and forgiving than listeners. So edit away. Make your author's words clear, precise, and user-friendly. Future editions of dictionaries depend on their sources, including published works. The quality of your dictionary's offspring may well depend on you.

—Peggy Smith (#111, 12/84)

*Charles Scribner's Sons, 597 Fifth Avenue, New York, NY 10017. 1984, 370 pp.

Test Yourself

On Metrics

What do the following prefixes stand for in metric terminology?

micro	deci	kilo	nano
milli	deka (deca)	myria	pico
centi	hekto (hecto)	mega	femto
tera	giga	atto	

(#14, 10/78)

Answers

micro: one millionth (10^{-6})
milli: one thousandth (10^{-3})
centi: one hundredth (10^{-2})
tera: one trillion (10^{12})
deci: one tenth (10^{-1})
deka (deca): ten (10)
hekto (hecto): one hundred (10^{2})
giga: one billion (10^{9})
kilo: one thousand (10^{3})
myria: ten thousand (10^{4})
mega: one million (10^{6})
atto: one quintillionth (10^{-18})
nano: one billionth (10^{-9})
pico: one trillionth (10^{-12})
femto: one quadrillionth (10^{-15})

(#15, 10/78)

Encouragement for the Editorial Temperament

"Every other author may aspire to praise; the lexicographer can only hope to escape reproach." Samuel Johnson's characterization of his calling applies as well to indexers, proofreaders, copyeditors, and all of us who skewer our life's bread with blue pencils. It helps us to hear, now and again, the epic tales of the heroes and heroines of our vocation—how Kate L. Turabian could cow a full professor, or how Thomas Wolfe would never have made it out of Asheville had it not been for Maxwell Perkins.

The next time the risk of reproach threatens to overwhelm, try reading a bit of Elisabeth Murray's wonderful biography of Sir James A.H. Murray, her "Grandfather Dictionary" (*Caught in the Web of Words*, Yale University Press, 1977). The card-carrying logophile will already know Murray as the greatest English lexicographer since Dr. Johnson. Murray edited THE dictionary, that work whose possession makes joining the Book-of-the-Month Club an excusable necessity.

In 1879, at age 42, Murray committed what he thought would be the next 7 to 10 years of his life to editing the (then called) *New English Dictionary on Historical Principles*. At his death 36 years later, the work had got as far as "S." The 12-volume *Oxford English Dictionary* (OED) was completed in 1928; a 4-volume supplement began appearing in 1972.

To read the story of Murray's life is to be at once delighted and inspired. To contemplate the magisterial scope of the OED and its importance to the English language is to be humbled. But after the reader hefts 15,487 quarto pages, peruses some half-million entries, and browses through the 1.5 million illustrative quotations selected from among nearly 6 million usage slips sent in by field readers—after all that—to discover that Murray edited *half of this himself* is to be stupefied.

The task of formulating even the typographical canons of a work such as the OED, let alone the mind-boggling problems of deciding what belonged in it or should be excluded, would be enough to induce a bad case of editorial hives. What distinguished Murray, and led to the ultimate success of his lexicon, was his absolute refusal to compromise his editorial standards. He preferred a production rate of zero to allowing less than his best effort to be printed. He appeared never to entertain the thought of "close enough is good enough." Though he engaged in repeated battles with the Delegates of the Oxford University Press, though he had to threaten resignation on several occasions, and though he had to face down one of the Victorian era's most formidable browbeaters, Benjamin Jowett, the Master of Balliol College, Murray remained unshakable. And he prevailed.

For Murray, editorial quality was an achievement purchased at the price of 36 years of 12-hour days. He wrote (longhand) an average of 20 to 30 letters a week to poets, writers, scientists, and authorities of all kinds inquiring about the meaning of words and terms. He and his staff ran down thousands of words to their Middle English roots, often producing trail-blazing philological and linguistic scholarship in the process. He faced and overcame the hopelessness that often accompanied such tasks as sorting out verbs like "set," which occupies more than 18 pages of the Dictionary and extends to 154 main divisions, the last of which (*set up*) has so many subdivisions that it exhausts the alphabet and repeats the letters down to *rr*.

Few today could aspire to, let alone match, his standard. But when the blue funk of frustration settles in, it is good to remember Murray. For him, the eternal editorial triangle of cost, time, and quality was never equilateral. Let the University Press rage about costs; let the public cool its heels forever waiting for the next fascicle; if it wasn't done right, it didn't go to the printer.

—Bruce O. Boston (#41, 4/80)

■ Dictionaries: Prescriptive or Descriptive?

If you think a usage or a spelling of a word is correct just because you find it in the dictionary, you may be misled. Many people still think of dictionaries as prescriptive—that is, as authoritative reference books that define and spell words to tell us what is correct and omit or label what is incorrect. But descriptive dictionaries, perhaps influenced by the prescriptive-descriptive dichotomy of structural linguistics, represent a different philosophy.

Editorial workers, however, need guidance. We need to know which word choices and spellings are wrong, which are right (meaning "standard"), and which are matters of style. We miss the prescriptions of traditional dictionaries that follow the word usage of established writers and, in light of that information, specify correct spelling and label usage as standard or substandard.

What Do Descriptive Dictionaries Do?

Descriptive dictionaries, of which *Webster's Third New International Dictionary* (G.&C. Merriam Company) is a prime example, describe the word usage of celebrities and of average people without making value judgments. In fact, *Webster's New Collegiate Dictionary*, based on *Webster's Third New International*, includes forms and spellings that can only be called incorrect (*ain't*, *restauranteur*, *momento*, *dependant*), listed without benefit of labels or with questionable labels. The classic example is the *Webster's Third* note for *ain't*: "though disapproved by many and more common in less educated speech, used orally in most parts of the U.S. by many educated speakers, esp. in the phrase *ain't I*?"

Of course a Merriam-Webster dictionary also includes correct spellings for all words listed; it just doesn't tell you which is traditionally considered correct or incorrect. Since this is the dictionary recommended by both the GPO and the Chicago style manuals, editorial workers who follow those styles might find a more authoritative dictionary helpful as a backup to avoid using the misspellings that a Merriam-Webster dictionary contains.

How Can You Tell If a Dictionary Is Authoritative?

The *Oxford American Dictionary* (OAD), *Webster's New World Dictionary*, *Random House College Dictionary*, and *The American Heritage Dictionary* are all advertised as authoritative, but some are more authoritative than others.

The OAD, probably the most prescriptive of the four, traces its ancestry to the *Oxford English Dictionary* and boasts of a "cheerful attitude of infallibility." The OAD provides hundreds of usage notes, includes few choices, and lists no misspellings.

Webster's New World Dictionary, Second College Edition, serves as the desk dictionary for *The New York Times*, Associated Press, and United Press International. *Webster's New World Dictionary* and *Random House College Dictionary* are generally prescriptive, although both include the misspelling *dependance*.

The American Heritage Dictionary, Second College Edition, is described as authoritative on the cover and as descriptive in the foreword. Its split personality may come from its Usage Panel, a diverse group whose responses to usage questions determine the content of the usage notes. The panel labels *ain't* nonstandard, apparently reluctantly, because a note adds, "*Ain't* has acquired such a stigma over the years that it is beyond rehabilitation, even though it would serve a useful function as a contraction for *am not* and even though its use as an alternate form for *isn't*, *hasn't*, *aren't*, and *haven't* has a good historical justification." The *American Heritage Dictionary* also includes the misspellings *restauranteur* and *dependance*.

Summary Advice

In using any dictionary, wherever it falls on the prescriptive-descriptive continuum, always choose the dictionary's first listing when you have a choice. In every dictionary, the first listing is correct; in some dictionaries, the second listing is incorrect. Some unfortunate listings in descriptive dictionaries, such as *momento* for *memento*, however, are alphabetical, so you can't tell which is right. It's a problem.

—Mary Bodnar (#92, 8/83)

Dictionary Recommendations and Queries

The Eye asked readers to recommend their favorite dictionaries. Among the responses are these:

One for Etymologists

Readers with an etymological bent may find the New College Edition of *The American Heritage Dictionary of the English Language* as engrossing as I do. Its appendix on Indo-European roots, sounds, and other features really opens one's eyes to the relationships among words that, at first glance, seem unrelated. And there are several articles on grammar, usage, pronunciation, dialects, and the origin of English that I found fascinating. (My copy is the 1976 edition; there may be later ones, with changes unknown to me.)

—Collier N. Smith, Boulder, CO

Editor's Note: The Second College Edition, 1982, does not have the appendix on etymology.

Finding the Date of Publication

We are a small publications department that writes and publishes technical manuals on the products our company manufactures, and we have a mixture of desk copy dictionaries and a 1968 unabridged edition of *Webster's Third New International Dictionary of the English Language*.

We are currently looking for an updated unabridged dictionary and are considering the 1981 edition of the one mentioned above. We would like to get the most recent dictionary; however, it is difficult to determine the publication (copyright) date from sealed copies in book stores, and catalog listings seem to omit this information.

—Charles T. Christensen, Atlanta, GA

Editor's Response: A recent copyright doesn't necessarily mean a recent edition; publishers routinely protect the work by updating the copyright without updating the dictionary. Unabridged dictionaries are revised only rarely; the 1968 volume you are now using is the current edition of that work. However, you can buy a publication called *6,000 Words: A Supplement to Webster's Third*, issued by the publisher in 1976, or buy the latest collegiate abridgment of that or some other dictionary.

'New World' Endorsement

I agree with AP, UPI, *et al.*, in preferring *Webster's New World*. I've used the *New World* for years, mostly because it has much clearer definitions and better etymology. (As an example, compare the definitions of "existentialism. . . .")

—Gerald A. Mann, Lanham, MD

Webster's New Collegiate:

ex-is-ten-tial-ism /-ˈten-chə,liz-əm/ *n* : a chiefly 20th century philosophy that is centered upon the analysis of existence and of the way man finds himself existing in the world, that regards human existence as not exhaustively describable or understandable in scientific terms, and that stresses the freedom and responsibility of the individual, the irreducible uniqueness of an ethical or religious situation, and usu. the isolation and subjective experiences (as of anxiety, guilt, dread, anguish) of an individual therein.

Webster's New World:

ex·is·ten·tial·ism (-shəl is'm) *n*. [Fr. *existentialisme* < *existenciel*: see prec.] a philosophical and literary movement, variously religious and atheistic, stemming from Kierkegaard and represented by Sartre, Heidegger, etc.: it is based on the doctrine that existence takes precedence over essence and holds that man is totally free and responsible for his acts, and that this responsibility is the source of the dread and anguish that encompass him—**ex'is·ten'·tial·ist** *adj*., *n*.

A Computer Dictionary

A dictionary I particularly like that deals with matters of computerdom is *The Random House Dictionary of New Information Technology*, edited by A.J. Meadows, M. Gordon, and A. Singleton, published by the Vintage Books division of Random House, copyright 1982. It's a 206-page paperback and is about the best I've seen. I recently wrote a chapter for a textbook on computers for Prentice-Hall, and this dictionary supplied explanations that simply were not available to me elsewhere.

—Alice Craig Harvey, Silver Spring, MD

Editor's Note: Another promising new technical dictionary by an author we know to be reliable is *The Illustrated Dictionary of Typographic Communication*, by Michael L. Kleper (Graphic Dimensions, 8 Frederick Rd., Pittsford, NY 14534, 200 pp., 1,000 definitions).

This book provides information on terms used in word processing, managing information, typesetting, telecommunication, photography, pasteup and art, and preparation.

A Little Experiment

LOGO•PHILE

There's a potato chip company whose advertising slogan used to be "Bet You Can't Eat Just One." I have a parallel problem with dictionaries. Every time I open one, whatever the reason, I rarely stop looking when I find what I went after. To me, dictionaries are like Disney World; they were made to wander around in.

Along that line, I have always thought that the most important characteristic of any good dictionary was its ability to keep you from doing more useful work. Having never subjected this a priori judgment to rigorous scientific scrutiny (my evidence has heretofore been completely anecdotal), and faced with the necessity to come up with a column, I devised an experiment. My hypothesis was that any single page of my dictionary, chosen at random, could keep me interested long enough to waste at least an hour.

I took my desk dictionary (*American Heritage*), let it fall open at random, and timed how long I could avoid other activity. Unfortunately, I was able to remain on p. 846 for only 27 minutes. But that's not the whole story.

Play by the Rules

There are some rules for doing this sort of thing that ought to be mentioned before the results are fully reported. Rule One: You have to stick with your choice. Abandoning your chosen page just because it happens to be one on which all the words begin with the same prefix is cheating. Rule Two: You must run through all the entries quickly and see how many words you either know or recognize. If "words known are more than words not known" you may be headed for trouble. Nevertheless, do not despair; there are plenty of byways to explore. But if "words not known are more than words known," congratulate yourself; you're in for a good long stretch. A more rigorous form of Rule Two is to substitute being able to give a fair definition of the word instead of just being able to recognize it. This rule may also be called the Humility Rule. Rule Three is to save the longest entry until last, sort of like the maraschino cherry in a Manhattan cocktail, unless you don't like maraschino cherries or don't drink, in which case it's OK to read the longest entry first. Rule Four: Don't take any notes. There's no point in using a dictionary to waste time if you're going to get fanatical about it.

From "Moll" to "Monad"

Page 846 runs from *moll* to *monad*. The most engaging (and longest) entry, the kind for which the *American Heritage* has been justly praised, is for *moment*. Eight main definitions are presented, the first two of which flatly contradict one another in sense: "1. a brief, indefinite period of time," and "2. a specific point in time, especially the present time." Alice's question to Humpty Dumpty comes to mind: "The question is whether you can make a word mean so many different things." Humpty Dumpty's response, of course, is probably the definitive commentary on all usage: "The question is, who is to be the master—that's all."

Definitions 7 and 8 of *moment* are special to physics and statistics. One of the two from physics I could understand: ("the rotation produced in a body when force is applied; torque"). The other one reminded me of why I majored in history. The one from statistics was, to be sure, as succinct as a dictionary definition should be: ("the expected value of a positive integral power of a random variable"). Having abandoned anything to do with what I call "the quantitative morass" when I parted company with second-year algebra, I did not tarry long with this lexicographical pearl, except to wonder about the connection between a "positive integral power" and the Latin root *momentum*, meaning "movement."

There follows a whole paragraph of synonyms, ranked according to duration in comparison with *moment*. *Moment* and *minute*, used informally, are regarded as of interchangeable length. An *instant* is shorter than either and also carries connotations of haste and urgency. *Second* may be used specifically or loosely as the equivalent of *instant*. *Trice*, *jiffy*, and *flash*, however, while they are of approximately the same duration as *instant* and may imply haste, need not imply urgency. I have a hard time believing that a *flash* isn't a lot faster than a *jiffy*, however.

Proof of the Hypothesis

The most interesting word on the page (an interesting word is a nonscientific word I don't know) was *momus*, a word particularly appropriate for editors because it derives from *Momus*, the god of blame and ridicule in Greek mythology. A *momus* is a carping faultfinder.

Momus was a delightful find because it inspired me to look up the god of which this word is the eponym, first in Bullfinch's *Mythology* then in Willard Espy's delightful book on eponyms, *O Thou Improper, Thou Uncommon Noun* (Clarkson, Potter, 1978). And with that, I shot the rest of the morning.

Q.E.D.

 (#105, 7/84)

Black Eyes

HEADLINE:

U.S. to spend $3 million on missing child center

Imagine what they'll spend when they find it.

HEADLINE:

Man Kills Self, Shoots Girlfriend

Ed. Note: For "Man" substitute "Former Magician"

(#103, 5/84)

THE FINE POINTS

I. PUNCTUATION

Although nobly titled, this section on "The Fine Points" of punctuation, spelling, and usage may be the source of more debate than other sections of this book. For it is on these three portions of the editorial track that the rubber really does meet the road (or the eraser the paper).

Alas, that argumentativeness seems to be part of the professional editor's DNA. More's the pity, because although the editor often knows better, the people the editor works for often think that on any given "fine point," there really is a "right" and a "wrong" spelling, punctuation, or usage. To plead, for example, that whether one uses a colon or a dash at a given point in a particular sentence is really debatable, availeth not. Conversely, to continue to insist that "the whole comprises the parts" and "the parts compose the whole" is likely to get you nowhere with a boss who just read in the morning paper that "Seventeen delegates from four states comprised the caucus."

Yet, for all that, editors are paid for answers, not ambiguities. Thus, the following section treats a variety of familiar knots in the editorial planking. Some you can cut right through, others you have to go around. But there will always be those for which the only intelligent solution is to choose a new board. In other words, rewrite.

The Serial Comma, Otiose or Essential?

American academic and literary styles call for the serial comma. Journalistic style omits this comma in a simple series. Here are some authoritative—but conflicting—guidelines on the subject.

Words Into Type: In a series of the form *a*, *b*, and *c* or *red*, *white*, and *blue* most publishers prefer a comma (sometimes called the serial comma) before the conjunction, whether the items of the series are words, phrases, or clauses. The consistent use of this comma is recommended, for in many sentences it is essential for clarity.

U.S. Government Printing Office Style Manual: The comma is used . . . after each member within a series of three or more words, phrases, letters, or figures used with *and*, *or*, or *nor*.

University of Chicago Press *A Manual of Style:* In a series consisting of three or more elements, the elements are separated by commas. When a conjunction joins the last two elements in a series, a comma is used before the conjunction.

H.W. Fowler, *A Dictionary of Modern English Usage:* The more usual way of punctuating such an enumeration as [*French, German, Italian, and Spanish*] is *French, German, Italian and Spanish*: the commas between *French* and *German* and *German* and *Italian* take the place of *ands*; there is no comma after *Italian* because, with *and*, it would be otiose. There are, however, some who favor putting one there, arguing that, since it may sometimes be needed to avoid ambiguity, it may as well be used always for the sake of uniformity.

Wilson Follett, edited by Jacques Barzun, *Modern American Usage:* A large body of opinion that includes nearly all newspapers insists on *a, b and c*—that is, they omit the last comma. A smaller body, numbering many of the most respectable book publishers, sticks to *a, b, and c*. . . . [Only one] argument for omitting the last comma . . . is cogent—the saving of space. In the narrow width of a newspaper column this saving counts for more than elsewhere, which is why the omission is so nearly universal in journalism. But here or anywhere one must question whether the advantage outweighs the confusion caused by the omission.

United Press International Stylebook: Omit the final comma in a simple series: The flag is red, white and blue. Use a final comma in a complex series: I had orange juice, toast, and ham and eggs for breakfast.

E.L. Callihan, *Grammar for Journalists:* When the conjunction, usually *and* or *or*, is used before the last word or phrase or clause in the series, no comma need be inserted before the conjunction. This is universal journalist style.

—Peggy Smith (#10, 8/78)

Bring Back My Hyphen to Me

In Neil Simon's play, "Chapter Two," the male lead writes crime stories under the pseudonym of Kenneth Blakely-Hill.

"Blakely hyphen Hill," he explains.

"Hyphen Hill?" a puzzled character asks.

"No, Blakely-Hill with a hyphen."

Wonderful! Here, finally, is someone who finds a hyphen worth mentioning. Hyphens should be mentioned. As each year passes, fewer and fewer hyphens are used. When it comes to compound adjectives, the hyphen is becoming an endangered species like Nile crocodiles and the New Guinea snake-neck turtle.

Nowhere is this omission of the hyphen (where it should *not* be omitted) more prevalent than in advertising. The television commercial says that if I take a certain tablet (name on request), I shall get "12 hour relief." A newspaper advertisement proclaims a sale in Filene's Basement in Boston, where—at bargain prices—I am promised "long sleeved dress shirts" and "double breasted suits" by "well known makers of fine clothes." Other ads speak of "all day dining," "all night parking" and "salt free peanut butter. . . ." In the news columns are references to "well deserved mention" and "first hand experience." (First experience with hands?)

On the way to Boston I see gasoline stations with "self serve islands," billboards touting "strong tasting" low-tar cigarettes, stores selling "wood burning" stoves. A restaurant next to the motel boasting "year round swimming" offers an "Italian style lunch." One sign, mysteriously, advertises "self storage."

Television titles are notoriously hyphenless. PBS, for example, introduced a series last year called "Non Fiction Television." Gateway Productions was advertising a program called "The 45 Billion Dollar Connection." Most blatantly hyphenless, of course, was the "Six Million Dollar Man."

Omission of the hyphen can be confusing. Take the phrase "first class recital." Was it the music class's first recital or was it a first-class recital, one which excelled? A careless headline spoke of a company's "first rate increase." The reference was not to the first increase in any rate but to a first-rate, appreciable increase in production. Hyphens make a difference.

Here I have a confession to make. For years, the CBS Evening News displayed a graph showing the "30 day" trend on the New York Stock Market. It hurt to see this, so I wrote about it to the executive producer. Not wishing to appear to intrude—after all, I had left the show—I posed as an aggrieved English teacher and signed the letter "Priscilla Sedgwick." It worked. The hyphen popped into place, and I experienced not only the satisfaction of seeing a spelling corrected on my favorite news program, but also, for the first time, a wondrous, intoxicating sense of viewer power.

On those increasingly rare occasions when hyphens *are* used, they frequently are misapplied. There is no hyphen in *Boston Herald American*. Nor in *New York Herald Tribune*, a paper fondly remembered though long gone. In 1968, the NBC Nightly News, in reporting the performance of the stock market, consistently hyphenated Dow Jones. Once more, Ms. Sedgwick took up her pen and wrote to the program's producer, and two days later the hyphen disappeared. Right now I'm looking at a newspaper story about a boy injured in an auto accident. The story says the boy is "the 10-year old son of Mr. and Mrs. Michael Ladd." There is no hyphen between *year* and *old*. There should be.

This mistake is commonplace. The writer senses a need for hyphens but doesn't know one hyphen is not enough. The writer simply is ignorant of the *function* of the hyphen in this instance, which is the amalgamation of three words to form one word, an adjective modifying the noun *son*.

Journalism Quarterly, one of this country's most scholarly publications, carried the text of an important address by James W. Carey, president of the Association for Education in Journalism. Reference is made in the text to a "long run effect." We are not told where this run took place, or what effect it had. All we know is that it was a long run, so it may have been a marathon.

I know this makes me vulnerable to the charge of being a smart aleck. But whatever *did* happen to the hyphen? We need it. Let's find it and bring it back—where it belongs.

—Edward Bliss, Jr., reprinted from *The Quill* (Nov. 1980)
published by The Society of Professional Journalists
Sigma Delta Chi

(#57, 4/81)

. . . Points of Ellipsis . . . Points of Contention . . .

Authors, editors, and style guides disagree on the number and spacing of ellipsis points (dots) to indicate omission from a quotation.

Number of Points

Earlier convention required four dots for ellipsis with a fifth dot added for the period at the end of a sentence. Many authorities now specify three dots with a fourth dot for the period. There is, however, a tendency toward using only three dots, whether a sentence ends or not.

Spacing of Points

Most authorities who add a dot for a period treat the first of four dots as the period and close up the first dot to the word before it. Others treat the last dot as the period and put space before and after each dot.

Although spacing specifications differ for typewritten and typeset copy, the variations can look something like the following examples:

To show any omission:

any . . . any
any ... any
any...any

To show omission from the middle of a sentence:

middle . . . middle
middle ... middle
middle...middle

To show omission after a sentence ends and before a new sentence starts:

end. . . . Start
end . . . . Start
end. ... Start
end....Start
end ... Start

To show omission from the middle of a sentence up to the start of another sentence (the last example is the only one different from the end-Start list):

middle. . . . Start
middle . . . . Start
middle. ... Start
middle....Start
middle ... Start

Prediction

Economic, technological, practical, and esthetic considerations will determine the future accepted mark of ellipsis. Considerations influencing the decision include ease for the reader; attractiveness of page design; use of spaced dots as computer codes; and need to lessen the available space, the time to check an author's accuracy, and the number of keystrokes.

We can expect to see three dots spaced like a three-letter word to mark any ellipsis: any ... any.

Advice

Meanwhile, what should editors, editorial typists, and proofreaders do?

Editors and editorial typists: if you have a choice, follow a sensible, conservative authority, such as *A Manual of Style* (University of Chicago Press) for typeset copy and, consistent with Chicago Press style, *A Manual for Writers* by Kate L. Turabian for typewritten copy.

Chicago style looks like this:

middle . . . middle
end. . . . Start
middle . . . Start

Proofreaders: be aware of the many acceptable possibilities and query when you see departures from any acceptable style.

—Peggy Smith (#24, 3/79)

Ask *The Eye:* Punctuation

The Question: Do Periods and Commas Go Inside or Outside Closing Quotation Marks?

For years I have been the office English major. I was always the one everyone came to on questions of construction, agreement, and when to use *s* apostrophe and when to use apostrophe *s*. Suddenly the rules have changed and I've become confused about when the periods and commas go inside the quotes and when they go outside. It seems they teach different groundrules on the subject than they did when I was in school. Could you please run a brief article on the subject so I can once again trust my judgment on periods, commas, and quotes?

—Judith Johnston

The Answer

The American printers' rule is to place commas and periods inside closing quotation marks for appearance's sake. American typographers and style guides generally follow this tradition. (Dashes, semicolons, question marks, and exclamation points go inside only when they belong to the quotation.)

Some British authors and printers place punctuation outside the closing quotation marks when an isolated word or incomplete sentence is quoted.

(#39, 2/80)

■ The Semicolon: Different Viewpoints

Commas and semicolons are not marks to be added to a completed sentence for artistic effect; they are as much a part of a well-rounded sentence as are correctly placed pronouns and adverbs.

—Richard D. Mallery

Punctuation, [Abraham] Lincoln said to Noah Brooks, was with him a matter of feeling rather than education. The semicolon he found to be "a very useful little chap."

—Carl Sandburg

The semicolon is a symbol of purism, classicism, anti-gaucherie. And for those who live in part for the niceties, the delightful touches, the savoir faire . . . for us it is a cause of importance.

—Al Englehard

It is almost always a greater pleasure to come across a semicolon than a period. . . . You get a pleasant little feeling of expectancy; there is more to come; read on; it will get clearer.

—George F. Will

Show me a man agonizing over whether to use a comma, a semicolon, or a period, and I'll show you a happy man. (I'll also show you a semicolon; in such debates the semicolon always wins.)

—Melvin Maddocks

Semicolons are pretentious and overactive. . . . Far too often, [they] are used to gloss over an imprecise thought. They place two clauses in some kind of relationship to one another, but relieve the writer of saying exactly what that relationship is.

—Paul Robinson

There is a 19th-century mustiness that hangs over the semicolon. We associate it with the carefully balanced sentences, the judicious weighing of "on the one hand" and "on the other hand," of Conrad and Thackeray and Hardy. Therefore it should be used sparingly by writers of nonfiction today.

—William Zinsser (#45, 7/80)

On Dashes, On Slashes

The Em Dash, or THE DASH

The em dash was born in the 17th century, about the time English punctuation was becoming syntactical rather than elocutionary in purpose. It is the best-known, and by many the only-known, dash. Its liberal use, compared with other dashes, may be partly attributable to its versatility, but the widespread recognition of a typewritten symbol for it also deserves credit. Most readers and typesetters understand that "word - word" or "word—word" in typed copy means insert a 1-em dash between the words.

This dash usually denotes discontinuity. In many cases, its use is discretionary—a matter of style (hence the name dash?). In such uses, some substitute punctuation or none at all may do the job as well. For example, an em dash *may* be used to

- set off a defining or enumerating complementary element of a sentence. But so might commas or a colon. "Once upon a time, there were three bears—Mama Bear, Papa Bear, and Baby Bear." Or, ". . . three bears: Mama Bear. . . ."
- enclose a parenthetical element that does not bear a close relationship to the rest of the sentence. But so might parentheses. "They lived—when they weren't out berry picking—in a house in the woods." Or, "They lived (when . . .)."
- precede such expressions as *that is*, *namely*, or *for example*, if a break in continuity follows. But so might a semicolon. "Each bear had its own equipment—that is, suitably sized furniture." Or, ". . . equipment; that is, suitably. . . ."
- precede a credit line, either separate or run-in; follow a run-in side head; separate run-in questions and answers; or emphasize elements or portions of text, if you want a change from bullets. But so might no punctuation at all.

Em dashes do have their unique uses, however. A dash *should* be used to follow an introductory phrase leading into two or more lines that complete the sentence, to indicate faltering speech, and to replace a colon after a question mark or exclamation point in the middle of a sentence.

With so many uses and so much choice about them, em dashes are frequently overworked. A dash is considered a strong punctuation mark, and a few go a long way. A page littered with dashes may leave the impression that the author has expository hiccups.

Paul Robinson, in "The Philosophy of Punctuation" (*New Republic*, Apr. 26, 1980) cautions on the use of dashes and parentheses: "[They] are syntactical defeats. They signify an inability to express one's ideas sequentially, which, unless you're James Joyce, is the way the language was meant to be used. Reality may be simultaneous, but expository prose is linear. Parentheses and dashes represent efforts to elude the responsibilities of linearity. They generally betoken stylistic laziness, an unwillingness to spend time figuring out how to put things in the most logical order. Needless to say, they also betoken a failure of discipline. Every random thought, every tenuous analogy gets dragged in. Good writing is as much a matter of subtraction as creation, and parentheses [and dashes] are the great enemy of subtraction."

The En Dash, the Family Cinderella

It is possible that only we fans of editorial esoterica know the en dash exists and how useful it can be. Others mistake it for a hyphen, because in typewritten copy, it *is* a hyphen. The en dash is the victim of technological discrimination: the typewriter has no symbol for it, and no convention has emerged to compensate for this omission. The en dash can be expressed typologically, but the copymarker should indicate each and every one for the typesetter by marking the appropriate hyphens "$\frac{1}{N}$."

The en dash does have several specific uses and can be highly helpful. It is not discretionary like some em dashes, but it is not entirely indispensable either; we can, and conventionally do, accept a hyphen in its place.

A major use of the en dash is to substitute for the word *to* in inclusive pairs of dates, times, page numbers, and the like; for example, 1980–81, pp. 35–38, or January–June. It is used even when the closing date has not arrived—"John Doe (1940–)." Do not use it when the phrase starts with *from* ("from January to June") or *between* ("between January and June"). The en dash is also used to separate combinations of numbers or letters: telephone 703–999–1234, or AFL–CIO.

This brings us to situations in which the hyphen–en-dash identity gets most confusing. An en dash should be used in a compound adjective in which one element has two words or is a hyphenated word, as in the preceding sentence. Of course, on a typewriter, we just wind up with a series of hyphens that implies the existence of a special kind of dash—a hyphen en dash. Similar implications may result when two related words make up the compound: labor-management (the management of labor?) or cost-benefit (some benefit deriving from costs?). Please IBM, Remington, Smith–Corona, et al., make us an en dash.

2-, 3-, and 5-Em Dashes, Rare Birds

The extra-long dashes are highly specialized. You may never need one. The 2-em dash indicates missing letters. Once, we often found such dashes in the middle or at the end of four-letter words (Go to H---l, or Go to H----), but by now authors have said to hell with it and use the words intact.

The 3-em dash is used to indicate a missing word. Another place to find flocks of 3-em dashes is in bibliographies, to indicate an author is the same as the one above.

Slashes, the Usurpers

The slash originated sometime in the 13th or 14th century as a form of light stop. In the late 15th century, according to the *Britannica Book of English Usage*, it "sank to the baseline, developed a curve," and became the modern comma—a much better use than most it has now. The GPO style manual, in fact, simply ignores the use of the slash.

The slash does have legitimate uses, but often it merely usurps the work of the much-neglected en dash—possibly because the slash has been awarded a place on the typewriter keyboard and thus is there for writers who feel guilty about misusing a hyphen. This is how we get labor/management, cost/benefit, and the infamous and/or. The Chicago style manual legitimizes this usurpation by suggesting that the slash may substitute for an en dash for periods or seasons extending over two successive calendar years (fiscal year 1980/81 or 361/60 B.C.).

The slash has several technical uses: It is one of the symbols for shilling; it distinguishes lines of poetry in text (The boy stood on the burning deck/ Eating peanuts by the peck/ . . .); it is used for fractions in text (mainly because the numerator-over-denominator form would require two lines); it replaces *per* to indicate rates (miles/hour); and it is used to separate month/ day/year in dates. We suspect that the highest and best use of the slash is to add a word omitted from rough drafts.

—Charlene Semer (#58, 5/81)

Ask *The Eye:* Apostrophe

The Question: To Apostrophe or Not?

I'm stumped. Baffled. Is there technically a correct, proper, and "only" way to show possessive on:

"The candidate should have five years of experience."
"The candidate should have five years experience."
"The candidate should have five years' experience."

I strongly support the last, but would appreciate some gospel on which to pontificate. You see it both ways in the classifieds and displays.

—John Breen, McLean, VA

The Answer

The simple answer to your question is, you can't go wrong using your first and last examples, but most authorities condemn the middle one. Here are some opinions you can cite:

Washington Post Deskbook: Use an apostrophe in established idiomatic phrases that take the possessive even though there is no actual ownership: *a day's wages, John's service, two hours' travel time, a stone's throw, for pity's sake, in case of the train's leaving, for old times' sake, week's end.*

Government Printing Office (GPO) Style Manual: The possessive case is often used in lieu of an objective phrase even though ownership is not involved: *1 day's labor* (*labor for 1 day*), *2 hours' traveltime, a stone's throw, 2 weeks' pay, 5 or 10 billion dollars' worth, for charity's sake.*

Associated Press Stylebook: Quasi Possessives: . . . *a day's pay, two weeks' vacation, three days' work, your money's worth.* Frequently, however, a hyphenated form is clearer: *a two-week vacation, a three-day job.*

Random House Dictionary: genitive case . . . used primarily to indicate that a noun is a modifier of another noun, often to express possession, measure, origin, characteristic, etc., such as *John's hat, man's fate, week's vacation, duty's call.*

The one source I found that permitted omission of the apostrophe hedged its advice by suggesting rephrasing to avoid the problem:

Words Into Type: In some expressions, the idea of possession is so remote that the apostrophe is unnecessary and the phrase looks and sounds fine without it. The former possessive noun then becomes an adjective:

A two weeks waiting period is found in the laws of Alabama (or, *a 2-week* . . .)

The judge imposed 60 days sentence (or, *a 60-day* . . .)

Descriptive or Possessive?

While we're on the subject of when to use apostrophes, most style guides recommend omitting an apostrophe in proper names and in terms where usage is more descriptive than possessive.

Washington Post Deskbook: Omit the apostrophe in proper nouns unless the possessive aspect is clear, but follow established usages. *Actors Equity*, *State Teachers College*, *Harpers Ferry* (but *White's Ferry*, *Pike's Peak*, *New Year's Day*, *Court of St. James's*, *Prince George's County*, *Mother's Day*).

Omit the apostrophe where usage is more descriptive than possessive: *printers union*.

Associated Press Stylebook: Descriptive Phrases: Do not add an apostrophe to a word ending in *s* when it is used primarily in a descriptive sense: *citizens band radio*, *a Cincinnati Reds infielder*, *a teachers college*, *a Teamsters request*, *a writers guide*.

Memory aid: The apostrophe usually is not used if *for* or *by* rather than *of* would be appropriate in the longer form: *a band for citizens*, *a college for teachers*, *a guide for writers*, *a request by the Teamsters.*

An *'s* is required, however, when a term involves a plural word that does not end in *s*: *a children's hospital*, *a people's republic*, *the Young Men's Christian Association*.

Words into Type: The apostrophe is frequently omitted in names of organizations or buildings where the idea of possession seems obvious. In the absence of clear proof that the construction is correct or deliberate, the copy editor should query: *Farmers Loan and Trust Company*, *teachers college*, *Peoples Savings Bank*, *Consumers Union*.

GPO Style Manual: Generally the apostrophe should not be used after names of countries and other organized bodies ending in *s*, or after words more descriptive than possessive (not indicating personal possession), except when plural does not end in *s*: *United States control*, *United Nations meeting, Southern States industries, Massachusetts laws, House of Representatives session, Congress attitude, editors handbook, technicians guide, merchants exchange, children's hospital,* but *Veterans Administration* (in conformity with enabling statute) when specifically requested on copy.

Peggy Smith's *Proofreading Guide and Reference Manual* characterizes possessives in which the apostrophe is omitted as "frozen." Examples include acronyms ("it is better style to avoid both apostrophe and *s* with acronyms," as in *CRS policies, HUD reorganization, GPO style*).

(#81, 11/82)

■ By No Means

Almost every time you omit even a single negative, you help your reader. *When the flash flood struck, there were no cars or people on the road.* An instant picture of cars and people filling the road comes to mind. Better: "When the flash flood struck, the road was empty."

"Say only what you want the reader to see," cautions novelist C.J. Cherryh. Wise advice. President Nixon said, "I'm not a crook," and readers remembered *crook.*

What do you see here? *The Senate Appropriations Committee rejected an amendment that would have killed the B-1 bomber.* What echoes in the mind is *killed the B-1 bomber.* What slips from the mind is *Committee rejected.* Both *killed* and *rejected* are negatives. When you must use such negatives, a couple of strategies will improve clarity.

- Break the sentence into two sentences. Put as few negative ideas as possible in each one. *An amendment was proposed to kill the B-1 bomber. The Senate . . . Committee rejected it.*
- Recast the sentence in the order events happened. The mind then has less backing and filling to do. *An amendment that would have killed the B-1 bomber was rejected by the . . . Committee.*

Even one negative sometimes demands rereading for understanding. The brain seems to stick as it shifts from forward to reverse to forward. In a British study of tests, the removal of simple negative forms greatly improved the scores of the test takers. One chemistry question originally read, "Which one of the following could *not* be the atomic weight of [three given isotopes of] the element?" Only 50 percent of the pupils got the correct answer.

The question was changed to "Which one of the following could be the atomic weight?" Now 62 percent got it right.

We often make our readers flunk reading. Consider the reader wading through the swamps of three negatives in the following passage. I have added italics.

> When you drive above 55 mph, you *reduce* your savings on fuel, of course—and you also *decrease* your ability to *avoid* crashing with another car in a fatal accident.

Here's another, also with three negatives. I failed to make sense of it:

> The justices *struck down*, 9-0, campaign-finance *restrictions* that a lower court said *prevented* national political parties from assuming some fund-raising power. . . .

Any sentence that begins with a version of *the court overturned a lower court's denial of* has the reader in deep trouble. Almost always, the higher court's overturning is the news, but let it come at the end of the sentence telling what was overturned.

Try this one (emphasis added):

> The First Circuit has now become the second federal appeals court to hold explicitly that 'communications *prohibited* by a protective order *restricting* the dissemination of information obtained through court-ordered deposition qualify for protection under the First Amendment.'

Can you tell what journalists won with that momentous decision? This sentence suffers from its lawyer language, nouns and adjectives made from verbs (*communications*, *protective*, *dissemination*, *information*, *deposition*, *protection*), but its main fault lies in the reversals the reader must do to get past the maze of two negatives.

—Ethel Grodzins Romm, in *Editor & Publisher*,
Jan. 23, 1982, reprinted with permission (#78, 9/82)

Test Yourself

Can You Spell the Top 50?

The 50 words in this test are among the most frequently misspelled words in English. What's more, these words are usually misspelled the same way by everyone.

Choose the correct spelling, a or b, for each word in the list below.

A *below-average* speller will get only 6 of the 50 right. The *average* speller will feel certain about the first 15 but have an even chance of being right on the rest. The *superior* speller will do well on the first 40 and after that will be wrong half the time. The *perfect or near-perfect* speller will know how to spell all 50 words. Words are listed in order of difficulty.

1. (a) grammer	(b) grammar
2. (a) arguement	(b) argument
3. (a) supprise	(b) surprise
4. (a) achieve	(b) acheive
5. (a) annoint	(b) anoint
6. (a) definately	(b) definitely
7. (a) separate	(b) seperate
8. (a) desirable	(b) desireable
9. (a) developement	(b) development
10. (a) existence	(b) existance
11. (a) pronounciation	(b) pronunciation
12. (a) occasion	(b) occassion
13. (a) assistant	(b) assisstant
14. (a) repitition	(b) repetition
15. (a) privilege	(b) priviledge
16. (a) dependant	(b) dependent
17. (a) irresistible	(b) irresistable
18. (a) consensus	(b) concensus
19. (a) accommodate	(b) accomodate
20. (a) occurence	(b) occurrence
21. (a) concience	(b) conscience
22. (a) commitment	(b) committment
23. (a) embarrass	(b) embarass
24. (a) indispensible	(b) indispensable
25. (a) allotted	(b) alotted
26. (a) liason	(b) liaison

27. (a) proceed (b) procede
28. (a) harrass (b) harass
29. (a) perseverance (b) perseverence
30. (a) ecstacy (b) ecstasy
31. (a) antiquated (b) antequated
32. (a) insistent (b) insistant
33. (a) exhillarate (b) exhilarate
34. (a) vacuum (b) vaccuum
35. (a) ridiculous (b) rediculous
36. (a) nickel (b) nickle
37. (a) oscilate (b) oscillate
38. (a) tyrannous (b) tyranous
39. (a) drunkenness (b) drunkeness
40. (a) dissention (b) dissension
41. (a) connoiseur (b) connoisseur
42. (a) sacreligious (b) sacrilegious
43. (a) battalion (b) batallion
44. (a) prerogative (b) perogative
45. (a) iridescent (b) irridescent
46. (a) inadvertent (b) inadvertant
47. (a) geneology (b) genealogy
48. (a) villify (b) vilify
49. (a) innoculate (b) inoculate
50. (a) dilettante (b) dilletante

(#13, 9/78)

Answers

1b, 2b, 3b, 4a, 5b, 6b, 7a, 8a, 9b, 10a, 11b, 12a, 13a, 14b, 15a, 16b, 17a, 18a, 19a, 20b, 21b, 22a, 23a, 24b, 25a, 26b, 27a, 28b, 29a, 30b, 31a, 32a, 33b, 34a, 35a, 36a, 37b, 38a, 39a, 40b (although *Merriam-Webster* lists choice a also), 41b, 42b, 43a, 44a, 45a, 46a, 47b, 48b, 49b, 50a.

(#14, 10/78)

Mnemonic Spelling

Can't remember how to spell *consensus*? Does *inoculate* have one *n* or two? Remember Roy G. Biv as the mnemonic for the color spectrum? Here are some spelling mnemonics, courtesy of *The Eye*.

affect, as v., *a*lter, sw*a*y; as n., psychological st*a*te
effect, as v., *e*stablish; as n., *e*nd r*e*sult
all right, two words; remember its antonym, *all wrong*
anoint, use *an oint*ment
balloon, two *l*'s as in ba*ll*
battalion, two *t*'s, one *l*, as in *battle*
capitol, building where state or federal government functions are carried out, *o* as in d*o*me
Connecticut, first I *connect*, then *I cut*
consensus, a con*sens*us makes *sense*
deductible, *i* as in *IRS*
dependent, take depen*dent*s to the *dent*ist
descendant, descend*an*ts come from *an*cestors
February, "*Br*! It's cold."
friend, a fri*end* to the *end*
grammar, bad gram*mar* will *mar* your progress
gray, *a* as in *A*merica
grey, the English spelling, *e* as in *E*ngland
inoculate, one *n*, one *c*, as in i*n*ject
memento, *mem* as in *mem*ory
minuscule, contains *minus*
piece, a *pie*ce of *pie*
privilege, a privi*leg*e gives you a *leg* up
recommend/recommendation, contain the word *commend*
rhythm, divide the six letters into two groups, each with an *h* in the middle
separate, break into *par*ts
stationary, st*a*nd still
stationery, writ*e* on it

vaccine/vaccination, the serum is measured in *cc*'s
vacuum, one *c* as in vacant
villain, the villain is *in* his *villa*

Silly but Memorable

May I share my mnemonic device for spelling harass, morass, and embarrass? Mr. and Mrs. Rass's child is learning to talk. She calls her father Ha (Ha Rass) and her mother Mo (Mo Rass). If you ask what family she is a member of she says, "I'm an Embar of the Rass family" (Embar Rass).

—Maria Bente (#113, 1/85)

More on Variant Spellings

Is the square cap worn by ecclesiastics a *biretta*, a *berretta*, a *birretta*, or a *beretta*? Is aluminum silicate *feldspar* or *felspar*? Is it *collectable* or *collectible*? Variant spellings can be the bane of a copyeditor's existence. To help sort out questions such as these, the National Council of Teachers of English has published a revised edition of *Variant Spellings in Modern American Dictionaries*.*

The dictionaries compared are the *American Heritage*, *Webster's New Collegiate*, *Webster's New World*, *Random House*, and *Funk & Wagnall's Standard College*. A fanciful example of the variety of variants is the following sentence, cited from the introduction: "In a *cozy* house *cater-cornered* from the palace, a finicky *caliph* who maintained that a *jinni* had revealed to him the secrets of the *cabala*, spent much of his time smoking *panatelas*—sometimes *kef*—and training his pet *parakeet*." Given the number of variant spellings of the underscored words, the sentence could be written 11,197,440 ways and still be correct.

(#111, 12/84)

**Variant Spellings* can be ordered from the National Council of Teachers of English, 1111 Kenyon Road, Urbana, IL 61801.

Black Eye

Yoga eases bachache, India's spaceman says

We have a lot of symphony for him.

—Submitted by Jeane Schultz, *Miami Herald*, April 24, 1984 (#105, 7/84)

How to Tell an -ible from an -able

Only a few hundred English words end in -ible, but they cause thousands of spelling mistakes daily.

There are no rules to tell you how to distinguish all the -ible from the -able words, but a few hints and a little etymology will help with most of the troublesome words.

Three Useful Rules

Rule 1. Use -able if the corresponding noun ends in -ation.

Corollary: Use -ant (not -ent), -ance (not -ence), -ancy (not -ency) if the corresponding noun ends in -ation. Examples: information/informant, domination/dominant/dominance, occupation/occupant/occupancy.

Memory device: Dr. Mabel is able to do the ablation.

This rule works for hundreds of words. The only exception I can find is a false one: sensation/sensible; the corresponding noun for sensible is sension (rare).

Among the spelling demons this rule exorcises:

- dispensation/dispensable/indispensable
- termination/terminable/interminable
- limitation/limitable/illimitable.

Rule 2. Use -ible if the suffix comes after soft *c* or soft *g*. Use -able if the suffix comes after soft *ce* or soft *ge*.

Memory device:

It is I (Who, me?),
It is I — B — L — E
  When soft *c* and soft *g*
  Are not followed by *e*.

Examples:

- deducible, forcible, eligible, intelligible
- effaceable, peaceable, changeable, chargeable.

Sorry, this rule does not help you decide between spellings such as forcible and forceable.

Rule 3. Use -ible if the suffix comes after *s* and if the corresponding noun ends in -sion.

Memory device: Sybil sions (shuns) her siblings.

This rule takes care of at least 125 words—a large proportion of those in -ible. There are very few exceptions.

Examples:

- accession/accessible/inaccessible
- admission/admissible/inadmissible
- repression/repressible/irrepressible
- vision/visible/invisible.

Exceptions:

- excisable, intraversable, manumisable, professable, versable
- revise/revision/revisable and supervise/supervision/supervisable (because revisible and supervisible mean visible again and highly visible).

Some words that follow rule 3 are also correct with -able: confusable and confusible, discussable and discussible, pressable and pressible, transfusable and transfusible. (*Webster's Third New International Dictionary* recognizes widespread interchange of -able and -ible suffixes: admissable, admissible; collectable, collectible; permissable, permissible; feasable, feasible.)

Rule 3 does not account for words with no *s* before the suffix:

- extension/extensible, but extendable
- persuasion/persuasible, but persuadable.

Latin and French Origins

Among the layers of languages that form English are Latin (from the Roman domination of England and from the Classical Revival of the Renaissance) and French (from the Norman Conquest).

Latin has four conjugations. The infinitives of verbs in the first conjugation end in -are; in the second, -ere; in the third, -ere; and in the fourth, -ire.

English words ending in -ible derive chiefly from Latin -ere, -ere, and -ire verbs, which form their adjectives in -ibilis.

Many -able words come from Latin -are (-abilis) verbs and from Latin by way of French. (In French, the regular ending -able is used for adjectives derived from all Latin verbs.)

-Able is a living suffix, used for nearly all coined words, many of which enter the dictionaries. -Able transforms verbs, nouns, and phrases to adjectives:

- The new grass is high enough to be mowable.
- His face is portraitable.
- Her house is not get-at-able by bus.

Sidelights

- Far more words end in -able than in -ible.
- A few words have different meanings in -ible and -able: passible (from passion—feeling, suffering), passable (from passage or pass); conversible (from conversion), conversable (from conversation).
- -able adjectives convert to -ably adverbs and -ability nouns (duration/durable/durably/durability); -ible converts to -ibly and - ibility (accession/accessible/accessibly/accessibility).
- For individual words that do not fit the rules, you can invent your own memory devices; for example: deductible takes an *i* as in *I*RS.

—Peggy Smith (#33, 10/79)

Letter to the Editor

-ible and -able Rules Not Comprehensive

Thanks ever so much for the article "How to Tell an -ible From an -able" in Issue 33 of *The Editorial Eye*. At first I thought that I might report your three rules in an end-of-page filler in the Feb. issue of *Word Ways*, but upon looking into the subject in a bit more detail this weekend, I find that it is an exceedingly involved one.

In particular, I decided to see how well your rules did against the commonest -able and -ible words, so I drew a sample of 115 different -ables and 37 -ibles from Kucera and Francis's list of one million words in English-language publications during 1961 (in particular, I took all -able and -ible words that appeared three times or more in this corpus).

In evaluation, I was somewhat strict about insisting that the corresponding -ation or -sion word should be known to the average (educated) reader (for example, I think that "sension" is so rare that the etymologically flawed "sensation" would be applied instead); on the other hand, I was liberal in allowing close relatives instead of exact substitutes (for example, "accreditation" instead of "creditation" to verify credit*a*ble).

Your rules are very accurate when they apply, but (alas) they applied to only about one-third of the -able and -ible words, leaving an awful lot to be covered by individual memory devices.

Anyway, I am now considering writing a full-dress article detailing these findings, with the likely conclusion that a simple -able vs. -ible set of rules that is comprehensive as well is almost impossible to find.

Is it possible that the discredited Furness rule about -able words remaining words when the suffix is dropped might be revived but only for cases in which the core word is a verb, and with the understanding that verbs ending in *e* must have the letter replaced (as in adorable—ador*e*)? In conjunction with your rules, this would help a lot.

—A. Ross Eckler (#36, 12/79)

III. USAGE

A Five-Star Book for Editors

SUCCESS WITH WORDS: A Guide to the American Language, prepared in association with Peter Davies. Pleasantville, NY: The Reader's Digest Association, Inc., 1983, 602 pp.

Eureka! I have found the book on language and usage I've been looking for. You may be skeptical of its authority because of its publisher's plebeian reputation, but you must admit that *Reader's Digest* understands plain English. And you may be put off by its title, but its subtitle explains its true worth.

You may also be repelled by its hard-sell, low-brow, direct-mail promotion:

> When it comes time to speak your mind or write a note, are you afraid to use that one zingy *right* word? . . . You don't have to be frustrated and insecure about words any longer. *Reader's Digest brings you new confidence.*

I have the feeling that *Reader's Digest* commissioned a peanut-butter sandwich, and when it got a gourmet meal it went ahead with its peanut-butter sandwich promotion. (Its ad in *The New Yorker* has more class and comes closer to my view of the book: "The most interesting thing to happen to the study of the American language since Noah Webster picked up his pen," it says. Well, let's not forget Mencken.)

Usage Problems

On the usage problems of standard English, the book stands with the great ones and above the good ones. It's as learned as Fowler, Nicholson, or Follett, but warmer and easier to use. It's as witty and practical as Bernstein, but more comprehensive. It's far better typographically than Copperud's irritating long lines and small type. And where Flesch is imperative, this book is courteous, explaining its recommendations so you can take them or leave them, knowing exactly what you're doing.

For example, a column on *center around* discusses the image of the circle with its center, radius, and circumference; tells us "we know that a *center*, of all things, cannot be *around* anything," but that the expression "doesn't seem to cause any trouble or misunderstanding—until the schoolteacher points out its awful illogic"; cites the phrase's use by Walter Pater, David Cecil, and Truman Capote, among others; and ends with this recommendation: "Relax. The logic of language is not as literal as the logic of the schoolroom."

Editorial Style

On the choices of editorial style, *Success With Words* has the fairest and wisest discussions I know of. More than five columns on abbreviation include the advice, "When in doubt, spell it out." An entry of 14 columns on capitalization explains that "capitalization gives importance, distinction, and emphasis"; that "one's use of capitalization is likely to vary with one's perspective"; that "each alternative may have its appropriate uses"; and that "effective writers will view it as a flexible instrument of style that can give special force and vigor to their writing."

An entry of five and one-half columns on number style starts like this:

> The key question here (which many people cheerfully neglect to ask) is whether to express a number in figures or in words. Many writers simply follow their whims; there is no pattern and no coherence to the way they treat numbers. However, even professional copyeditors who care about such things—when confronted with a style decision in this area—have been known to become paralyzed. Some simply turn numb. (Some even turn number.)

Encyclopedic Coverage

The book is an encyclopedia compared with those that cover only usage and literary style. You will find entries on the following topics:

- All the North American regional dialects, including Hawaiian English (*hybolic* means pompous, bombastic), Central and Prairie Canadian (*swither* means to hesitate), and Pennsylvania German-English (*smutz* means to kiss or caress).
- Sources of our vocabulary, including Old English (*answer* comes from *andswaru*, literally back-swearing), Latin (*stupid* comes, via French, from *stupidus*, meaning dazed), and Japanese (*honcho* is a Japanese word meaning squad leader).

- Fallacy, with 11 columns on deceptive logic "to help us understand and guard against the subtle seductions of rhetoric . . . in a world awash with misleading rhetoric."
- Literary forms and styles such as figures of speech, including six and one-half columns on the glories and abuses of metaphor: "Perhaps the British writer George Orwell had the last word on mixed metaphors. They are, he observed, 'a sure sign that the author is not interested in what he is saying.' "
- Contributors to the language, including Shakespeare, Noah Webster, and the Bible (with a chart comparing leading Bible translations).
- Sports terms, including those of golf (now I know the difference between a *birdie* and an *eagle*) and horseracing (so that's where *parlay* comes from).
- Gender treatment, including several enlighted and useful articles. For example, a column on *chairman* points out that because *chairperson* is sometimes applied to female officeholders only, its use at best "suggests a halfhearted attempt at change" and "at worst, it turns *person* into a code word for *woman*, suggesting that the *-man* word is the term that bestows real status." The article then discusses "the magic of metonymy" through which *Capitol Hill* means the U.S. Congress, which meets there; the *White House* means the President, who lives there; and *the chair* can mean the presiding officer who sits there, a use "standard since the 17th century." The recommendation:

Chair is a better choice than *chairperson* because it is shorter and because it has been in the language so long. Or, entirely different titles may be used, such as *president* (of an organization), *presiding officer* (at a meeting), *convener* (of a convention), or *coordinator* (of a project or committee).

- Special vocabularies such as political, legal, heraldic, equestrian, and publishing terms. The publishing glossary has this delightful introduction:

> The publishing world has long been viewed by the general public as one inhabited by gentle, professional types—an ivory tower. It is perhaps in reaction to this oversimplified conception that people in publishing have, over the years, developed a professional jargon of peculiarly violent cast.
>
> One begins with relatively harmless maritime images—of galleys and mastheads, of rivers and casting off—but before long one encounters broadsides, sinkage, and widows.
>
> Back on shore there are dummies and nuts running around, armed with bullets and slugs, and other inferior characters (some with bastard titles) on

the skids and running ragged in gutters. There are linecuts and bleeds, cropping and blind stamping. Operative terms in this world include *kill*, *delete*, and *blow up*. Chase leads to crash and lockup, and then inexorably to hanging heads and dead matter. For the doubtful, there is foul proof. But for the truly fortunate, there is perfect binding.

Recommendation

Buy this book; browse through it; enjoy it; learn from it; put it with the other classics in the genre; and use it as your first reference.

—Peggy Smith (#95, 10/83)

Absolute Qualities

Most editors know it is generally unwise to modify *unique,* but other adjectives that denote absolute qualities also need watching. My list includes *vital, essential, critical, favorite, extreme, perfect, excellent, complete,* and *adequate*.

Of course things can be *nearly perfect* or *almost complete,* but *very vital* or *particularly essential* are tautologies. Similarly, a patient's condition is either critical or it isn't; to describe it as *extremely critical* is redundant.

Authorities differ on the degree to which they accept comparison of absolutes. Fowler's *Modern English Usage* states that *unique* can tolerate *quite, almost, nearly, really, surely, perhaps, absolutely,* or *in some respects,* but not *more, most, very, somewhat, rather,* or *comparatively*.

Opdycke, in *Harper's English Grammar,* notes that many absolutes, when used in a "relative or approximate sense," are compared by the best writers and speakers. "If you say that a thing is more complete or more perfect than another, you may quite properly mean . . . that neither is absolutely complete or perfect, but that one is more nearly complete or perfect than the other."

Wilson Follett's *Modern American Usage,* edited by Barzun, cautions against comparison or partition of absolutes in general. For example, this source says that "*essential* means *indispensable,* and does not admit of *more* or *less,* or even of *so.*"

Yet, with respect to *perfect,* Follett/Barzun notes that the Constitution's preamble speaks of "creating a more perfect union" and continues, "Usage has in fact authorized *more perfect* and *less perfect,* it being understood, perhaps, that nothing on earth achieves perfection and that the degrees of approximation to it deserve to be named."

It strikes me that *equal* belongs in the list of absolutes, and perhaps that the modern comparisons of it (*more equal* treatment under the law, for example) are probably acceptable under the same general reasoning that Follett/Barzun applies to *perfect.*

Sometimes the writer can replace the problem word with one that can readily be modified. For example, one can use the *most important* of the points instead of the *most vital.*

—Priscilla Taylor (#30, 7/79)

■ Tricky Diction

Iran, commentators and politicians tell us, has been flaunting international law. "Flaunt" or "flout"—the confusion of one word for another—is termed an impropriety and is a problem of diction—the choice of the correct, clear, effective word.

Mrs. Malaprop in Sheridan's *The Rivals* is the archetype of the users of ludicrous impropriety, known as malapropism. "You lead and I'll precede you," she says. "If I reprehend anything in this world, it is the use of my oracular tongue, and a nice derangement of epitaphs."

Modern American Usage by Wilson Follett, edited by Jacques Barzun, lists "dangerous pairs" of easily confused words. "The richer a language is and the more symmetrical its 'architecture,' the more pairs and triplets will occur to betray the unseeing . . . [but] all can be differentiated with the aid of a dictionary," the book points out.

Many other books on usage discuss commonly confused words, such as lie and lay; hanged and hung; emigrant and immigrant. Some improprieties are simply a matter of misspelling a homonym—altogether, all together; it's, its; born, borne.

"All I Know Is What I Read in the Papers . . ."

Professor Philip Herzbrun of Georgetown University has discovered one way wrong words are perpetuated.

Herzbrun noticed that students often defended their misuse of language by saying that they had "seen it in the newspaper" (and occasionally providing citations).

When Herzbrun also found that far more students were regular readers of newspapers than of magazines or unassigned books, he decided to monitor usage in *The Washington Post,* the paper most read by his students.

From the *Post,* Herzbrun compiled a list of improprieties that coincided with those in freshman compositions, excluding any one-time occurrence from either source. He disregarded "vagaries of verbal taste"—imprecise usage such as "amount" for "number," "less" for "fewer," "media" for "medium," and "aggravate" for "annoy." Such woolliness, he felt, did not cause definite misunderstanding.

Each entry on Herzbrun's final list was an example of the obliteration of a distinct meaning "which must be preserved if sanity is to prevail in the institution of language." (As if to confirm Herzbrun's worst fears, when an article about his work appeared in *Georgetown Today* magazine, it was headed "The Literary Crisis at Ground Level Zero"—a misuse of "literary" for "literacy," followed by a heavy-handed mixed metaphor.)

Although Herzbrun disclaimed any attempt to blame either newspapers or students, *The Washington Post* was concerned enough to reprint part of his list. Even more concerned, we reprint it all:

THE HERZBRUN LIST
(in alphabetical order, mistaken word first)

abrogated-arrogated
adverse-averse
affect-effect
erring-errant
eruption-irruption
essay-assay

appraise-appris(z)e
assignment-assignation
avoid-evade
beside-besides
bite-bight
compliment-complement
contemptible-contemptuous
council-counsel-consul
credible-creditable-credulous
defies-deifies
delusion-illusion
demure-demur
depreciate-deprecate
discrete-discreet
dispense-disburse
disprove-disapprove
dissemble-disassemble
distinguished-distinctive
economical-economic
emerged-immersed
eminent-immanent-imminent
enormity-vastness or hugeness
equivalence-equivocation
forthright-forthcoming
founding-foundering
fulsome-abundant
gentile-genteel-gentle
haul-hale (into court)
historical-historic
hitherto-heretofore
homogenous-homogeneous
imply-infer
indite-indict
inequity-iniquity
Jacobin-Jacobite-Jacobean
libel-liable
evoke-invoke
exalt-exult
excessively-exceedingly
exorcized-excised
expiate-expatiate
flaunt-flout
loathe-loath
luxurious-luxuriant
martial-marital
mislead-misled
moral-morale
obtuse-abstruse
omnivorous-omnifarious
oppose-appose
parameter-perimeter or border
peaceful-peaceable
persecuted-prosecuted
persistent-insistent
perspicuous-perspicacious
phase-faze
pour-pore
precipitous-precipitate
preclude-include
predominate-predominant
presently-now
presentment-presentiment
rebound-redound
sanguinary-sanguine
sensual-sensuous
site-cite
slight-sleight
specially-especially
toxin-tocsin
troop-troupe
verbiage-wording

(#38, 1/80)

Test Yourself

On Anatomical Adjectives

Match the adjectives with the nouns in the following lists:

Nouns				Adjectives	
1. arm	____	14. head	____	a. aural	n. hemal
2. back	____	15. kidney	____	b. brachial	o. hepatic
3. bladder	____	16. lip	____	c. buccal	p. labial
4. blood	____	17. liver	____	d. capillary	q. lingual
5. bone	____	18. mouth	____	e. carpal	r. oral
6. cheek	____	19. nose	____	f. caudal	s. osteal
7. chest	____	20. skin	____	g. cephalic	t. pectoral
8. ear	____	21. sole	____	h. ciliary	u. pedal
9. eyelash	____	22. tail	____	i. cubital	v. plantar
10. foot	____	23. tongue	____	j. dental	w. renal
11. forearm	____	24. tooth	____	k. dermal	x. rhinal
12. forehead	____	25. wrist	____	l. dorsal	y. vesical
13. hair	____			m. frontal	

Answers

1. b	6. c	11. i	16. p	21. v
2. l	7. t	12. m	17. o	22. f
3. y	8. a	13. d	18. r	23. q
4. n	9. h	14. g	19. x	24. j
5. s	10. u	15. w	20. k	25. e

(#95, 10/83)

Fowler's Fanciful Names for Errors to Avoid

"The conferring of a name on a type of mistake, making it recognizable and avoidable, is worthwhile if the mistake is common," said language authority H.W. Fowler. Here are some Fowlerisms from *Modern English Usage* to help you avoid grammatical and stylistic errors.

Abstractitis. Giving such prominence to abstractions as to make vague who is doing what to whom, and even to cause perplexity as to what is being said. Example: "The examination of the problems concerning the structure and working relationships in the organization has brought in discussions about balanced decentralization versus centralization."

Battered ornaments. Stale literary pretensions, including

- elegant variations (labored avoidance of repetition, as "daughter of Eve" for "woman")
- outworn metonymies ("the grape" for "wine")
- foreign tidbits ("*dolce far niente*")
- hackneyed phrases ("at this point in time"; "in terms of")

Cannibalism. A mixed construction in which a word is logically required twice but is used only once, thereby swallowing its own kind: "The Assembly was undecided as to which country the sanctions should be applied." (The preposition "to" has swallowed a second "to".)

Cast-iron idiom recast. Changes in established idiom that create awkwardness or impair meaning: "He contented himself by (instead of 'with') saying . . ."; "He had every motive in (instead of 'for') doing so."

Legerdemain with two senses. The use of a word twice in the same sentence (or of a word that has a double job to do) without observing that the sense required the second time is different from the sense in which the word was first used: "As a child he showed no sign of becoming the musical genius for which his name will long be remembered." ("Genius," the antecedent of "which," is a person, not a quality.)

Object shuffling. Failure to discriminate between verbs requiring a direct object and verbs requiring a noun attached to them by a preposition: "instill with courage" (for "instill courage"); "prefix a name with a title" (for "prefix a title to a name").

Out of the frying-pan. Illogicalities arising from efforts to avoid what are assumed to be faults in grammar: "Praise is welcome, by no matter whom bestowed" (to avoid ending a sentence with a preposition); "When the story comes objectively to be told" (to avoid what has been mistaken for a split infinitive).

Pairs and snares. Words likely to be confused: "consequent" and "consequential," "definite" and "definitive," "purport" and "purpose."

Side-slip. Diversion of a sentence into a mixed construction by the disturbing influence of what has been said on what is about to be said, often brought about by the word "of": "The primary object was not the destruction of the ship, or of the ammunition, or of whatever military cargo was there, or even of killing or capturing the crew."

Sturdy indefensibles. Idioms that, although well understood, fail the test of grammar or logic: "It's me"; "Don't take that too literally"; "She's the best swimmer of anyone I know."

Swapping horses. Changing a word's sense in the middle of a sentence (as in legerdemain with two senses). Changing a sentence's subject: "Half of the truck's weight could be reduced and yet carry the same load." Shifting from one construction to another in the middle of a sentence: "Knowing your commitment and compassion, your humanitarian principles and your interest in protecting individual liberty and freedom have made an outstanding contribution to furthering the cause of human dignity."

Unequal yokefellows. Mistakes in the completion of constructions: "Hardly had we closed the shutters than the storm broke" ("than" instead of "when"); "Their ages ranged between 6 to 60" ("to" instead of "and"); "Either he did not know or was lying" ("Either he" instead of "He either").

Walled-up object. An object of two verbs that is enclosed between one of the verbs and a phrase belonging exclusively to that verb: "We urge all readers to buy and make this book their own"; "A reward will be paid to the person who finds and returns the purse to its owner."

Wardour street. The affectation of rarely used, poetic, or archaic expressions to establish the writer's claim to taste and style (named for a London street once known for antique furniture): "albeit"; "anent"; "aught"; "haply"; "thither."

(#45, 7/80)

Black Eyes

Experiments with Parents

SUBSTANCE ABUSE AWARENESS SEMINARS

WHO: Adolescents Experimenting with Drugs and Their Parents

—*McLean High and SPTA Report to Parents*, contributed by Lois Dean

(#44, 6/80)

Literati Lean Less on Latin Language

Latin words and phrases are losing either their italics or their place in many nonlegal publications in the United States. Relatively obscure expressions, such as *ceteris paribus,* are rarely accepted now, and many common ones, such as *ad nauseam,* have become naturalized and are no longer italicized.

The All-Out Attackers

William Strunk, Jr., and E.B. White (*The Elements of Style*) strongly oppose Latin terms:

> The writer will often find it convenient or necessary to borrow from other languages. Some writers, however, from sheer exuberance or a desire to show off, sprinkle their work liberally with foreign expressions with no regard for the reader's comfort. It is a bad habit. Write in English.

Even in scientific writing, tolerance is waning. Lois DeBakey, long an advocate of clear medical and scientific writing, denounces the use of Latin or other foreign expressions in scientific reports as "an offensive affectation." She charges, "When the reader sees such artifices, he suspects that the writer is using a fancy veneer to camouflage inferior substance."

The University of Chicago Press Approach

The Chicago Manual of Style recommends printing most common Latin expressions (*ibid*., *et al*., *ca*., *passim*) in roman type. In citations, it recommends that the short title of a book or article replace *op. cit*. and *loc. cit*. after an author's name—a suggestion readers will welcome, especially when the author is responsible for more than one work cited.

Chicago also suggests that *e.g., i.e.,* and *etc*. be used inside parentheses or in tables or footnotes. *For example, that is,* or *and so forth* (or *and the like*) should be substituted in running text.

Chicago recommends that *sic* continue to be italicized, however, because of the word's "peculiar use in quoted matter."

GPO Style

The *Government Printing Office Style Manual* recommends that, in nonlegal work, words such as *ante, post, infra,* and *supra* be italicized only when part of a legal citation. Otherwise these terms, as well as the abbreviations *id., ibid*., *op. cit*., *et seq*., and other foreign words, phrases, and their abbreviations are to be printed in roman type.

The Opposing Point of View

To daunt your readers, you can ignore the plain English advocates and stud your prose with foreign phrases.

Latin, says *The Phrase Dropper's Handbook* by Beaudouin and Mattlin (Doubleday, 1976), is the queen of snob languages. Latin helps you "to keep up with the sophisticates, to put down the phonies, to put in with the scholars, and to get out alive."

Among the Latin maxims the book recommends are *Timeo Danaos et dona ferentes* (I fear the Greeks even when bearing gifts)—useful for foreign affairs discussions; *Quis custodiet ipsos custodes*? (Who shall guard the guards themselves?)—applicable to everything from police corruption to the teaching of English; and *De gustibus non est disputandum* (There is no disputing about tastes)—equally applicable to those who recoil from Latin and those who use it to seem more learned than they are.

—Priscilla Taylor (#37, 1/80)

Test Yourself

On Latin Abbreviations

Spell out each of the following Latin abbreviations and give an acceptable English substitute:

1. e.g. 2. et al. 3. et seq. 4. ibid. 5. id. 6. i.e. 7. loc. cit.
8. N.B. 9. op. cit. 10. q.v. 11. sc. 12. s.v. 13. viz.

Translate the following:

14. ad hominem 15. a posteriori 16. a priori 17. ceteris paribus
18. de novo 19. in extenso 20. in extremis 21. infra 22. modus operandi
23. pari passu 24. passim 25. per contra 26. supra

(#37, 1/80)

Answers

1. *e.g.*—exempli gratia, for example.
2. *et al.*—et alii, and others; —et alibi, and elsewhere.
3. *et seq.*—et sequens, and the following.
4. *ibid.*—ibidem, in the same place.
5. *id.*—idem, the same.
6. *i.e.*—id est, that is.
7. *loc. cit.*—loco citato, in the place cited.

(#38, 1/80)

8. *N.B.*—nota bene, note well.
9. *op. cit.*—opere citato, in the work cited.
10. *q.v.*—quod vide, which see.
11. *sc.*—scilicet, namely.
12. *s.v.*—sub verbo, under a word (or —sub voce, heading).
13. *viz.*—videlicet, namely.
14. *ad hominem*, appealing to a person's feelings or prejudices rather than to the intellect; in logic, a supposed argument against something but in fact an attack on the person rather than the merits of his position.
15. *a posteriori*, inductive.
16. *a priori*, deductive; presumptive.
17. *ceteris paribus*, other things being equal.
18. *de novo*, over again; anew.
19. *in extenso*, at full length.
20. *in extremis*, in extreme circumstances; at the point of death.
21. *infra*, below.
22. *modus operandi*, a method of procedure.
23. *pari passu*, at an equal rate or pace.
24. *passim*, here and there, used particularly in footnote references when no specific page reference is given.
25. *per contra*, on the contrary.
26. *supra*, above.

■ Identical To/Identical With

Which is correct—"identical *to*" or "identical *with*"? The language research service that G.&C. Merriam Company offers to owners of its *Webster's New Collegiate Dictionary* accepts both usages:

Since the meaning of the word is not affected by the use of *to* or *with,* we merely need to count the number of citations for each usage. At present, it appears that *with* has a 2 to 1 edge, but *identical to* is quite firmly established in standard English. . . . Either choice, in the absence of other "rules," will do just fine.

(#47, 9/80)

Identical With or Identical To?

With all due respect to the G.&C. Merriam Company, frequency of use (number of citations) does not dictate the *correctness* of usage. I've picked this bone with them before, and their response is interesting: "We don't pretend to be an authority on the use of language" (a paraphrase of Dr. Fred Mish). To whom I asked—and continue to ask—"then to whom can we turn?"

I ask you to find someone willing to take a position of authority (I hope that that authority is not only willing but able). When you find that "someone," please share the knowledge with us.

—John Holtz

"To whom can we turn? As long as we do not have the counterpart of the French Academy, we have a changing language. You can take your pick from among the able people who take positions on questions of usage. Here, for example, are opinions on the problem from two respected authorities.

IDENTICAL   Takes preposition *with* or *to*.

—*The Careful Writer,* by Theodore M. Bernstein (Atheneum, 1979)

identical. . . .Idiom calls for *with*.

—*Modern American Usage,* by Wilson Follett, edited and completed by Jacques Barzun and others (Warner, 1974)

(#49, 10/80)

Is "Try And" Good Usage?

The consensus overwhelmingly validates *try and.*
—Roy H. Copperud, *American Usage and Style, The Consensus* (Van Nostrand Reinhold, 1980)

Yes, But. . . There is in fact a shade of difference between [*try and* and *try to*]. *Try to* is unmistakably purposive. Nobody thinks of saying *I will try and climb Mount Everest*: I will *try to* is compulsory. But the very casualness of form in *try and* makes it worth preserving for occasions when no definite time or effort of will is stipulated. *He knows we want one; he'll try and pick one up for us.*
—Wilson Follett, edited by Jacques Barzun,
Modern American Usage (Warner, 1974)

Not Always Use of *try and* colloquially, especially when it adds force to the meaning of a sentence, has gained some acceptance. . . . But unless they are quoting someone, journalists working for newspapers and most magazines will always use *try to.*
—E.L. Callihan,
Grammar for Journalists (Chilton, 1969)

No *Try.* Takes the infinitive: "try to mend it," not "try *and* mend it."
—William Strunk, Jr., and E.B. White
The Elements of Style (Macmillan, 1979)

(#56, 3/81)

Compare to, Compare with

What are the appropriate times to use compare *to* and compare *with*? The Language Research Service offered by G.&C. Merriam Company to owners of *Webster's New Collegiate Dictionary* has this to say:

> The general, more or less traditional, rule . . . has been [to] use *compare with* when things are examined for similarities or differences and *compare to* when one thing is likened to another or shown to be in the same class with another. . . .
>
> This traditional distinction . . . does not reflect the actual state of language used by professional writers.
>
> An analysis done some years ago . . . for *compare to* and *compare with* in the different senses for the period of the early 1940s showed just about an equal number of examples of each use. In the 30 years since then, the files show that usage is still almost evenly divided between *compare to* and *compare with* in the sense of "liken." Yet if we examine only the writings since 1960, we find that all of the citations for this use are *compare to*. Maybe the effect of the usage books is finally being seen. In the sense of "evaluate two things to determine where they are alike and where different," the *compare with* examples have a very slight edge (only about 5 percent), but the margin of difference seems to be rapidly closing.
>
> So from our standpoint, there is no appreciable difference in usage between these, and either is perfectly suitable—unless a particular publishing house has its own traditional rules.

(#57, 4/81)

Ask *The Eye:* How to Use Comprise

The Question: How to Use "Comprise"?

Do you think that in an issue of *The Eye* you could deal with the proper usage of the word "comprise"? I think it is one of the most misused words I've come across.

—Amy Berk, Chicago, IL

The Answer

For a capsule definition of a disappearing nicety, it's hard to improve on Strunk and White (*The Elements of Style*):

Comprise. Literally, *embrace.* A zoo *comprises* mammals, reptiles, and birds (because it embraces, or includes, them). But animals do not comprise (embrace) a zoo—they *constitute* a zoo.

(The misuse has reached some dictionaries, which list *comprise* and *constitute* as synonyms, usually, however, after the preferred definitions.)

(#81, 11/82)

Ask *The Eye:* Everyone/Their

The Question: Is Ungrammatical Compromise the Answer to Irresistible Force?

Is the increasing use (more in ads, sometimes in text) of the possessive pronoun "their" gradually undermining the likes of William Strunk, Jr.'s *The Elements of Style* (revised by E.B. White in 1959), virtually the bible on style? [Strunk and White's advice is to change "Everybody thinks they have a sense of humor" to "Everybody thinks he has a sense of humor."]

Women's liberation has made giantess strides, but are we headed for a case of the irresistible force vs. the immovable object and resultant ungrammatical compromise? Is Will Strunk passé?

. . . I assume today's sensitive editors are trying to avoid the awkward "his/her" situation—as well as the ladies' brow-furrowing upon seeing solely "his."

I recently edited/proofed a draft from our company president to all employees. His senior VP had drafted: ". . . my thanks to each employee and their family . . ." Determined, I hastily rewrote it ". . . to all employees and their families."

Have you noticed a subtle but seemingly inexorable swing to "their" as a cover-up?

—An editorial manager in Virginia

The Answer

You have raised two related issues, one concerning specific nouns ("each employee") and one concerning indefinite pronouns ("everybody," "anybody"). There is no question that it is ungrammatical to use a plural pronoun to refer to *each employee*, and your plural solution neatly avoids the generic *he* (which, as you imply, has certainly come under attack in recent years) and the *he/she* construction (which everybody agrees is awkward).

Authorities disagree, however, about whether (or when) it is all right to use *they* and *their* to refer to indefinite pronouns. According to Roy H. Copperud (*American Usage and Style: The Consensus*), *anybody, anyone, each, either, everybody, everyone, nobody, no one, somebody,* and *someone* are all technically singular pronouns, but plural references to these words are common. ("Everybody shouldered their pack and moved on.") Four authorities whom Copperud consulted approved the plural reference outright; four others permitted it in conversation but disapproved of it in writing. Random House called it nonstandard and Harper rejected it. (Nobody seems to have pointed out the problem with a singular *pack*.)

In a section on what he calls the "adolescent they," however, Copperud ridicules the use of a singular verb with the plural pronouns *they* or *their*. "The church welcomes all students to participate in the varied programs they offer." (Use "it offers.") "The street will be blocked at night to prevent anyone from parking their cars there." (Use "his car" or "to prevent drivers from parking their cars," Copperud advises.)

Merriellyn Kett (in *The Business Writer*, June 1983) notes that before the rules of grammar were formalized in the 19th century, it had been quite common to use *they* in a sentence such as "Anyone can do it if they try hard enough." She then argues that *anybody* is "psychologically plural even though we know it takes a singular verb." She adds, "If we insist upon defining *they* as exclusively plural, then *they* fails to agree with a singular, sex-indefinite antecedent like *anybody* by one feature: number. On the other hand, *he* fails to agree with a singular, sex-indefinite antecedent like *anybody* also by one feature: gender." Kett used all this discussion to introduce her theme: strategies for avoiding sexism (writing in the plural, revising the sentence, eliminating the pronoun, repeating the noun, using a synonym for the noun, and so on).

(#93, 9/83)

■ Redundancy: Empty Calories for the Mind

LOGO•PHILE

Writers are like fatties; they have to work at their verbal waistlines every day. The equivalent of junk food for the writer is redundancy, and the job of the editor is to count calories and impose diets. The temptation to gorge on empty calories arises from motives both noble ("I want to give just the right shade of meaning") and base ("The metaphor is so good I can't bear to give it up"). But the temptation must be resisted.

In Many Guises

Redundancy takes several forms. One is tautology, in which the same idea is repeated in different words without adding to sense or rhetorical effect:

"The foreman said only one additional worker has been added to the night shift." Another is periphrasis or circumlocution—talking around the subject. A common example is the *not un . . .* construction, as in "She was not unsympathetic to his overtures." This way of putting things runs the not unreal danger of becoming not unarch after a while. The passive periphrastic tries to pass off excess baggage for elegance, as in "His former plan was made the overall, guiding framework for a new attempt."

Another form of redundancy is plain overwriting. Consistently using constructions like *at this point in time* for *now* or *in the immediate vicinity* for *near* is simply overkill.

Another contribution to the linguistic spare tire is the pleonasm. Pleonasms are to ideas what chocolate sauce is to the brownie—too much of a good thing. Several seem to be making the rounds, some predictable and harmless, others more troublesome. Most writers and editors are alert to the fact that *unique* should not be qualified. But English suffers a body blow every time a congressional committee delves into the *true facts*, or the school board reaches a *shared consensus*, or the company adopts a *recent innovation*.

Thinking it Through

Part of the problem, of course, is that people don't think through the full meanings of the words they use. Usage authority Roy Copperud points out, for example, that words like *custom*, *experience*, *events*, *records*, and *history* are basically tied to the past. Using *past* to modify any of them is pleonastic. Similarly, *plans*, *prospects*, and *developments* are tied to the future; phrases like *advance planning* and *advance reservations* are one word too long.

When the connotations of a word are ambiguous, context usually supplies clarity. *Records* do not have associations only with the past, as any sports fan will tell you. But when some pole vaulter clears 20 feet, the achievement need not be designated a *new* record; the adjective is superfluous.

A Free Gift

So, for what it's worth, here's some advance warning. The ups and downs of the writing life may put a smile on your lips or a frown on your forehead—either can be the end result. But above all, remember to maintain your personal friendships. Beware situations of close proximity, however; they have a way of eventuating in outcomes that remain perpetual for all time. In that case, the best thing you can do is maintain your equanimity of mind and avoid redundancies, again and again.

 (#100, 3/84)

■ Oxymorons

LOGO•PHILE

"Turn it inside out and you may be able to find another use for it," my old logic prof used to say. In that spirit, the LOGO*PHILE turns to the oxymoron. The last LOGO*PHILE dealt with some forms of redundancy, such as the pleonasm, a rhetorical figure in which the nominally obvious is adjectivally belabored, as when the *widow woman* goes to the *funeral service*, after her husband has run afoul of the *lone gunman*.

Inside-Out Pleonasm

By turning the idea of the pleonasm inside out, you get the idea of the oxymoron. Ask any 10 people to guess what an oxymoron is and 8 of them are likely to tell you it's a new detergent. But the word is actually a combination of two Greek words, *oxys* (*sharp*) and *moros* (*dull*). The term is thus itself an oxymoron, a *sharp dullness* in the metaphorical sense of being *clever–foolish*. An oxymoron is something like a neatly tied together contradiction, as when Chaucer calls poverty a *hateful good*, and Yeats refers to ". . . the murderous innocence of the sea."

The fact that writers of this stature use them to such good effect already differentiates oxymorons from pleonasms, which are almost always excess verbal baggage. Oxymoronic expressions gain force from the seeming absurdity they bring to mind. It is this forcefulness that brings them to the front rank of effectiveness among figures of speech. They work especially well in poetry ("No light, but rather darkness visible": Milton), politics ("the loyal opposition"), and humor ("My wife has a whim of iron": Oliver Herford). Oscar Wilde's masterly oxymoron, "He hasn't a single redeeming vice," shows that oxymorons can be ironic as well as funny.

Handle with Care

But as the great Fowler warns, "the figure needs discreet handling or its effect may become absurd rather than impressive." Or, he might have added, it may quickly degenerate to the level of cliché, as in *paper tiger*, *open secret,* and *the beginning of the end.*

The oxymoron is particularly useful in constructing definitions, as in Eugen Rosenstock-Huessy's recasting of a definition by Goethe. Goethe wrote that "architecture is frozen music"; Rosenstock-Huessy, a sociologist, insisted that "architecture is frozen sociology."

Oxymorons are found not only among the most cultured and literate. The Hollywood producer, Samuel Goldwyn, was famous for his oxymorons (both deliberate and innocent), and many of them have crept into everyday parlance: "I can give you a definite maybe," "Let's have some new clichés," and "Include me out."

What is all this in aid of? Well, think of it this way. The next time a conversation turns to airline food, military intelligence, or contemporary rock music, at least you'll know what name to call it.

 (#101, 4/84)

Weeds

LOGO•PHILE

If a weed is only a plant growing somewhere you don't want it, then jargon is the weedpatch of language. Thus, I don't hold with Fowler, who defines jargon as "talk that is considered both ugly sounding and hard to understand." Ugliness is in the eye of the beholder, and while a word like "byte" may be ugly to some, it is elegant to a computer programmer, for whom it expresses a precise and therefore clear meaning. It isn't that jargon is noxious in itself, it's that, like crabgrass, the dratted stuff keeps rooting where it doesn't belong.

Jargon creates two difficulties, both of which endanger clear understanding. The first is seldom mentioned: jargon deflects the attention of the reader away from the subject at hand and onto the writer. And, truth to tell, this is why most of us lapse into jargon; we succumb to the temptation to parade our command of various and arcane vocabularies. But the business writer who lapses into computerese while discussing marketing risks losing the reader's attention and respect. Or, as Dick Cavett puts it, "Anyone who uses the words 'parameter' and 'interface' should never be invited to a dinner party."

The Style of Jargon

The second difficulty is a more common complaint. Jargon, because it is language misdirected, soon becomes soporific and finally narcotic. It depends on a prose style that sooner or later becomes a candidate for the putdown C. Wright Mills made on the writing of fellow sociologist Talcott Parsons: "Talcott writes with ink of opium on pages of lead." Jargon prefers the noun to the verb; its building blocks are smothered verbs and the prepositional phrases that trail in their wake. Among the most common constructions of jargon-laden writing is the all too familiar: "the (choose any verb)-tion of (choose any noun)." Thus, like the builders of the Tower of Babel, the architects of jargon court the confusion of tongues as they stack their nominalizations one atop another. The style of jargon uses bricks without the mortar of thought, and in the end, the sentences and paragraphs simply collapse.

On examination, both these problems turn out to have a moral dimension; both are a refusal to apply standards, in the one case to the writer and in the other to the product. Allowing the weeds of jargon to grow all over the garden is basically a refusal to say that this is good writing and that is bad writing. The writer's willingness to make such distinctions and the implicit trust of the reader that the writer will make them are part of the moral bond between them, and jargon threatens the integrity of this bond.

Two Responses

The conventional response to the moral problem of jargon is a kind of moralism, a "tsk-tsk-ing" of the kind that most of us learned from our eighth-grade English teachers. We hear their echoes today in the tough cadences of those Kojaks of the English language, Edwin Newman and John Simon. But the cure of moralism is no cure at all and is often worse than the disease. It changes so little and risks so much good will from people who might otherwise be disposed to curb their jargoneering; self-righteousness is a taste only angels can afford to cultivate.

But there is another way. Richard A. Lanham, in his intriguing little book, *Style: An Anti-Textbook* (New Haven: Yale University Press, 1974), suggests that a more fruitful approach is to think of jargon as an effort toward a real style, however clumsy. His point is not that we indulge ourselves in a kind of linguistic Grundyism, but that we start translating jargon into real English, and thereby get some fun out of all the special little lingoes each of us dabbles in from time to time. His advice is to stop being linguistic police and to start becoming connoisseurs of jargons.

Perhaps Lanham is right. Once we start thinking of jargon not as a collection of misplaced weeds but as a garden of metaphors, waiting to be dug up and repotted, we might just begin to get a new perspective, and spread a little beauty around the place. There are plenty of flowerbeds out there, and, who knows, by transplanting a weed or two, and indulging in a little cross-pollinating, we may discover something new. Perhaps we need to take seriously the possibility that Gregor Mendel and Luther Burbank can be our role models as well as E.B. White and Lewis Thomas. Nothing immoral about that.

 (#107, 8/84)

■ The Fuzzy *With*

Have you ever noticed how people use *with* to mean so many things other than *with*? As a preposition, *with* has well over a score of distinguishable meanings. But inexperienced writers often use the word loosely.

- *With* is sometimes used as a kind of two-chain to attach to a sentence a thought that would be treated more clearly and grammatically as an independent clause following either a semicolon or *and.* Example: "English and history are his majors, *with* a minor in economics." Better: ". . . ; his minor is economics."

- Fowler (*Modern English Usage*) suggests that *with* came into popular usage to replace *as to* and *in the case of.* Example: "With pipes, as with tobacco, William Bragge was one of the most successful collectors."
- Barzun (*Simple & Direct*) gives an example in which *with* strays from the literalness of "Come *with* me" to a more elliptical meaning: "*With* her relatives gone, she could start her housework." Better: "Without her relatives, . . ."
- Another of Barzun's examples points to the error of ascribing to *with* the conjunctive power of *and.* In the book jacket blurb ". . . married *with* two children," the preposition *with* has been substituted for more than one word and more than one part of speech. Better: ". . . married, Smith has two children."

The editorial solution is to query the "withness" of the *with.* In the sentence "Most of the victims were older, *with* ages ranging from 55 to 65," what is *with* what? Nothing is *with* anything. Substitute *their* for *with.*

(#111, 12/84)

■ Brush Up Your British

Adventurous editors who want to work overseas should steel themselves for considerable divergence between American and British usage. British usage is preferred not only in the United Kingdom but in many international organizations. (In the United Nations system every editor has a copy of the *Concise Oxford Dictionary* in front of his nose.)

Some of the differences in spelling are well known: "connexion," the "our" endings ("colour," "favour," "honour"), and the "re" rather than "er" endings ("centre," "theatre," "metre").

The English have a penchant for the softer "s" (as opposed to "z") in such words as "analyse," "criticise," and "humanise." They also like to double their l's, as in "marvellous," "traveller," "shovelling," and "jewellery." Some British forms, like "cheque," are starting to wilt, but one especially hardy bureaucratic perennial is "programme."

In punctuation, probably the most common departure from much American practice is the omission of the final serial comma, e.g., "Russia, Bulgaria and Czechoslovakia voted against the resolution."

There are a few grammatical quirks. The English prefer "got" as a past participle to "gotten"; they also tend to use plural verbs with collective noun subjects ("The Government are planning to introduce a minibudget"). One surprising form, though it is likely to be encountered only in speech, is "eat" (pronounced "et") used as the past tense of "to eat."

English names for many things differ from American ones. An Englishman speaks of petrol, not gasoline; or paraffin, not kerosene. He will refer to the windscreen, bonnet, mudguard, and boot of his car; not to its windshield, hood, fender, and trunk. In his apartment (or flat) he will allude to taps, not faucets; points, not outlets or sockets; and he will watch the telly rather than the TV.

Confusion can arise over words with similar sounds and meanings but with different spellings: the English prefer their own "rumbustious" to the later American coinage "rambunctious."

Possibly Misleading Expressions or Oops! Say What You Mean

Certain expressions may have disconcertingly different meanings in the United States and the United Kingdom. By now you should all know that to "knock up" someone in England means simply to wake that person, but the American meaning has doubtless given rise to much innocent merriment over the years.

A more serious trap for the editor is the phrase "to table a motion," which in England means precisely the opposite of what it means here, i.e., to bring the motion forward for discussion. British English in fact is so rich in these indigenous expressions that the BBC has employed an American translator to render English into his native tongue.

Vulgar language brings its own difficulties, although it is to be hoped editors will not encounter them in their professional functions. The American slang word "bum" is in England simply a rude word for posterior; whereas the American euphemism "fanny" is English slang for the female derrière.

The American vulgarism "ass" means only "fool" in England (where it is usually preceded by "silly"); whereas the English spelling of the American meaning may be found in Doctor Johnson's definition of a politician as "an arse that everyone has sat on but a man." And to call a woman a "bitch" is not a serious insult in England; to call her a "cow" means war.

Many Americanisms have passed into British English, and prevailing linguistic winds are westerly. But in this imperfect world it is likely that the English will go on using their own language for many years to come, and would-be overseas editors should welcome the chance to enrich their own culture instead of waiting for the disappearance of other cultures.

Useful Publications

A good way to acquire a nodding acquaintance with British English is by an occasional dip into the *Concise Oxford,* as well as *A Dictionary of Modern English Usage* and its companion volumes, *The King's English* and *A Dictionary of Modern American Usage* (to see what the English consider distinctively "American").

An even better way is to read some quality English newspapers and periodicals—*The Times* (when it is publishing) and *The Economist,* which, despite its offputting title, has the liveliest prose style among English weeklies.

—Trevor Leamington-Jones (#20, 1/79)

Editor's Note: We have refrained in the foregoing article from our usual practice of stamping out biased language because the author assures us that in the United Kingdom the masculine pronoun has no ideological significance. He adds that he is even in doubt these days about its sexual significance. We therefore let it stand, without endorsement, as a further example of British usage.

Postings on the Refrigerator Door LOGO*PHILE

According to Jim Quinn, the refusal to judge English usage is the basis for all contemporary study of the language, "which has long since concluded that if you are a native-born speaker of English, you never make a mistake in grammar because you don't know how: grammar is what you say."

This amazing statement appears on page 11 of Quinn's *American Tongue and Cheek* (New York: Random House, 1980). (The book was reviewed in *The Eye* in Issue 63.) Quinn's book is billed as a "populist guide to our language"; it reads like a tongue-lashing of the "pop grammarians," among whom Quinn numbers not only Edwin Newman, John Simon, Theodore Bernstein, and William Safire, but also Wilson Follett, Eric Partridge, and H.W. Fowler! On the grounds that Quinn's point of view and research methods constitute a direct attack on what this newsletter stands for, the LOGO*PHILE is taking another look.

The idea that native speakers cannot err, though astonishing to many, is not new. Quinn is quite right that it lies close to the center of the entire discipline of modern linguistics. I believe he is wrong to insist that grammar is only a map of possible utterances in a language. It is also a guide to the standards that enable us to discriminate how well utterances communicate meanings. The logic of Quinn's position seems to me to have the same power as the logic of tautology, because that's where it leads. If grammar is merely what we say, then grammar becomes coterminous with its subject, in which case it disappears entirely.

Grammar

If it is anything, grammar is a set of ordering principles, as the medieval curriculum recognized when it grouped grammar with logic and rhetoric to form the basis for the study of all knowledge. If, as Quinn seems to think, grammar is purely descriptive and should not be used prescriptively, then how are we to trust the relationship that language constructs between the reality we experience and our communication of that reality? Against what do we measure utterances to make sure they are language and not nonsense? How do we know that "I do my work" is a better sentence than "I does my work," even though many native speakers would use such a sentence and be perfectly well understood? The word *language*, if it means anything at all, carries with it the idea of a commonly agreed upon process that is ordered by commonly agreed upon rules.

Because that's what language is—a human invention for ordering reality and communicating about it—you cannot abandon that order without eventually paying a price for it in the form of garbled communication and mangled meanings. At a slightly more complex level, you cannot use plural verbs with singular subjects because if you do, you violate a consensus about the logical relationship between language and reality. Languages have singulars and plurals because reality comes at us that way, and we have to have some way of dealing with that fact.

Change

Quinn himself, in mounting his argument, follows closely the basic premise his argument denies. He uses words and puts them in relation to each other according to long-established conventions. If he didn't, he would not be understood. More to the point, his book would not have been published. But he is quite right in reminding us that these are conventions, and that conventions change. The real issues are change, rates of change, who decides what changes are acceptable, and which changes threaten to destroy the superstructure that holds language in place for all of us. For better or for worse, the commonly agreed upon answers to those questions lie largely in the hands of the people most of us believe are best at using language. If you want to find out the best way to hit a baseball, you ask someone like George Brett. If you want to find out the difference between *flout* and *flaunt*, you ask someone like H.W. Fowler. The fact that Brett and Willy Mays are going to disagree on some of the fine points of hitting ought not stop us from soliciting their advice. Nor should the fact that each struck out occasionally. The fact that "average speakers" do not always agree in their speech with usage authorities and prescriptive grammars is not an argument for abandoning standards.

Much of Quinn's book is given over to remonstrances that usage authorities tend to be adamant about what's right and what's wrong; that is, the book goes to the level where change is most vigorously debated. Here we encounter such usage questions as whether *between you and I* is acceptable, whether *gift* is a verb, the "real" meaning of *fulsome*, whether you can use *over* to mean *more than*, and the like. Here is where he inveighs against the "pop grammarians" for their prescriptiveness. In every instance his approach is to select citations from the *Oxford English Dictionary* showing either that some great writer used the word in question in exactly the sense now frowned upon by some "pop grammarian," or that the usage he himself is championing was in use in centuries past. When Babe Ruth hit a home run, he did not follow the method advocated by George Brett OR Willy Mays. Big deal.

Research Method

Quinn's research method reminds me of nothing so much as the 9-year-old who discovers that *ain't* is in the dictionary and proceeds to pepper his speech with it for a week, to the consternation of his maiden aunts. This kind of research is a kind of linguistic "flashing," testing to see if someone will call the police. And when they do, I imagine Quinn's likely defense would be to quote a 3x5 card that would say something like "While at Oxford, John Milton once mooned one of his professors."

Even college sophomores know that the appearance of something in print is not an argument for its truth. The same difficulty develops in theological circles, where proving points by quoting isolated verses of Scripture (proof-texting) has been a discredited form of argumentation among scholars for a very long time. The point is not that we ought to be able to say *between you and I* because the locution appears in *The Merchant of Venice* (III.ii.321). The point is that good writing and correct speech use the objective case for personal pronouns where it is called for, and that trespassing the boundaries of standard grammar and usage should only be done for good reason. These border crossings are not an argument for a different norm; in fact, they reinforce the norm precisely because they are seen as violations.

Good usage is decided by good writers and by people who take the trouble to learn how to use language well. And that "well" is all-important because it implies standards; it says that grammar and language are not the same thing. Good language is like good art. An artist takes the trouble to learn how to use the tools of color, light, line, and perspective. Good writers get into print; good artists get into galleries and museums. For Quinn, art becomes like the first-grade scrawls of a child on the refrigerator door. They don't become art because they've been hung.

 (#114, 2/85)

Subject Index